Spectacular Politics

Spectacular Politics

LOUIS-NAPOLEON BONAPARTE

AND THE *FÊTE IMPÉRIALE*,

1849–1870

MATTHEW TRUESDELL

New York   Oxford   ·   Oxford University Press   1997

Oxford University Press

Oxford   New York

Athens   Auckland   Bangkok   Bogota   Bombay   Buenos Aires
Calcutta   Cape Town   Dar es Salaam   Delhi   Florence   Hong Kong
Istanbul   Karachi   Kuala Lumpur   Madras   Madrid   Melbourne
Mexico City   Nairobi   Paris   Singapore   Taipei   Tokyo   Toronto

and associated companies in
Berlin   Ibadan

Copyright © 1997 by Oxford University Press, Inc.

Published by Oxford University Press, Inc.
198 Madison Avenue, New York, New York 10016

Oxford is a registered trademark of Oxford University Press

Library of Congress Cataloging-in-Publication Data
Truesdell, Matthew.
Spectacular politics : Louis-Napoleon Bonaparte and the Fête
impériale, 1849–1870 / Matthew Truesdell.
p.   cm.
Includes bibliographical references and index.
ISBN 0-19-510689-X
1. Napoleon III, Emperor of the French, 1808–1873—Influence.
2. France—Politics and government—1848–1870—Social aspects.
3. France—Cultural policy.   4. Symbolism in politics.   5. Mass
media and public opinion—France—History—19th century.   6. Rites
and ceremonies—France—History—19th century.   I. Title.
DC278.T78   1997
944.07—dc20   96-27986

1 3 5 7 9 8 6 4 2

Printed in the United States of America
on acid-free paper

For

Audrey

and

Caroline

Preface

This is the story of how Louis-Napoleon Bonaparte dazzled and se-
duced the French populace with spectacular celebrations, a lavish
court, a beautiful and caring empress, and stirring military pageantry. First
as president of the Second Republic and then as Emperor Napoleon III,
this man ruled France for twenty-one years, longer than any other modern
leader. He owed this astounding longevity not to military might or personal
charisma but to a canny politics of image and what we might today call
"marketing," which he pursued, in large part, through these spectacles.
Through them, this first "democratic despot" reached out to a mass audience and presented himself as the culmination of French history, the guarantor of prosperity and stability, and the embodiment of the national will.

But this is also the story of how Louis-Napoleon's spectacles generated
opposition and contradiction. Their very success drove his opponents—
republican and legitimist alike—to try to destroy the monolithic façade of
the imperial shows by disrupting official celebrations, by interpreting those
celebrations in their own ways, and by finding ways to put on their own
public shows. Moreover, the *fête impériale* itself was riven with internal
contradictions: there was no single Bonapartist version of French history,

the Universal Expositions were far from universal, and the emperor's military playacting sat uneasily with the image of the nation-in-arms.

To flesh out both Louis-Napoleon's use of festivity and the ways those efforts were challenged, I have organized this book topically and chronologically. The first chapters cover the years of the Second Republic and the Decennial Republic, the year-long interlude between the coup d'état of 1851 and the formal restoration of the Empire in 1852. Here, I show how Louis-Napoleon used spectacle to undermine the Republic and replace it with a restored Empire. The next chapters turn to the Second Empire itself and take a more thematic approach. Chapter 3 looks at the political use of evocations of the past in historically oriented spectacles, such as the baptism of the Prince Imperial and the 15 August celebrations. Chapters 4 and 5 then turn to the deployment of more modern images of progress and prosperity, both in the imperial celebrations generally and in the Universal Expositions in particular. The sixth chapter takes a different angle by examining the seemingly unspectacular but nonetheless well-publicized charitable work of the Empress Eugénie, work that put on display the supposed goodness and solicitude of that sovereign. Chapter 7 looks at the more masculine image of the emperor that was projected in military pageantry, and chapter 8 examines the use of imperial spectacle in the French provinces. The final chapter describes oppositional festivity during these years, and especially the Republican use of funerals and funerary commemorations as a means to challenge the Napoleonic regime.

Many people helped me over the course of this project. I would particularly like to thank Susanna Barrows for her patient and incisive criticism and her unflagging enthusiasm for French history. Without her guidance and encouragement, this book would never have been written. I am also grateful to the many others who have read and commented on various parts of the manuscript, including Carol Armstrong, Antoine de Baecque, Girish Bhat, Alon Confino, Lynn Hunt, Ben Lapp, Martin Jay, Audrey Sung, and all of the members of the University of California at Berkeley French dissertation group during my time there. Additionally, Maurice Agulhon, Pierre Nora, Pascal Ory, and Madeleine Reberioux took the time to speak with me about this project in France. I would also like to express my gratitude to the French government for making possible a year of research in Paris with a Chateaubriand Fellowship and to the editors and anonymous reader at Oxford University Press.

Oakland, California   M. N. T.
November 1996

Contents

Spectacular Politics

Introduction

With the Revolution of 1848 and the broadening of the suffrage to include all adult men, France entered the world of democratic politics. But democracy, as the French quickly discovered, did not guarantee tranquillity. Indeed, it seemed to bring ever more complicated problems as the different politicians and divergent political visions of the age clashed, sometimes violently, in their competition for popular approval. Out of this, however, emerged one undisputed master of the new political game: Louis-Napoleon Bonaparte. This book examines how Louis-Napoleon, first as president of the Second Republic and then as Emperor Napoleon III, developed and refined the use of public spectacle as a powerful instrument for dealing with a political system based on universal male suffrage and a society that put ever more trust in the value of popular opinion.

Throughout the 1850s and 1860s, the subjects of this study—officially supported ceremonies and celebrations either carried out at least partially in public or widely if vicariously experienced through the press—occurred with dazzling frequency. A yearly holiday on the birthday of the First Emperor, spectacular visits to the provinces, elaborate inaugurations, enormous military reviews, two Universal Expositions, an imperial marriage and baptism, visits from foreign royalty, and a variety of other gala events comprised what has come to be called the *fête impériale*. But these events were more than just amusements; they were also among Louis-Napoleon's key tools in the projection of powerful images before a mass audience, images that portrayed him as the ideal leader for the age—the providential savior of the country and the guarantor of a peaceful, prosperous, and glorious future. Although these efforts ultimately failed to establish a legitimacy sufficiently powerful for the Empire to survive military defeat and the capture of the emperor at Sedan in 1870, it should be remembered that Louis-Napoleon headed the French polity for twenty-two years, longer than any other leader in the modern period.

The importance of studying official celebrations in order to gain a full understanding of the political life of the past has been increasingly recognized by historians.[1] Placement, decoration, staging, costumes, symbols, speeches, and other elements are carefully combined to make such manifestations effective political tools to legitimate—directly or indirectly—leaders, regimes, and systems. At least in the late modern period, they are, in essence, political propaganda, but they are political propaganda of a very particular sort since they work not only through verbal argument in the form of speeches but also through emotionally resonant symbols and images. They also reach enormous numbers of people, and their "messages" are usually easily grasped, even by the illiterate. Bernard Ménager, for example, has shown that festivals served as important and effective conduits for the transmission of Bonapartist sentiments over the course of the nineteenth century.[2]

Official celebrations can be seen as ritual activities that legitimate political authorities by linking them to what Clifford Geertz terms "the structures of meaning through which men give shape to their experience."[3] But because the nature of legitimacy, the object legitimated, and the audience before which the spectacle is performed all vary greatly, ritual legitimation works in vastly differing ways in different ages and societies. A medieval prince whose authority was based on fealty or divine right, in other words, had very different symbolic requirements from those of a modern republican democracy. Even when two ceremonies seem identical on the surface, they may still operate very differently since different ages and societies may give different meanings to the same symbols. As David Cannadine puts it, "Even if the text of a repeated ritual . . . remains unaltered over time, its 'meaning' may change profoundly depending on the nature of the context."[4]

By far the most important contextual change for European politics in the nineteenth century was the rise of popular sovereignty. Historian George Mosse has described what he calls a "new politics" that emerged when popular sovereignty, as given form in the concepts of the general will and the nation, became a "secularized religion." According to Mosse, from about 1800 onward, political leaders promoted national myths and symbols and developed a secular liturgy that

> attempted to draw the people into active participation in the national mystique through rites and festivals, myths and symbols which gave a concrete expression to the general will. . . . The chaotic crowd of the "people" became a mass movement which shared a belief in popular unity through a national mystique. The new politics provided an objectification of the general will; it transformed political action into a drama supposedly shared by the people themselves.[5]

Elsewhere, Mosse uses the term *Caesarism* to refer to this new politics of mass democracy, especially when practiced by individual leaders. Oddly enough, however, though the modern use of the term *Caesarism* appears to have begun with Pierre-Joseph Proudhon's criticism of Napoleon III, Mosse does not seem to see the Second Empire as truly within that tradition. He focuses instead on the Third Republic and asserts that the new politics went "beyond the plebiscite as both Napoleons had understood it."[6] This remark does not do justice to the politics of the second Napoleon. The plebiscites of Napoleon III were part and parcel of the new politics. If rites and ceremonies were its "liturgy," plebiscites were its revealed truth, the proof that Louis-Napoleon represented what was known even officially as the "national will."[7]

The crucial turning point for this new politics in France, then, was not the foundation of the Third Republic in 1870 but the institution of universal male suffrage by the revolutionaries of 1848. This new politics had been gradually taking shape since at least the eighteenth century, when the primary purpose of even dynastic and military celebrations became, as one historian has put it, "to place the relationship between power and population on an affective mode."[8] And during the Revolution, as Mona Ozouf has shown, the revolutionaries attempted to use festivals to transform passive subjects into citizens who could provide the foundation for a renovated society and wholly new forms of politics. The First Empire, Restoration, and July Monarchy returned to monarchy and monarchical forms of celebration, but they also moved increasingly—especially with the July Monarchy—away from a simple mimicry of the Old Regime and toward the use of new celebrations aimed at winning the allegiance of the nation as a whole. Only under a government that openly relied on a truly democratic franchise as the source for its legitimacy, however, could the new politics come to full fruition. Such a system was born in 1848.

The Revolution of 1848 brought France an explosion of public ritual and celebration. Indeed, in Paris, as Maurice Agulhon has pointed out, no fewer than eight major celebrations took place in just nineteen weeks.[9] Public festivity quickly became an important part of republican politics in the provinces as well, as both new celebrations and traditional festivals given new content emerged as vehicles for popular participation in the political process.[10] But events soon overtook this flurry of activity. The violence of the June Days dulled whatever euphoric and effervescent edge these manifestations had ever had and brought in its wake the beginning of the repression that would eventually close them down almost entirely. Even more important, December 1848 saw the election to the highest post in the country of a man who would challenge the Republic's domination of the festal stage.

When he came to power in 1849, Louis-Napoleon Bonaparte was a political outsider whose only real strength was his apparent popularity with the mass of the French electorate. He soon learned that he could use public celebrations—even seemingly apolitical ones—to tap into that support. Thus, as *L'Illustration* noted in 1851, "when the president of the Republic wants to strengthen his political position, he chooses with a special predilection those grand occasions that, by their nature and object, seem furthest from any political concern."[11] In these "grand occasions," Louis-Napoleon did not simply bask in the spotlight of celebrity, he plied the French people with visions of national glory, social harmony, peace, and prosperity.

These visions were often communicated through the spoken word. Napoleon III himself had a clear full voice that carried well, an important consideration in the days before amplification, though his speeches were also posted publicly and printed in the press the next day. Most important, he had a knack for coming up with the felicitous phrase, the emotionally appealing slogan that summed up his policy in simple terms and was infinitely repeated in newspapers, speeches, songs, and poems, in a sort of nineteenth-century equivalent of the sound bite. The most successful of these slogans, "L'Empire c'est la paix" (The Empire means peace), pronounced at Bordeaux in 1851, immediately became a rallying cry for all those who wanted to restore the Empire. Louis-Napoleon had neither Bossuet's eloquence nor Lamartine's emotional range, but his ability to package his ideas in short, appealing verbal slogans made him one of the most successful political orators in French history.

The celebrations also worked through visual spectacle. For many at the time, elaborate ceremonies and the apparatus of court etiquette were part of the necessary elevation of power. The people, in this view, "respect above all that which is surrounded by an appropriate splendor and the consideration that is due it."[12] Although it was an Englishman, Walter Bagehot, who gave this idea its most profound examination in his study, *The English Constitution* (1867), it was, at least in a general sense, quite common among Frenchmen, especially during the Old Regime. As Jean-Marie Apostolides has noted, "For the intellectuals of the seventeenth century, spectacle was a necessity intrinsically linked to the exercise of power; the monarch must astonish *[éblouir]* the people."[13] But this view was by no means dead during the nineteenth century. Indeed, according to Flaubert, one of the "received ideas" of the age was that decorum, or ceremony, "gives prestige" and "strikes the imagination of the masses."[14] The men of the Second Empire acted on this axiom by producing stunning spectacles clearly designed to attract and astonish large crowds, crowds that themselves served as "proof" of the regime's popularity and, therefore, of its legitimacy.

In addition to simply astonishing the spectators, these affairs used emotionally charged symbols to move them in particular ways. As Emile Durkheim noted in a famous passage, "It is a well-known law that the sentiments aroused in us by something spontaneously attach themselves to the symbol which represents them."[15] Thus, symbols that referred to highly emotive concepts such as the nation or the First Empire tended to conjure up the emotions associated with those concepts. This in turn invested the celebrations themselves with a degree of emotional appeal difficult to attain through other sources of communication. The symbols used were also multivocal; they could be interpreted in more than one way and thus could achieve what David Kertzer calls "solidarity without consensus."[16] In this respect, a symbol like the tricolor flag or an image of the First Emperor could be expected to appeal to a wide variety of people, even people with very different conceptions of what the flag or the emperor really stood for.

Louis-Napoleon's most common symbols were those that evoked the First Empire. By using Napoleonic eagles and bees and by emulating First Empire celebrations, Louis-Napoleon directly linked his regime with its illustrious predecessor. Sometimes this linkage also went beyond general association and articulated an interpretation of French history that portrayed the First Emperor as bringing the best of the Old Regime (authority, order, monarchical principles) together with what was worth preserving from the Revolution ("principles of 1789"). Through these historical symbols and interpretations, Louis-Napoleon not only tapped into the strong emotional resonance of the First Empire but also laid claim to one of the most important manifestations of the national community: its memory.

For all the historical appeal, Louis-Napoleon never forgot that his claim to the nation remained directly linked to popularity. Not only was the regime legally and morally founded on universal male suffrage, but also the democratic society of the age imbued popularity itself with a particular power. When individuals are equal, Alexis de Tocqueville noted, "not only does [the individual] mistrust his own strength, but even comes to doubt his own judgment, and he is brought very near to recognizing that he must be wrong when the majority hold the opposite view. There is no need for the majority to compel him; it convinces him."[17] Thus, one of the most important political functions of public celebrations was the underscoring of Louis-Napoleon's popularity. For the *Te Deum* celebration for the plebiscite of 1851, for example, the number of "yes" votes was emblazoned on the façade of the cathedral of Notre-Dame. More commonly, however, Louis-Napoleon's popular mandate was physically and symbolically embodied in the crowds of spectators who came out to see him.

The regime went to great pains to ensure the presence and enthusiasm of large crowds at these events. The lavish decorations, fireworks, concerts, popular amusements, and other attractions all naturally tended to draw crowds. The authorities also sometimes closed schools and offices on the day of a celebration or planned the celebration for a Sunday, when people did not have to work. Another tactic, one often used on official excursions, was to bring supporters of the regime in from outlying areas. For Louis-Napoleon's 1852 visit to Bordeaux, for example, the official deputations from the department of the Gironde as a whole amounted to some 3,000 people.[18] This number alone could not fill a city like Bordeaux, but almost all would have been dedicated imperialists, and when added to Louis-Napoleon's local supporters and the many others who came on their own, they would have provided a significant kernel of enthusiasm to excite a much larger crowd. This was important since even at his most popular, Louis-Napoleon never enjoyed the unanimous support that the spectacles were supposed to prove.

At times, the regime resorted to using "cheerleaders" to whip up enthusiasm by mingling with the crowd, loudly cheering, and yelling out pro-imperial slogans. Unfortunately, we have few sources of information about the use of this tactic, in part because the Paris police and municipal archives for the period were destroyed during the Commune. Nonetheless, some official records of hired cheerers do exist,[19] and witnesses, not all of them hostile to the regime, sometimes described seeing them.[20] Moreover, the practice is strikingly similar to the use of the "claque" in the theaters of the time. This was a group of spectators hired to cheer at plays and other performances in order to prompt the audience on. Although often ridiculed, the claque seems to have been effective at drumming up enthusiasm. One performer who hired such a group was "glad to notice that the public 'followed suit,' and that the bravos emanating from the pit radiated through the whole house." [21]

The regime's canny use of the media allowed the celebrations to reach a vastly larger audience than their immediate spectators. Descriptions and images of the celebrations spread throughout the country through daily newspapers, illustrated weeklies like *L'Illustration* and *Le Journal illustré*, books, and inexpensive broadsheets and programs, often roughly illustrated. The regime's use of the media gives Second Empire spectacle something of the flavor of what Daniel Boorstin has called "pseudo-events," which are not spontaneous but are "planted primarily (not always exclusively) for the immediate purpose of being reproduced." [22]

Certainly the regime did much to ensure full media coverage, including arranging special access to ceremonies for members of the press, inviting sympathetic writers and press magnates to the palace, subsidizing newspapers, bringing writers along free on provincial trips, and allowing artists from the illustrated journals to see decorations before they were opened to the general public. The regime also had an official newspaper, *Le Moniteur universel*, that provided extremely detailed accounts of the spectacles. Perhaps most striking is that by putting on such spectacular and seemingly important (i.e., "newsworthy") shows at the same time that it censored criticism, the regime effectively made even newspapers that did not support it into vehicles for its propaganda. This was especially true for the increasingly widely distributed illustrated papers.[23] A weekly like *L'Illustration*, for example, would have been incomplete had it not included illustrations of major state spectacles. Thus, even though the editor of *L'Illustration* was no friend of Napoleon III, he regularly carried engravings and accounts of celebrations that effectively glorified the regime.

This canny and concerted use of the media allowed Second Empire spectacles to reach far beyond the actual crowds that witnessed them. If, as one scholar has argued, "part of what constitutes modern societies as 'modern' is the fact that the exchange of symbolic forms is no longer restricted primarily to the contexts of face-to-face interaction, but is extensively and increasingly mediated by the institutions and mechanisms of mass communication," [24] then the Second Empire was very modern indeed.

In addition to dangling the carrot of spectacle, the regime adroitly brandished the stick of repression.[25] "Organizing a cultural hodgepodge into a workable polity," as Clifford Geertz has noted, "is more than a matter of inventing a promiscuous civil religion to blunt its variety. It requires either the establishment of political institutions within which opposing groups can safely contend, or the elimination of all groups but one from the political stage." [26] The Second Empire chose the latter of these two options. Under a more open political system, its spectacles would have lost much of their impact since opposition groups could have disrupted the official celebrations, challenged the descriptions and interpretations in the Bonapartist press, held their own counterdemonstrations, and ridiculed the pompous nature of the *fête impériale*. Indeed, especially at the beginning of the period, before the repressive system was fully in place, and at the end, when the repression was lifted, such challenges occurred. But throughout much of the period examined here, opposition was extraordinarily difficult. The regime maintained a virtual monopoly on public discourse; it had what one commentator on Eastern Europe before 1989 has called a "semantic occupation of the public sphere."[27] Through its use of various repressive laws (censorship, prosecution of "seditious cries," etc.), the regime controlled not only what happened in public but also what was said about it and the ways in which it was interpreted.

Because of the repression, it is difficult to trust even the seemingly independent press as a source of information about certain aspects of celebrations, above all the attitudes of spectators. Any doubts about the popularity of the emperor's reception were sufficient to bring down the wrath of the regime. The newspaper *Phare de la Loire*, for example, was reprimanded by the imperial censor simply for having written that "the emperor gave a speech which, according to the Havas agency, several times brought forth shouts of *Vive l'Empereur!*," the formula, "according to the Havas agency," being deemed to express doubt about the emperor's popularity.[28]

With the official and subsidized press, we fare even less well than with the independent press, since those papers almost invariably claimed that crowds greeting the emperor were overwhelmingly enthusiastic. But even if the actual attitude of the crowd remains hidden in these reports, they often tell us much about what the Empire saw as important in its spectacles: chiefly the continuing popularity (and thus legitimacy) of the emperor. The welcome the emperor received at the inauguration of the boulevard de Sébastopol in 1858, for example, was said by one Bonapartist newspaper to have "once again proved that . . . nation and emperor think and act with the same confidence and the same sympathy. The nation still recognizes in him its elected."[29] In the Bonapartist view, then, these spectacles brought people and ruler together in a privileged moment of recognition that demonstrated Napoleon III's continuing legitimacy. The crowd stood for all of France in paying homage to the emperor.

Reports to Paris by local prefects and prosecutors on the state of public opinion in their areas offer another possible source of information, but one with weaknesses similar to the press reports. As the correspondent for the London *Times* noted in 1868: "Prefects are generally too optimist. They do not like to displease their chief on whom they depend; and, in his turn, the Minister prefers giving a pleasing account of things."[30] The same, of course, was true of prosecutors and other officials. Not only were all of these men responsible to some extent for the attitudes of their regions; they were also generally ardent supporters of the regime and thus psychologically predisposed to interpret public opinion in a favorable light. Still, it would not have looked good had some serious insurrection fallen on the heels of a report of ardent local support for the regime, so these reports probably did not wander as far from the truth as the accounts in the press.

Another way to approach crowd attitudes is through private memoirs and journals. Here, republicans often described as cool and apathetic the same crowds that the Bonapartist press and officials described as spontaneously enthusiastic. Such accounts often offer a useful corrective to the official ones, but they are plagued with some of the same problems. Republicans were as predisposed to see apathy as Bonapartists were to see enthusiasm, and there is an unfortunate dearth of truly independent French observers who commented on the crowds. What is fascinating about the issue, however, is precisely that the observations vary so widely and divide so cleanly along political lines. This politicization of descriptions of the crowds demonstrates the central importance of these crowds to political legitimacy in mid-nineteenth-century France. They were crucial—and manipulable—pieces of evidence not only for the general popularity or unpopularity of Louis-Napoleon but also for his ability to represent the will of the nation as a whole. As such, it should hardly be surprising that dispassionate, objective observations of the crowds are difficult to find.

A final corrective is provided by foreign sources. A number of foreign visitors to France during this period commented on the crowds at the spectacles, especially in the years from 1848 to 1853, when the political situation was evolving rapidly. More complete are foreign newspapers. The London *Times* is especially good, since its correspondents knew France well and covered French news quickly and fairly completely. Though foreigners were by no means free of prejudice, their biases were at least different from those of the French journalists.

We will never know, then, how the people who watched these celebrations "really" felt. Certainly some came to show support for Louis-Napoleon and others to oppose him. But many probably sought and found simple diversions, pleasant and festive escapes from the tedium of daily life. And still others probably came to gawk at the high and mighty, drink with friends, or earn money selling refreshments. But no matter what drew them, they were counted, assessed, and analyzed by various political commentators. The masses had entered politics, whether they knew it or not.

ONE

The Divided Republic

In several days of rioting in February 1848, the people of Paris overthrew the July Monarchy of King Louis-Philippe and began an experiment with democracy called the Second Republic. The months that followed the February riots were a strange and uncertain period. The volatile new Republic, although decidedly a creature of the left in origin, soon veered decisively to the right. April elections for the Constituent Assembly resulted in a stunning victory for the moderate republicans over their more radical rivals. In June, three days of lethal street fighting in Paris decimated the left and brought on a political reaction that included restrictions on freedom of the press and the suppression of secret societies. Then, in December, in the Second Republic's first presidential election, voters chose a man whose sole credible claim to their attention was his very unrepublican name: Louis-Napoleon Bonaparte.

When he moved into the presidential palace, Louis-Napoleon had no major political party behind him and few supporters among the political elites. His power stemmed directly from his popularity with the great mass of French voters, a popularity predicated in the first instance on the simple fact that his name evoked one of the nation's most glorious epochs. To continue to garner popular support after the election, however, he needed more than name recognition. He needed to present himself convincingly as a fit ruler of France, as a man who could bring peace and prosperity while simultaneously ensuring that neither glory nor the national interest was allowed to flag. He soon found that public ceremonies and celebrations provided an ideal vehicle for projecting such an image. As time went on, he also began to use celebrations to undercut the Republic itself and to lay the groundwork for its eventual overthrow.

Louis-Napoleon's ultimate success in this matter was intimately tied up with the failure of the republicans to establish workable national celebrations of their own—celebrations that might have focused public attention on the Republic as an expression of the national will. This failure resulted primarily from the political division between radical and conservative republicans. The radicals (also known as the "reds" or *démoc-socs*) were highly committed to democratic principles and to the idea that the Republic should introduce broad social policies benefiting the masses. The conservatives (sometimes called the *burgraves*), on the other hand, were far less committed to democracy and were not committed at all to social programs. At worst, they were closet legitimists, men such as Adolphe Thiers and Comte Molé, whose very acceptance of the Republic was tenuous. At best, they were genuine republicans who wanted to establish a government that was responsible to the people but whose fears of "disorder" and "socialism" made them unable to cooperate with the radicals.

Although part of Louis-Napoleon's appeal was based on his social policies (he had written a pamphlet entitled *The Extinction of Pauperism*), on most issues he had more in common with the conservative republicans than with the radicals. Indeed, the early part of his presidency was characterized by collaboration with the right, especially when it came to repressing the left. But there were also differences between Louis-Napoleon and the conservatives, differences that rose to the surface whenever the perceived threat from the left receded. As Maurice Agulhon put it: "Bonaparte and the *burgraves* were alternately in alliance or in opposition, depending on whether the red peril, their common adversary, appeared imminent or distant."[1]

On 20 December, the day of the new president's oath of office, almost all of the 900 members of the Constituent Assembly packed into their chamber.[2] Representative Waldeck-Rousseau read a long report declaring that Louis-Napoleon had received more than 74 percent of the votes cast in the election. The head of the provisional government, General Cavaignac, then formally resigned his powers, and Armand Marrast, the president of the Assembly, proclaimed "citizen Charles-Louis-Napoleon Bonaparte" president of the Republic "from this day until the second Sunday of May

1852." Marrast then called for Louis-Napoleon to come forward and take the oath of office.

Dressed in black and wearing his grand cordon of the Legion of Honor as well as his representative's rosette, the new president mounted the tribune. Marrast read the oath of office: "In the presence of God and before the French people represented by the Assemblée nationale, I swear to remain faithful to the one and indivisible democratic Republic and to fulfill all of the duties imposed upon me by the Constitution." To this, Louis-Napoleon responded in a clear voice: "I swear it."

The ceremony might have ended here, but rather than stepping down from the podium, Louis-Napoleon took out a sheet of paper and read a short speech declaring his faith in the Republic and his desire to "strengthen democratic institutions." "I will consider," he solemnly announced, "as enemies of the fatherland all those who try to change, by illegal means, that which all France has established."

The Assembly applauded him. He might have refused to take the oath unless the new Constitution were ratified by plebiscite, as the hard-line Bonapartist Fialin de Persigny had advised him.[3] Instead, he not only had taken the oath but also had voluntarily added a ringing declaration of allegiance to the Republic. Not all doubts were assuaged, however. Upon leaving the tribune, Louis-Napoleon approached General Cavaignac, a conservative republican and his closest rival in the presidential election. The new president held out his hand. Accounts vary as to whether Cavaignac actually refused to shake Louis-Napoleon's hand or just hesitated enough to make his disapproval clear.[4] Either way, the ceremony clearly ended on a sour—but prophetic—note.

The oath of office was no minor formality. In it, the republicans, hatchets buried for once, had attempted to give the Republic—the sovereign people—the kind of central symbolic place the king had enjoyed previously. Under the monarchy, every public functionary had been required to take an oath of allegiance to the king. The Constitution of the Republic, however, abolished such oaths for all public servants, with the crucial exception of the president. And the president, of course, did not pledge fidelity to an individual but to "the one and indivisible democratic Republic." Moreover, it is significant that he took the oath before the National Assembly. Symbolically, then, the oath placed the president in a markedly inferior position to both the Republic and the Assembly. He did not stand as a source of power in his own right but drew his power from the people, as represented by the National Assembly.

The president's next major public appearance, however, struck a very different note from the oath-taking ceremony. Just four days after the oath, the president reviewed the troops of the Paris garrison dressed in the uniform of a general in the National Guard.[5] Since Louis-Napoleon had never held rank in the French National Guard, and since the Constitution of the Second Republic expressly prohibited him from commanding troops, this was both an assumption of unearned military rank and a violation of the Constitution.[6] To radical republicans, the review clearly indicated that Louis-Napoleon was plotting a military restoration of the Empire, an idea that quickly became a staple of the radical press. In Louis-Napoleon's favor, it should be noted that National Guardsmen were not line soldiers but middle-class volunteers more closely associated with the Second Republic than with the Empire. But a Bonaparte wearing a military uniform and reviewing troops was bound to have imperial overtones, no matter what branch of the service was represented.

Moreover, Louis-Napoleon went out of his way during the review to underscore his ancestry. In an incident that became the subject of a number of popular engravings, Louis-Napoleon shook hands with General Petit, an officer who had served under his uncle. "General," he is supposed to have said, "my uncle shook your hand at his last review; I am happy to be able to shake it at my first." Since Napoleon I's final review held a special place in the imperial memory, this well-publicized incident linked Louis-Napoleon to his uncle in a particularly evocative way and made him seem to be taking up the imperial cause.

Political divisions between the radical *démoc-socs* and the conservative "party of order" also came into play during this period, especially in connection with establishing a new annual holiday for the Republic. The radicals favored fixing the celebration on 24 February, a date that emphasized the revolutionary origins of the new regime, and proposed the requisite legislation in the National Assembly on 14 February. They wanted an immediate vote, but Minister of the Interior Léon Faucher requested a day's delay to allow the government to propose legislation on the subject.[7]

In the Assembly the next day, Faucher read a proposal for establishing a celebration on 24 February, the date favored by the radicals. Rather than a day full of rejoicing, however, he proposed that the holiday be "consecrated with a funerary service celebrated in all the communes of France in memory of the citizens who died for the Republic." This approach was the brainchild of Charles Blanc, minister of fine arts. In a letter to Faucher, Blanc argued that the festivals of the Republic needed to be founded on something different in both theory and practice from monarchical spectacle. "The anniversary of 24 February 1848 cannot be celebrated . . . with the forms and extravagances of the monarchy," Blanc wrote to Faucher. "It is necessary that the festivals of the Republic, through their seriousness, make citizens remember the new rights conferred on them by the Revolution."[8] Faucher's proposal, however, also provided for a less sober day of "public rejoicing." But that celebration was reserved for 4 May, the date of the official proclamation of the Republic by the duly elected Constituent Assembly. In essence, then, the government's proposal viewed the February Revolution as worthy of commemoration but insufficient for the foundation of a new regime. It adroitly used the radical republican focus on sacrifice to separate the radicals themselves from the Republic.

Though the government defended its proposal as an appropriate and serious tribute to the Revolution of February, it did not manage to fool the radicals, who were infuriated. "It is not with a day of glorious commemoration, but with a day of mourning that you want to consecrate the anniversary of the victory of the people," responded Ferdinand Flocon, a prominent *démoc-soc.* "You can efface the days of February from your official calendar, but you will never efface them from the recognition of the people or from the memory of France."[9] At issue here, then, were two different visions of the foundation of the Republic: a radical vision that gave prominence to the revolutionary moment of February and a conservative one that saw the Republic as stemming from the legal proclamation of a representative body.

As it finally emerged from the debate, the law was a compromise that declared both 24 February and 4 May "jours feriés et fêtes nationales." But the two holidays were not really equal, since the government proceeded to make the first anniversary of 24 February into the memorial it had originally proposed. For the main service, the archbishop of Paris held mass in the Church of the Madeleine, the interior of which had been draped in black and provided with a cenotaph, around which sat the widows and orphans of those killed in the revolt. Both the president and the members of the Assembly attended, as did the other important bodies of civil servants. After the absolution, a *Te Deum* was sung, and at that point the black mourning decorations were removed from both the Madeleine and the July Column, beneath which the dead of 1848 had been buried alongside the dead of 1830.[10] After the ceremony, the public was allowed to enter the church and file past the cenotaph. Many also visited the Place de la Bastille to leave wreaths at the base of the July Column or attended one of the less spectacular funerary services that had been decreed for all the parishes of France.

A little over two months later, the approach of the anniversary of the fourth of May found the government preparing a more festive but still restrained celebration. It had secured a 200,000-franc credit after a stormy session in the legislature, in which the radicals had unsuccessfully demanded that the celebration include a declaration of amnesty for all of those convicted after the June Days. A large part of the money went into decorating the Place de la Concorde, for which architect Théodore Charpentier designed an elaborate structure at the base of the obelisk (see figure 1.1). Classically garbed goddesses of Liberty, Equality, and Fraternity, each

Figure 1.1. The decoration of the Place de la Concorde, 4 May 1849, from *L'Illustration,* 5 May 1849. (Doe Library, University of California, Berkeley)

some fifteen feet tall, adorned three sides of the structure. On the fourth side, Peace and Religion flanked a staircase leading to a platform on which stood an altar.

At ten o'clock the rumble of cannon fire from the Hôtel des Invalides announced the departure of the members of the National Assembly, who walked in procession to the Place de la Concorde and took places around the obelisk. Following the Assembly onto the Place were the ministers of the government and a group of over 800 ecclesiastics who marched from the Madeleine. Louis-Napoleon, accompanied by his war minister and General Changarnier, arrived last and took a place at the foot of the altar next to Boulay de la Meurthe, vice president of the Republic, and Marrast. A hundred and one cannon shots heralded a rousing *Te Deum*, sung by the choir of the Conservatory of Music from the platform. Then came the orison, the thanksgiving, and the thrice-repeated *Domine salvum fac Rempublicam*, the traditional prayer for the reigning sovereign, now with "Rempublicam" replacing the name of the king.[11] All in all, it seemed a strongly republican show.

After the officials were finished, the Place de la Concorde was opened to the public. That evening the whole area from the Madeleine to the Assembly and the entire Champs-Elysées were brilliantly illuminated. Louis-Napoleon attended a banquet at the Hôtel-de-Ville, an ostensibly republican affair with republicans, republican symbols, and republican toasts abounding. But even all of this was not enough to efface the memory of the monarchy. According to one municipal official, "Following the example of the kings, who were considered as if in their own palace and masters of the house when they came to the Hôtel-de-Ville, the president of the Republic was placed in the middle of the table, in front of the grand fireplace that one saw to the left of the entrance and in front of the apartments reserved, in similar circumstances, for the sovereigns."[12] Ceremonial forms derived from the monarchy and clearly remembered as such, then, were being used to honor the new president even at the first celebration of the birthday of the Republic.

This royal carryover can be seen in several different ways. On one level, it was merely a function of political jockeying for power. It was natural for the city to flatter Louis-Napoleon, the president of the Republic, and what was more flattering than putting him in the place of the king? Yet the question also cut much deeper. The conservative republicans of 1849 were committed to an authoritarian republic (if there was to be a republic at all), and their only models for the representation of that authority came from the monarchy.

One of the first to realize the seriousness of this problem was the Russian intellectual Alexander Herzen. Visiting France in 1849, Herzen argued that the monarchy had been based on the representation of a "sacred authority" that separated the government from the people:

> Both solemnity and splendor *[éclat]* are indispensable to a monarchy; the majestic representation and royal purple are as necessary to the monarch as the robe is to the priest. Monarchic authority must announce itself at every step, must always be visible; it must constantly remind the individual that he is insignificant in comparison with it, that he is a *subject* and obliged to sacrifice the best part of himself and above all to submit in everything.[13]

Herzen found that the Republic "has emancipated the state from the Orleanist dynasty, but it has not freed the individual from the state; on the contrary, it has left the individual weak and powerless before the royal purple-cloaked specter of representation."[14] Herzen realized that the politicians of 1849 might have been willing to do without the monarchy, but they were not willing to do without authority. "The party of order," as a modern historian put it, "was not only *in* power, it was also very much the party *of* power."[15] The problem was how to represent that power. Unwilling to rethink the representation of political power, as the French Revolutionaries had, the conservative republicans fell back on many of the forms and manners used by the monarchy. In many cases they simply substituted the symbols of the Republic for those of the monarchy. The same prayer used for the king in public ceremonies was now used for the Republic, for example, and new public buildings were now decorated with the letters "RF," just as the monarch's initials had traditionally been placed on the public buildings erected during his reign.

The symbolic changes that accompanied the shift from monarchy to republic, then, were surprisingly meager and probably too minimal to create in the populace a conception of itself as the essential sovereign entity in the state. Despite the experience of several revolutions, the French at mid-century were not yet such a people, and the narrow measures of the conservative republicans were unlikely to foster the kind of fundamental reconceptualization necessary to make them one. Given a long enough period of time, the Second Republic might still have managed to instill republican democracy in French consciousness, if only by dint of long familiarity. But time, of course, was something the Republic lacked.

Between the summer of 1849 and the summer of 1850, Louis-Napoleon and the conservative republicans frequently found themselves working together against their mutual opponents: the radicals. From the perspective of political spectacle, the principal result of the repression was to further handicap the radical leaders, the president's only real rivals for the affection of the masses.

The repression began in earnest with the crushing of the last large *démoc-soc* manifestation on 13 June, 1849. The radicals, under the leadership of Alexandre Ledru-Rollin, had opposed the government's Italian policy and called for a demonstration in the streets of Paris. But the government responded by sending out troops to rout the demonstrators and then passing a series of restrictive laws. The aftermath of the demonstration saw radical leaders forced into exile, left-wing newspapers and cafés closed down, and twenty-one representatives removed from office.[16]

The repression specifically targeted public manifestations of support for the radicals. The government moved against republican banquets and songs and placed firmer controls on local festivals in what one historian has called a "systematic closing of opportunities for public political expression."[17] By the spring/summer of 1850, the repression extended to much that had previously been considered essential to the Republic. In March, for example, the Assembly passed the Falloux Law, giving the Church enormous power over education, that is, the training of future voters. Two months later, it placed new hurdles in the way of smaller newspapers by increasing the stamp tax and required publication deposit. Worse, it passed the law of 31 May, which struck at the very principle of universal suffrage by imposing technical voting qualifications that disenfranchised almost a third of the electorate. Many Bonapartists, however, knowing well that the source of their own strength lay with the masses, refused to participate in this particular piece of legislation.[18]

Along with the repression went the demonization and marginalization of the left. Bonapartists concurrently played up the socialist menace to society and minimized its following among the French people as a whole, the vast majority of whom were supposed to support Louis-Napoleon. "The socialists constitute an imperceptible minority in the face of a visible majority," said a Bonapartist newspaper, but they nonetheless wanted to "eradicate society," something they could only do "by surprise, by cutting society's throat while it slept."[19] Louis-Napoleon himself was adept at portraying the radical republicans as demagogues and rabble-rousers, rabid revolutionary socialists without support among the populace. In his proclamation concerning the 13 June rally, for example, he characterized the demonstrators as merely "a few agitators who still dare to raise the standard of revolt against a legitimate government because it is the product of universal suffrage."[20]

The president's descriptions of himself contrasted sharply with his presentation of the left. During a mid-July visit to the fortress at Ham, where he had been confined after his 1840 attempt to overthrow the state, he crowed that he had been "elected by all France" and was "the legitimate head of this great nation."[21] In a marked shift from his speeches in the first half year of his presidency, he now rarely mentioned the Republic. "There is no one who is not struck," wrote a republican newspaper apropos of the president's summer trips, "by the strange affectation with which the president avoids pronouncing even once the word Republic."[22] In contrast to February, then, when he had said that *the Republic* should provide a "neutral ground" for all parties to work for the greatness of France, he now described *himself* as "legitimate," the "recognized head of the great nation," and as "uniting under the same flag all men devoted to the country."[23]

This focus on Louis-Napoleon as the representative of the entire nation was underscored by the increasingly large crowds that turned out at his public appearances. According to a sympathetic newspaper, he drew 30,000 to Ham in July and 150,000 to Le Havre in August.[24] At the sight of the president, these masses supposedly cheered him wildly and yelled out "Vive Louis-Napoléon!" and "Vive le Président!" Bonapartist press accounts made these crowds into proof of Louis-Napoleon's ongoing popular mandate. After the defeat of the 13 June rally, for example, when the president took a turn on the boulevards, *Le Dix Décembre*, a particularly ardent Bonapartist newspaper, wrote:

> The popular enthusiasm reveals itself to us in all its magnificence. . . . [Louis-Napoleon] is carried along in the acclamations of the people and of the army as if in a triumphal whirlwind. From the boulevard, from the windows, from the adjacent streets, a long cry of love and faith rolls and continues; the hot sun of June seems to crown with a new halo the Elected One *[l'Elu]* of six million Frenchmen, a man who wants to be, who must be, the savior of this nation of 36 million souls.[25]

Reports such as this helped Louis-Napoleon make the cheering masses a stand-in for the country as a whole. His crowds seemed to give material substance to the abstraction of an entire people, a nation, unified behind him. With Louis-Napoleon, then, the crowd was, to use George Mosse's phrase, "transformed . . . into a coherent political force."[26]

The press played a central role in this transformation by providing a means for Louis-Napoleon's appearances to reach not just the hundreds or thousands of French people who actually saw him but also the millions who had access to newspapers. In order to ensure adequate and sympathetic press coverage for his events, Louis-Napoleon both subsidized Bonapartist papers, such as *Le Dix Décembre*, and carefully cultivated his relations with the larger-circulation independent publications, many of which (*Le Constitutionnel*, *La Patrie*, and *Le Pays*, for example) openly supported him. Louis-Napoleon provided journalists with entry tickets for celebrations and paid their way on official trips. As the Maréchal de Castellane noted of the presidential voyage in August 1849, "Journalists—some of the papers have sent three of them—have left with the convoy. All their expenses are paid; not only does the train carry them for nothing, but they have cards for lodging, lunch, dinner, etc. Clearly we will have plenty of accounts of the trip." [27]

Nor was it only the tame press that provided these accounts. Due to the seeming importance of many of Louis-Napoleon's appearances, even relatively hostile newspapers often had to cover them. Thus, despite the fact that Paulin, the editor of *L'Illustration*, the most important illustrated journal of the period, was no Bonapartist, he included illustrations of most of the ceremonies. According to Jean-Noël Marchandiau, author of a recent history of *L'Illustration*, Paulin attempted to show his disapproval by depicting Louis-Napoleon as a very small part of a much larger scene. [28] But only an extraordinarily perceptive reader could have read disapproval into the lavish, full-page illustrations Paulin often included, many of them portraying Louis-Napoleon in a very flattering light; with enemies like Paulin, Louis-Napoleon hardly needed friends.

A few newspapers, however, did openly contradict the Bonapartist accounts of Louis-Napoleon's receptions. When the president visited Le Havre in August 1849, for example, the Bonapartist papers emphasized the huge crowd and the warmth of the reception: "Shouts of 'Vive Napoléon!' rang out from every side," reported the *Moniteur*. [29] In complete contrast, the opposition papers reported that the president's reception was cold and that prorepublican calls by far dominated all the rest. [30] Humor was another tool in this effort to undermine the Bonapartist barrage. Accounts in the republican press often stressed the comical side of the celebrations—inept National Guardsmen reviewed by the president, bad food, and so forth. [31] Satirical illustrations, especially those in the periodical *Charivari*, also attempted to counterbalance the impressions of presidential popularity and importance. These sources generally portrayed the crowds as either curious but apathetic or supportive of the Republic, and they usually interpreted any enthusiasm for Louis-Napoleon as the product of threats, intimidation, or bribery.

The radicals placed direct responsibility for this manufacturing of Bonapartist enthusiasm at the doorstep of the Société du Dix Décembre, a group named for the date of the 1848 presidential election that maintained nominally charitable status to avoid the ban on political meetings. Founded in the fall of 1849, this organization soon took on immense proportions in the eyes of Louis-Napoleon's opponents.[32] According to *La Presse*, by some accounts the organization numbered 60,000, who were "enlisted, provided with arms, and ready to act on the signal of their leaders."[33] These attacks took bitingly comical form in a series of lithographs by Honoré Daumier published in *Charivari* in the summer and fall of 1850. Daumier portrayed members as ruffians carrying out their "philanthropic duties" by beating up those who refused to shout "Vive l'Empereur!" or making a new member take an oath to clobber any Parisians who did not shout it. In another, Ratapoil, Daumier's personification of the Bonapartist menace, leads his disreputable "general staff" in the same cry at a military review (figure 1.2).

The Bonapartists, however, maintained that the Société du Dix Décembre was merely a private philanthropic organization.[34] The truth about the society is elusive, but given the name of the organization and the many high officials associated with it, one suspects that the republicans were

Figure 1.2. Honoré Daumier's view of one of Louis-Napoleon's military reviews from *Charivari*, 1 July 1850. (Bibliothèque Nationale, Paris)

closer to the mark than the Bonapartists. Clearly the president did not maintain a private army 60,000 strong, much less travel about the countryside with such a group. But cheerleading was not unknown at such affairs, and some squelching of dissident voices clearly did take place. According to the republican press, for example, upon the president's return to Paris in September 1850, members of the Société du Dix Décembre shouting Bonapartist slogans beat up republicans who tried to shout "Vive la République!"[35] Although the initial Bonapartist press reports recorded only "unanimous acclamations" in support of the president, later reports indicated that something had taken place, though in their version the society was still not implicated.[36] The Société du Dix Décembre, then, seems to have been primarily a Bonapartist political club, one of the functions of which was to organize public support for the president.[37]

Local officials also sometimes attempted to counteract the effects of the presidential spectacles. These officials organized the receptions and other activities on Louis-Napoleon's trips outside of Paris, and most seemed to compete with each other in flattering the president. "All that they used to do for a visiting monarch," commented *Le National*, "they do for him."[38] Sometimes, however, officials committed to the Republic would attempt, more or less subtly, to subvert the visit. In August 1849, for example, Louis-Napoleon inaugurated both a new railroad line and a hospital at Angers. The republican prefect, however, attempted to undercut Louis-Napoleon's ovation by leading the president on a long trek outside of the city to the hospital inauguration and by giving a distinctly republican address at a rather lackluster celebratory dinner. The prefect was removed from his post soon after Louis-Napoleon returned to Paris.[39]

More modestly situated French people also attempted to destroy the impression of a crowd/nation unified behind the president at his every appearance. A republican locksmith from the Eure, for example, cast Louis-Napoleon's troop reviews in a very different light from the official version when he claimed that at one review the president had told the soldiers to sharpen their bayonets and sabers "in order to make more sausage meat." He was fined and sentenced to two months in prison.[40] A slightly less dangerous way to challenge the president was to shout something besides "Vive le Président!" or "Vive Louis-Napoléon!" The cry, "Vive la République démocratique et sociale!" was a favorite, but by mid-1850 it was considered a "seditious cry" and could bring a prison sentence.[41] A simple "Vive la République!" worked better. By standing in opposition to the personal cheers for Louis-Napoleon, this cheer for the Republic clearly voiced support for the left. Yet since it voiced support for the current form of government and did not call for radical change, it was hard to repress.

The repression cast a pall on the celebration of the second anniversary of the February Revolution in 1850. The official circular from the minister of the interior to the prefects requesting them to make plans for the celebration made clear that nothing more than minimal conformity with the law was required. "The law consecrates the anniversary of 24 February," it read. "We cannot better celebrate it than by asking the Church to pray for the citizens who died in the struggle and to call the blessings of heaven on the destiny of France."[42] In Paris, most of the municipal authorities attended the official mass in Notre-Dame, but the national authorities were conspicuous only by their almost complete absence. Fewer than ten representatives, among them Jules Favre, showed up for the ceremony.[43]

Following the advice of their leaders,[44] republicans remained calm during the celebration. In Paris, however, they did at least show their support for the Republic by leaving wreaths beneath the July Column on the Place de la Bastille. A riot almost broke out the next morning when it was discovered that the police had removed all of the wreaths during the night. In the face of popular indignation, the police backed down. Claiming that the removal had been the work of one misinformed officer, they quickly moved to replace the wreaths.[45] In the provinces, things were sometimes even worse for the republicans. Most mayors in the Gironde, for example, seem to have forbidden all unofficial banquets and public meetings for the day.[46] All in all, it was clear that the attitude of the public authorities was now firmly against the February anniversary and all that it represented.[47]

If the February celebration demonstrated growing hostility toward the left, the May celebration showed the progressive generalization of that hostility to include the very idea of the Republic and a hint of what might replace it. Although grander in style, the tenor of the celebration was markedly less republican than it had been the year before. Gone, for example, were the curvaceous statues of Liberty, Equality, and Fraternity. Instead, the decor commemorated the 1798 Egyptian adventure of the first Napoleon. Huge statues of pharaohs and sphinxes were erected around the obelisk (see figure 1.3) and accompanied by the words, "Bonaparte, général en chef de l'expédition," along with the names of the principal battles of the campaign. Triumphal arches dedicated to science, agriculture, fine arts, and industry also decorated the Place de la Concorde, as did uplifting allegorical statues of subjects such as Commerce, Painting, and Strength. Finally, a series of small plaques bearing the names of some of the liberal monarchists associated with the Revolution of 1789 were put up, though this was only mentioned in the left-wing papers.[48] By 1850, then, the Republic had almost been banished from its own party.

A cartoon in the satirical magazine *Charivari* gives a sense of what

Figure 1.3. The decoration of the Place de la Concorde, 4 May 1850, from *L'Illustration*, 4 May 1850. (Doe Library, University of California, Berkeley)

seemed to be happening to the festival of the Republic. Brought before a police commissioner and accused of having yelled, "Vive la République!," a bewildered worker declares:

—It's true, commissioner, thinkin' it was the festival of the Republic, I said to myself, I'm gonna yell *Vive la République!*

—With all the consequences?

—No, no! I yelled without consequences. . . . I didn't know it was gonna land me in the lockup!. . . Next time I promise I won't yell anything anymore. . . . I won't even yell long live my wife the second it bothers the government.[49]

Beginning in the summer of 1850, Louis-Napoleon turned his attention to finding a way around the constitutional requirement that he step down as president in 1852. He initially tried to persuade the Assembly to revise the Constitution to enable him to run for a second term of office, claiming that the vast majority of Frenchmen favored such a change. When that failed, he began to consider less legal methods of extending his term of office. Public celebrations played an important part in these efforts. The crowds provided evidence of popular support for revision, and it was a military review that triggered the "Changarnier Affair," which allowed him to place one of his own men at the head of the Paris garrison, a necessary first step toward the coup d'état.

Louis-Napoleon's public appearances took on an ever more populist tone during these months. While inaugurating a railway line, he declared that his "most sincere and devoted friends are not in the palaces but the thatched huts" and said that he was working to "ameliorate the lives of workers."[50] He also went beyond words and acted out this supposed solicitude for the unfortunate through staged acts of generosity to workers when visiting factories and by visiting sickbeds at hospitals. Even his military dinners pointedly included noncommissioned as well as commissioned officers. The president's most concerted efforts to play to the masses, however, occurred during two extended provincial excursions.

The first trip, through southern and eastern France, targeted radical republican strongholds. Bringing out supportive crowds in restive cities like Reims and Lyons assured the middle classes that Louis-Napoleon was a credible alternative to socialism—that he could guarantee social tranquillity by wooing the working class away from the radicals. Thus, the accounts of the trip in the Bonapartist press constantly underscored the president's popularity among workers by stressing the large number of *blouses* in the crowds cheering the president and by stressing his popularity in supposedly hostile areas such as Trévoux, which, according to the official government newspaper, was previously "noted as being socialist."[51] The trip, a Bonapartist newspaper smugly reported, was "a great review of public opinion, of "true, natural public opinion" taken at the source."[52]

Whatever the rhetoric, however, Bonapartist officials had to work hard to make this true, "natural public opinion" say what they thought it should say. Prefects, for example, might arrest a few known dissidents and anyone traveling without a passport. But they could not arrest everyone in any given city who might disrupt the spectacle. Thus, Interior Minister Baroche instructed prefects to bring in large numbers of peasants. "The best means of neutralizing the bad influence that [the workers' associations] exercise," Baroche wrote to the prefect of the Marne, was to bring into the cities "as many people from rural areas as you can."[53] Even here, not just anyone was allowed to come. Local officials could often eliminate people of "bad intentions" simply by refusing to give them railway passes.[54] Visits to cities of questionable politics were also sometimes kept very short, as at Reims, where the president spent only two hours.

Even with all of these precautions, there were still problems. At Dijon, Lyons, Colmar, and elsewhere, dissident voices yelled out republican slogans. And at a public ball in Besançon, the president encountered a major disturbance and General Castellane drew his sword to protect the president before the police arrived to calm things down. The results, according to *Le Moniteur officiel*, "could have been disastrous." The Bonapartist papers either neglected to mention or glossed over most of these incidents. The *Moniteur*, for example, turned the Besançon manifestation to Louis-Napoleon's advantage by playing up the dangerousness of foreign agitators. It blamed the trouble on that "race of furious communists," the several thousand Swiss watchmakers residing at Besançon, and maintained that "the mass of the population of the city of Besançon is excellent; its opinions are quiet and it loves order."[55]

In addition to stressing Louis-Napoleon's popularity among the workers, the voyages played up his ties to the First Emperor. He wore a general's uniform, reviewed troops, decorated former imperial soldiers, paid homage to Rude's famous statue of Napoleon rising from the dead, and chose 15 August, birthday of the Great Emperor, to enter Lyons in uniform, mounted on a prancing white charger. As his speeches made clear, however, the Napoleon I he was trying to evoke was not the haughty and authoritarian emperor but the savior of the principles of 1789, the "faithful champion of the rights of all peoples."[56] Louis-Napoleon adroitly linked this liberal image of his uncle to his own cause. "I am not," he said in Lyons, "the representative of a party, but the representative of the two great national manifestations which, in 1804 as in 1848, wanted to save through order the great principles of the French Revolution. Proud of my origin and of my flag, I will remain faithful to them; I will give myself entirely to the country, whatever it demands of me, abnegation or perseverance."[57] This was Bonapartist rhetoric at its best. The president presented himself as in favor of both order and the principles of the revolution, as both the national choice and the imperial heir. Most important, he proclaimed himself above the fray of party rivalries because he represented the "people": "If reprehensible ambitions were to be rekindled and threaten to compromise the tranquillity of France, I would be able to reduce them to powerlessness by once again appealing to the sovereignty of the people, for no one has a better right to call himself its [the people's] representative than I do."[58]

By mid-1850, then, Louis-Napoleon had made public appearances into a formidable political weapon. With the left weakened by repressive laws and the right unable to field a popular alternative, the president dominated public attention, even though he was still far from controlling the press and had relatively few politicians committed to his cause. He had forged out of his public appearances a vehicle not only for expressing his opinions but also for underscoring his seemingly overwhelming popularity. He had made the state foot the bill by getting the Assembly to vote him 250,000 francs a month to cover his display expenses.[59] Not everyone, however, was ready to concede defeat. What became known as the "Changarnier Affair" initially began as an attempt by General Changarnier, the legitimist commander-in-chief of the army in Paris, to curtail the president's political use of military reviews.

In a series of reviews in September and October 1850, Louis-Napoleon made a point of supplying the troops with postreview refreshments, including wine, champagne, and cigars.[60] The president's critics denounced these luxuries as an attempt to seduce the army to the cause of overthrowing the Republic in favor of a restored Empire, but the real problem was that the troops seemed to respond to Louis-Napoleon's ministrations. At each review, a number of soldiers cried out, "Vive Napoléon!," "Vive le Président!," and even "Vive l'Empereur!," as they passed the reviewing stand. At the final review on 10 October on the plain of Satory near Versailles, a number of cavalry regiments cried out, "Vive l'Empereur!," with great enthusiasm, while others, following the orders of General Neumayer, Changarnier's second-in-command, remained silent. Afterward, General Hautpoul, Louis-Napoleon's minister of war, was pointedly transferred to

Rennes. Changarnier reacted to this slap in the face by issuing an order of the day recalling military regulations prohibiting the shouting of slogans while bearing arms. It was a clear challenge to the president's authority.

Louis-Napoleon initially backed down before Changarnier's offensive. He made Hautpoul governor of Algeria and brought in a more popular replacement. In addition, his 12 November message to the legislature was a conciliatory declaration of his willingness to abide by the Constitution and the decision of the Assembly on its revision. Finally, he dissolved the Société du Dix Décembre after it was accused of plotting to assassinate Changarnier and André Marie Dupin, the president of the Assembly, even though the supposed plot was almost certainly a fabrication.[61]

Changarnier exulted in his apparent victory, even boasting to Prefect of Police Carlier that he would have Louis-Napoleon taken to the prison of Vincennes.[62] But his victory was short-lived. On 9 January 1851, Louis-Napoleon, tired of the cat-and-mouse game, pounced. He relieved Changarnier of his command, at the same time triggering a major political crisis. The conservative majority vehemently protested the president's action and voted to censure the government, which, in any case, had resigned. No matter; Louis-Napoleon simply appointed new ministers, undistinguished men who would meekly submit to his will. A majority in the Assembly voted against the new government, but the Assembly had no power to force the ministers to resign. What had begun, then, as an attempt to curb Louis-Napoleon's manipulation of military reviews had ended with a presidential triumph over one of the few men capable of standing in the way of a coup d'état.

Meanwhile, the "de-republicanization" of the republican anniversaries continued apace. Twenty-four February 1851 was still officially a "fête nationale," but the government paid it scant attention. Only at the Place de la Bastille was the day celebrated as anything like a commemoration of the February Days. There, as in previous years, thousands of workers gathered to give speeches and leave wreaths of everlasting red flowers at the foot of the July Column.[63]

In contrast to its studied neglect of 24 February, the government made the 4 May celebration into a much more elaborate show, albeit an equally unrepublican one. Sixteen statues of great Frenchmen, along with a giant female figure of "France distributing laurels" by Diebolt, decorated the Champs-Elysées; an enormous Neptune graced the Pont de la Concorde; and decorations, pavilions, illuminations, concerts, and other amusements occupied the various public spaces of Paris. Unfortunately, as *L'Illustration* remarked, "reminders and images [of the Republic] are not anywhere to be seen."[64] Indeed, other than a modest "Liberté, Egalité, Fraternité" inscribed on the base of the pedestal of Diebolt's France, republican symbols were almost entirely missing. With the exception of Marshal Ney, the statues depicted prerevolutionary heroes such as Richelieu, Joan of Arc, and Condé. Diebolt's France, as Maurice Agulhon has noted, was crowned with laurel leaves rather than with a Phrygian cap.[65] And the fireworks from the Chaillot Hill that evening depicted the siege of Rome, that is, the fall of the Roman Republic at the hands of the French troops. At any rate, rain poured down the entire day, dissolving the plaster statues, extinguishing the illuminations, and making everyone miserable except that most devoted of Bonapartists, Victor-Fialin de Persigny, who gleefully regarded the ruin of the festival as an omen of what was to come for the Republic.[66]

During the first half of 1851, Louis-Napoleon did not let the campaign for revision flag, though it is doubtful that he could have believed any longer that the Assembly would pass such a measure. True, a majority of conservatives favored revision—some because they saw it as the only way of avoiding a coup d'état, others because they saw it as a way of averting a possible victory of the left in the presidential election. But revision required a three-quarters majority, and more than a quarter of the Assembly was clearly hostile to the president.

Louis-Napoleon, however, had a number of good reasons for continuing to work for revision. The campaign made him far more the center of attention than would lame duck status and thus allowed him to publicly pave the way for a coup d'état. It also would later allow him to say that he had exhausted the legal means of continuing in power before turning to illegal ones. Finally, by getting as much support as possible for revision, he could make it appear that his opponents were a tiny minority standing in the way of the national will. Thus, after revision failed by a vote of 446 for and 278 against, Bonapartists argued that only 97 men the number needed to reach a three-quarters majority for the measure had thwarted the will of the entire nation.

So Louis-Napoleon once again began traveling around the country, beating his own drum and dropping hints that he might not step down as constitutionally required. Inaugurating a statue of Jeanne Hachette, a fifteenth-century heroine who had saved Beauvais from the Burgundians, he linked her spirit with that of his uncle and drew the grave lesson that "in extreme danger Providence often makes one individual the instrument of the safety of all." Given the fears and uncertainties of 1851, harping on providential saviors could only have one meaning: there was another in the making.

After the definitive failure of revision in late July, Louis-Napoleon began actively planning the more drastic measures he had been hinting at. For the most part this entailed ensuring that the right men were in the right positions, writing declarations, and deciding what to do in case of resistance. Celebrations also played a role by helping to prepare public opinion for the big event. When Louis-Napoleon ceremonially set the first stone of Paris's new central food market, Les Halles, for example, he told the largely working-class crowd that "with the support of the good citizens and the protection of heaven, we will be allowed to erect in France the foundations on which to raise a social edifice solid enough to provide shelter against the violence and capriciousness of human passions." [67]

These were hardly, as one historian has noted, the words of a man who believed his days in office to be drawing to a close. [68] Indeed, this symbolic statement of concern for the Parisian populace came just two days before the date originally scheduled for the coup d'état, and Charles Merruau, general secretary of the Hôtel-de-Ville, did not think it a coincidence. Louis-Napoleon, Merruau believed, was convinced that a gesture of solicitude would help to keep the working classes of Paris on his side after the coup d'état. [69]

As it turned out, the coup was delayed until December, and Louis-Napoleon had time for two more major public appearances as president of the Second Republic, appearances at which he stressed the threats to national tranquillity from the *démoc-socs* on the one hand and the monarchists on the other. "A vast demagogic conspiracy is being organized in France and in Europe," he warned in his annual message to the Assembly at the beginning of November. [70] And just a week prior to the coup, at an awards ceremony for the French exhibitors who had received medals at the Great Exhibition of 1851, he complained that the Republic was "constantly troubled by demagogic ideas on the one side and monarchical hallucinations on the other!" [71] Such problems seemed to call for drastic measures.

Although celebrations played a role in preparing for it, very little about the actual coup d'état was festive. On the morning of 1851 December 2, Parisians awoke to find posted proclamations announcing the dissolution of the legislature, the restoration of universal suffrage, and the preparation of a new Constitution to be ratified by plebiscite. Troops occupied strategic locations, and a number of important members of the Assembly were arrested.

At about ten in the morning, Louis-Napoleon decided to take a tour on the boulevards, perhaps hoping to inspire one of those "long cries of love" from the population. If so, he must have been very disappointed. He was greeted with cries of "Long live the Republic," and according to some accounts, shots were fired. The triumphal march ended with a hasty retreat to the Elysée Palace, from which Louis-Napoleon did not venture for several days.

The Second Republic failed, at least in part, because it did not manage to create a set of symbols and institutions that would be above political disagreement. Democracy, as Claude Lefort has noted, requires "an institutionalization of conflict. The locus of power [in a democracy] is an empty place, it cannot be occupied—it is such that no individual and no group can be consubstantial with it—and it cannot be represented." [72] Symptomatic of the Second Republic's failure in this respect was its inability to create republican forms of festivity that were viable alternatives to the monarchical forms that gave central symbolic place to one man. An abrupt transition from monarchy—even relaxed constitutional monarchy—to democracy is never easy. When people are accustomed to seeing the monarch as the source of all power, replacing that monarch with an "empty place" can be a wrenching and difficult process.

This problem was compounded in 1848 by the deep divisions between radical and conservative republicans. Indeed, republicans were so divided that they did not even succeed in establishing a yearly holiday but had to found two, one for the right, the other for the left. Thus, what should have been a unifying national ritual was itself representative of the basic underlying differences that continued to split the nation. Against this backdrop of division, Louis-Napoleon presented himself as above party political strife. Moving into the central symbolic place heretofore accorded the monarch and emptying the yearly holidays of their republican content, he turned the celebrations of these years into a key tool for the subversion of the Republic.

TWO

The Decennial Republic

The *Fête Impériale* before the Empire

L ess than three weeks after the coup d'état, Louis-Napoleon asked the French electorate—once again enlarged to include all adult men—to allow him to draw up a new constitution, and a very large majority of 7.5 million voted in his favor. For the Bonapartists, the plebiscite was, as Prefect of Police Charlemagne-Emile de Maupas put it, "a veritable national festival."[1] The 7.5 million votes seemed to prove conclusively the reality of Louis-Napoleon's popularity—the same popularity they so frequently had seen manifested in the celebrations of the Republic. For Bonapartists, the divided nation of the Republic seemed to have found in Louis-Napoleon a means of coming together as a unified community.

The results of the plebiscite baffled even Louis-Napoleon's most savvy opponents. "How can we respond to 6 or 7 million votes?," wondered George Sand: "They were a bit extorted it is true. The vote without the right to choose, without the right to meet, to consult, or to be heard is a real dodge. But, after all, no one was forced to vote yes, and the great majority voted yes. One does not buy or intimidate 6 to 7 million men."[2] The plebiscite fell far short of modern standards for open and free democratic elections. Soldiers and sailors voted in open registers—a system clearly more conducive to intimidation than to independence—and some

34

outright cheating by government officials certainly took place in the counting process. Moreover, in the days prior to the plebiscite, the government curtailed almost all means of expressing opposition to voting "yes," while letting loose a barrage of Bonapartist propaganda describing the coup d'état as necessary to prevent socialist revolution.[3]

But it would be a mistake to see the plebiscite as entirely rigged—as the cynical con game of an unscrupulous and unpopular adventurer. In the first place, as Sand noted, the sheer numbers involved make such a scenario highly unlikely. Louis-Napoleon did not hold the reins of state firmly enough to have carried out truly massive fraud, and he had not held them long enough for Bonapartist propaganda to have so thoroughly effaced the memory of other political possibilities for so many people. Moreover, other indicators of Louis-Napoleon's popularity—prefects' reports, for example—do exist, while there is little evidence of widespread dissatisfaction with the results of the plebiscite.

Nonetheless, a truly free and open plebiscite would not have favored the president quite so lopsidedly. And anything other than a crushing victory would have given the lie to Louis-Napoleon's pretensions to represent the whole nation and would have made it much more difficult for him to effect sweeping change and ultimately to declare himself emperor. The mandate of modern democratic dictators such as Louis-Napoleon has to rest on more than obtaining a mere majority of the vote. An essential part of the legitimacy of such rulers is the claim to be above politics and petty party squabbles. They must be, as a sympathetic deputy once called Louis-Napoleon, "the image of the entire people."[4] And the plebiscite was one of Louis-Napoleon's most important pieces of evidence that he fit this bill. Although the government's efforts to manage the plebiscite may not have been necessary for a simple victory, they certainly increased the margin of that victory and thereby made Louis-Napoleon's claim to national representation credible, or at least more credible than it would have been without such efforts.

Given the monumental importance of the plebiscite to the regime, it was only to be expected that that event would provide an occasion for public celebrations reinforcing its message. Thus, shortly before Christmas, architects Viollet-le-Duc and Jean-Baptiste Lassus were assigned the task of decorating the cathedral of Notre-Dame in Paris for a major *Te Deum* celebration to take place on the first of January.[5] But while Paris was to have the most spectacular ceremony, the festivities were not to be limited solely to the capital. To celebrate the national savior, the Bonapartists had to have something approaching national participation. So a few days after Christmas, Louis-Napoleon wrote to all of the bishops of France requesting that *Te Deums* be sung in all of the country's cathedrals "in order to call the blessings of Heaven on France and on the great mission that has been confided to me by the French people."[6] Circulars to the prefects and to the bishops from Hippolyte Fortoul, minister of public instruction and religious sects, expanded this instruction by ordering that *Te Deums* be held in all French churches (i.e., not only the cathedrals). The entire nation, then, was to share in this ceremony, which would, as Fortoul's circular put it, "thank God, whose protective hand has so visibly extended itself over France."[7]

In Paris, Viollet-le-Duc and Lassus received their instructions directly from Louis-Napoleon's half-brother, the Duc de Morny, and they sent him a detailed description of their plans.[8] The architects' major problem was that they only had eight days to complete their work. They did not, however, lack funds. Ultimately, the decoration of Notre-Dame cost 125,000 francs, about two-thirds of the 190,000 francs allocated for the whole celebration.[9]

Thematically, the decoration of Notre-Dame mingled the national with the personal.[10] The architects hung the interior of the old cathedral with rich red velvet embroidered with gold "N"s, and they erected tribunes along both sides of the nave to provide extra seating for dignitaries and for the mayors of the *chef-lieux* of the departments, who had been invited as national delegates (see figure 2.1). From the upper part of the nave hung ninety flags, each bearing the name of a department, and below these were placed the coats of arms of the principal French cities. But the center of attention remained Louis-Napoleon. Beneath a large velvet canopy in the transept, a platform was erected for him with a prie-dieu and a "seat of honor" that the Austrian attaché prematurely but understandably dubbed a "throne."[11]

References to Louis-Napoleon and to the plebiscite also marked the exterior of the cathedral. Above the main entryway hung a large awning bearing the letters "L-N" for Louis-Napoleon. ("RF"s were entirely absent despite France's nominal republican status.) More "L-N"s and a large number of tricolored oriflammes were erected on poles on the plaza in front of the cathedral, and large painted representations of Charlemagne, Saint-Louis, Louis XIV, and Napoleon decorated the cathedral's two towers. Most strikingly, splashed across the front of the cathedral in large gilded letters just above the entry was the number 7,500,000—the number of "yes" votes in the plebiscite.

It was one of the coldest days of the year. Blocks of ice floated in the Seine, and a thick, wet fog hung in the streets. The chilly weather did not, however, deter a large crowd of intrepid spectators from turning out for the show. At ten o'clock, the Invalides cannon marked the beginning of the

Figure 2.1. Interior of Notre-Dame Cathedral for the *Te Deum* of 1 January 1852. (Bibliothèque Nationale, Paris)

celebration by slowly booming out seventy-five times—ten times for each million "yes" votes in the plebiscite. It had not yet finished at 11:30, when Louis-Napoleon, in the uniform of a National Guard general and accompanied by a number of high officials and a military escort, left the Elysée Palace to make his way to the cathedral. The archbishop of Paris met the president at the entrance to the cathedral and escorted him ceremonially to his place in the transept.[12]

As soon as Louis-Napoleon had taken his seat, 300 hundred singers and 200 hundred musicians executed a march composed by Jean-François Lesueur for the coronation of Napoleon I. After the march came the religious service and more rousing and historically resonant music, including more pieces from Napoleon I's coronation. The ceremony ended with a new variation of the traditional prayer for the monarch, one that aptly symbolized the ambiguous nature of the new regime. For now, instead of three *Domine salvum fac Rempublicams*, there was only one, and following it came a *Domine salvum fac Ludovicum Napoleonem*.[13]

At the close of the hour-long ceremony, Archbishop Sibour, once again following the cross and accompanied by his clergy, re-escorted Louis-Napoleon to the door of the cathedral. The president climbed back into his carriage and the official procession re-formed. But instead of returning to the Elysée Palace, where it had started, the procession now made its way to the Tuileries Palace, the traditional palace of the French monarchs, which would henceforth be the official residence of the president. If, as Louis Girard has remarked, "to occupy the royal palace in Paris is the sign of the monarch,"[14] Louis-Napoleon seemed already to have assumed his uncle's place. But it is significant that the royal Tuileries would only be Louis-Napoleon's *official* residence; for the time being, his *actual* residence continued to be the presidential Elysée.

Similar compromises marked many other aspects of the new regime. The new Constitution maintained the Republic in name but gave Louis-Napoleon far-reaching powers and a ten-year term of office—hence the term decennial republic often used for this period. It also required all public functionaries, judges, and military officers to swear both obedience to the Constitution *and* fidelity to the president.[15] In a like vein, the president's profile soon replaced the figure of the Republic on French coins, but the words "République française" were maintained. Louis-Napoleon—now often tellingly called the *Prince-Président*—was clearly moving toward restoring some form of monarchical government in France, but he was not yet burning all of his bridges.

A few months later, the government took a further step toward a new empire when it reestablished the figure of the imperial eagle on the flagstaffs of the army. That decision prompted a long and elaborate military ceremony in which Louis-Napoleon distributed new battle standards on staffs topped with gilt eagles to the various units of the army. The battle standard eagles, a chief symbol of the First Empire, had originally been distributed by Napoleon I on the Champ-de-Mars on 5 December 1804, just three days after the coronation. After that, distributions of battle standards became a standard ritual for new French rulers. Louis-Philippe, for example, had distributed standards topped with the symbol of his regime, the Gallic rooster,[16] and the Second Republic had distributed standards bearing the initials "RF" at the Feast of Fraternity in 1848.

Louis-Napoleon's government intended its distribution to be as public as possible. At the wish of the president himself, the space allotted to reserved tribunes was to be kept to a minimum in order to give the general public greater access to the event.[17] Helped by a compliant sun, the strategy seems to have been effective; although accounts differ as to the enthusiasm of the crowd, its impressive size is undisputed.[18] Spectators began gathering at about nine in the morning, those well connected enough to have tickets taking their assigned places and the others either renting space from private property owners in the nearby streets (a proposition sufficiently lucrative that one such owner supposedly removed his roof and rented out his attic)[19] or crowding together on the edge of the field. Shortly before eleven, the area began to fill up with troops—an enormous number of them—taking their places for the ceremony. Altogether, there were some 60,000 soldiers from 48 infantry battalions, 56 cavalry battalions, and assorted other military units, all decked out in their dress uniforms.

The religious display was almost as impressive. All of the clergy of Paris (some 1,000 ecclesiastics) had gathered in full canonical regalia at a church a short distance from the Champ-de-Mars. Just before eleven, they left the church in procession, carrying the Cross of the Chapter before them and singing the hymn *Veni Creator*. After reaching the Champ-de-Mars, the clerics took places on and around an elaborate canopied altar platform, decorated not only with religious symbols but also with Napoleonic eagles and "N"s. Steps led up on three sides to the top of the platform on which the altar table itself was located. As Archbishop Sibour mounted the steps just before noon, a twenty-one-gun salute announced the departure of Louis-Napoleon from the Elysée Palace.

On horseback and wearing his usual general's uniform, the president and his military escort made their way down the Champs-Elysées, across the Pont d'Iéna, and onto the Champ-de-Mars, where trumpets and another gun salute greeted them. The president reviewed the troops (an activity that consisted primarily of galloping up and down between the rows of soldiers) and then took his place on a temporary pavilion that had been decorated with reminders both of the plebiscite in the number 7,500,000 and the inscription "Vox Populi, Vox Dei" and of the Bonapartist dynasty in a large eagle above the president's seat. The colonels from the various army regiments then came forward and took places on both sides of the steps. Each of the colonels approached the president in turn and received from his hands a new regimental standard. Like the other ambiguous symbols of this uncertain period, the new standards bore the words "République française" and the initials of Louis-Napoleon. The famous gilt eagles topped the staffs.

After the standards were distributed, the president made a short speech praising the army as the protector of the nation and the First Empire as a period of national glory. Napoleon I's eagle, he said, was "the most striking illustration of the regeneration of the grandeur of France." It had disappeared during the period of France's "misfortunes" but was now restored "as the symbol of our independence, as the *souvenir* of an heroic epoch, and as the sign of the nobility of each regiment." After the address, the colonels descended from the presidential tribune and took new places next to the altar platform for a mass accompanied by music from the military bands and a booming cannon to mark the elevation of the host. Once mass was completed, Archbishop Sibour proceeded toward the edge of the altar, around which the flagbearers had gathered. He chanted a prayer and sprinkled holy water on each of the standards before returning to his seat. The colonels approached the altar and knelt before the archbishop, flags in hand. When they had taken their places, Sibour read a short address in Latin and gave the gathering a general blessing, after which the president descended from his tribune and mounted his horse. The president placed himself a short distance in front of the tribune, where the military units paraded past him before proceeding out through the gate to the Ecole Militaire.

The Distribution of the Eagles celebrated a seeming regeneration of the French nation under the guidance of a new, popularly elected Napoleon. France, the distribution implicitly declared, had recovered from its "misfortunes" and was once again a dynamic and confident world power. The great Champ-de-Mars, filled with tens of thousands of armed men receiving a symbol of France's military glory from a vigorous young leader, was a palpable demonstration of refound national greatness. In this respect, the Distribution of the Eagles assured all concerned that under Louis-Napoleon France had successfully traversed a period of social and political conflict and was once again the powerful nation of the First Empire.

The same brash assertion of solidarity with the First Empire marked the new regime's choice of annual holiday. As during the First Empire, that celebration was held on Napoleon I's birthday, 15 August—which also happened to be the date of the Assumption, one of the chief festivals of the Catholic Church. During the Restoration and July Monarchy, other celebrations replaced the 15 August event, but the day continued to be observed in secret by groups of Bonapartists who gathered for convivial dinners that often included songs and poems celebrating the First Emperor.[20] After Louis-Napoleon became president of the Second Republic, 15 August was observed with a mass at the Invalides chapel and by the leaving of wreaths at the Vendôme Column, but in 1849, committed Bonapartists were already asking for something much more lavish.[21]

The decree-law declaring 15 August an official holiday made the First Emperor a symbol of national unity. "Considering that the celebration of political anniversaries recalls the memory of civil discord," the law read, "and that it is our duty to choose from among the festivals the one whose consecration tends best to unite everyone in the common sentiment of national glory, in the future, the only one recognized and celebrated as a national festival *[fête nationale]* is the anniversary of 15 August."[22] The mid-nineteenth-century Bonapartists, then, attempted to elevate the birthday of Napoleon I above the stature of a "political anniversary," a term clearly meant for the republican holidays of 24 February and 5 May. They saw such holidays as divisive, while 15 August would "unite everyone in the common sentiment of national glory." In other words, 15 August was to be an annual reminder that what unified France as a nation in the nineteenth century was the glorious memory of the First Empire.

Although the new 15 August celebration was taken directly from the First Empire, its ideological underpinnings differed greatly from those of its model. While the original holiday simply followed Old Regime precedent in providing a festival glorifying the reigning sovereign, the use of the past inherent in the new holiday broke fresh ground in French ceremonial history. All previous French regimes had celebrated either a foundation date or the current ruler. What is striking about the new holiday, by contrast, is that it sought to rally the nation around the memory of a supposedly historically significant date. In this it presaged the later establishment of Bastille Day during the Third Republic more than growing out of earlier holidays.[23]

The government put on a lavish show for the first 15 August celebration, a show that cost some 900,000 francs, more than any other 15 August celebration.[24] In charge was Fine Arts Director-General Auguste Romieu, a consummate political opportunist and man-about-town who had thrown in his lot with Louis-Napoleon after the election of 1848. Romieu had earned his high position not through administrative ability but through two books, *L'Ere des césars* and *Le Spectre rouge de 1852,* in which he helped lay the ground for the coup d'état by calling for a new Caesar to save society from an impending *jacquerie*.[25] Nonetheless, he had put some thought into the role of celebrations. As he wrote in *Le Spectre rouge,* "France loves glamour, splendor, stories of military exploits; she loves military festivals and still remembers the old carrousels. It is in vain that they have tried to soften her with a sorry regime of speeches and elections."[26] Romieu, seconded by the architect Théodore Charpentier, who had worked on several of the republican anniversaries, attempted to put this philosophy into effect in August 1852.

The decoration was predictably Napoleonic.[27] Eagles, a principal symbol of the First Empire, were everywhere: a giant one surmounted the Arc de Triomphe (visible in the distance in figure 2.2) and four more topped the Vendôme Column. Other decorations included sixty-two seven-meter-high fountains decorated with statues along the Champs-Elysées, eagles and "N"s atop the lampposts of that same thoroughfare, and a large equestrian statue of the First Emperor at the rond-point. At the Marché des Innocents, an enormous ballroom, large enough to hold 20,000 people, was erected over the entire square. The elaborately ugly principal façade of this tempo-

Figure 2.2. Louis-Napoleon reviewing troops on the Place de la Concorde, 15 August 1852, from *L'Illustration*, 21 August 1852. (Doe Library, University of California, Berkeley)

rary edifice was a sort of nineteenth-century rococo fantasy that juxtaposed eagles and "N"s with fish, cattle, and other symbols of the market (figure 2.3). In the interior of the ballroom, Louis-Napoleon's men made their domination of France manifest by setting a large eagle directly atop the square's chief artistic and historical attraction, Pierre Lescot's Renaissance fountain.

The celebration began with an official mass at the Church of the Madeleine followed by a military review on the Champs-Elysées. The rest of the day was devoted to more popular entertainments. Two temporary theaters erected on the Champs-Elysées gave free performances, as did a number of

Figure 2.3. The exotic façade of the ballroom at the Marché des Innocents, 15 August 1852, from *L'Illustration*, 21 August 1852. (Doe Library, University of California, Berkeley)

Figure 2.4. Napoleon I crossing the Alps in the fireworks show for 15 August 1852, from *L'Illustration*, 21 August 1852. (Doe Library, University of California, Berkeley)

regular theaters. Other attractions included greased poles, military bands, a regatta, and an elaborately staged naval combat on the Seine. After dark there were illuminations, an important part of most celebrations in those days before electricity. Thousands of the small colored bottle-lights filled with oil called *lampions* were strung on monuments and along major thoroughfares. A spiral of them twisted its way up the Vendôme Column, and a double row hung as garlands along the Champs-Elysées.

The night's real attraction, however, was an extraordinarily ambitious fireworks, show that depicted Napoleon crossing the Saint-Bernard Pass and the siege of the Bard fortress (figure 2.4). According to the description in *Le Constitutionnel:*

> The cannons roar. Besiegers and besieged exchange balls and bombs, all in fireworks, of course. The assault is made and the French are victorious. They blow up the stronghold they have taken. Then begins the passage of the French army. Napoleon, mounted on a white charger and dressed for battle, surveys the passing troops from atop a mountain. Infantry, cavalry, and artillery pass before him. . . . Soon snow begins to fall; it is a rain of fire that falls from all sides into the river and produces a most picturesque effect.[28]

Historically, the siege had not been quite such a glorious feat of French arms. One small fort, after all, had managed to stop the entire French army for four days, throwing Napoleon's plans into some disarray. The history lesson of 15 August, however, was not concerned so much with accuracy as with addressing what *Le Constitutionnel* called "the impressionable imagination of the masses."[29] The 15 August celebration transformed the history of the first Napoleon into myth and then presented it as a spectacular amusement designed to stimulate enthusiasm for a second Napoleon, one who would soon follow in the footsteps of his uncle by declaring France an Empire.

The first 15 August celebration, however, did not go off quite as well as expected.[30] For one thing, the organizers had not allotted enough time for the statues and other ambitious projects to be done properly, and the roughness of the work was evident.[31] Even more damaging was the weather; wind and rain wreaked havoc on the celebration, dousing *lampions*, carrying off decorations, and making the Seine too choppy for the regatta and naval maneuvers to be held as intended. The storm also ripped away the canvas roof of the ballroom on the Marché des Innocents, forcing a two-day postponement of the ball. It did not help the fireworks display either. A strong gust of wind carried away the mountain on which Napoleon's charger stood, so instead of gallantly bestriding the Alps, he seemed to be unsteadily suspended in mid-air.[32] Even so, one observer still found the celebration "fort belle" and noted that "the crowd on the quais and the Champs-Elysées was immense."[33] Still, the event must have been a disappointment to the authorities and above all to Romieu, who was eventually removed from his post as head of fine arts and made general library inspector, and to Charpentier, who never again had responsibility for a major celebration.

The report on the celebration in the official newspaper, however, did not mention the problems. The paper recounted the whole affair as if it were an unqualified success, even including details of canceled events as if they had taken place. The report was so patently mendacious that when Paulin, editor of *L'Illustration*, repeated it, complete with engravings of the celebration as it should have been, it was clear, according to one historian, that he was mocking the administration.[34] Most newspapers, however, did admit, if only obliquely, that everything had not gone entirely according to plan. Even the strongly Bonapartist *Le Constitutionnel* noted the poor weather. "The 15 August celebration," its report said, "was one of the most magnificent that Paris has ever seen. Only two things were missing: the sunshine of August and a clear sky."[35]

Problems also cropped up in the provinces. In some places, the weather created problems, but elsewhere, conflicts between religious and political authorities found public outlet in the celebration. Fortoul had written to the bishops and archbishops two weeks before the celebration to order that *Te Deums* be sung in all churches on the fifteenth, which, of course, meant once again singing the *Domine salvum fac Ludovicum Napoleonem.*[36] Not all members of the clergy complied, and in one case, the curé actually locked the procession of officials outside the church during mass.[37] These squabbles stemmed from a variety of sources, including legitimist clergy, personal conflicts between priests and mayors, and resentment of the fact that the Feast of the Assumption seemed to have been "profaned" by politics.[38] On the whole such problems were relatively rare, but the seriousness with which the government took them is indicative of the significance it attributed to the celebration.

The government's appetite for celebrations, however, was not dulled by the disappointments of 15 August. Less than a month later, Louis-Napoleon was off on another official voyage, the most important of his career and the most significant such excursion of the era. The presidential voyage of September–October 1852 is a prime example of the intimate connection between celebration and politics during this period, for it was to lead directly to the final overthrow of the last vestiges of the Republic and to the reestablishment of the Napoleonic Empire in France.

The voyage began with a gala departure from the Austerlitz train station on the afternoon of 14 September and ended over a month later, on 16 October, when the president and his entourage arrived back in Paris, having made a grand tour through central and southern France by train, boat, and carriage.[39] Perhaps the most striking aspect of Louis-Napoleon's itinerary is that it took him directly through the regions that were most hostile to his rule. Indeed, he visited the very areas that, just nine months previously, had opposed his coup d'état with what Ted Margadant has called "the largest provincial uprising in nineteenth-century France."[40] And while the widespread repression had eliminated the leaders of the revolt (and probably most of the followers), Bonapartists still viewed the areas with trepidation. Minister of War Saint-Arnaud, for example, who accompanied Louis-Napoleon throughout the whole trip, wrote back several times expressing fear of what might happen in these "mauvais départements."[41]

Saint-Arnaud's anxiety proved unfounded. Vigilant local officials redoubled their efforts to squelch possible sources of trouble in their districts before Louis-Napoleon arrived, even managing to uncover a supposed assassination plot in Marseilles.[42] In any event, no untoward incidents marred the voyage. For Bonapartists, the trip was an unqualified success. What made it so successful was the fact that cries of "Vive l'Empereur!" and

"Vive Napoléon III!," which had until then been relatively rare, suddenly seemed to emerge as the cheer of choice for the crowds that greeted Louis-Napoleon along the way. But what was behind this new movement of support for the reestablishment of the Empire? Was it, as official press reports at the time claimed and as Minister of Police Maupas later argued, a completely spontaneous expression of the popular will?[43] Or did the administration wittingly or unwittingly help things along?

In his memoirs, the Duc de Persigny, then minister of the interior, recounts that at a meeting with the president and cabinet ministers prior to the trip he argued the necessity of the administration's "putting itself at the head of Napoleonic sentiment." He was convinced, he says, that "the Empire was in the aspirations of the great popular masses," but that without government leadership, they would remain quiescent and "the trip through the Midi, that could so easily be the triumph of the Empire, would become itself an argument in favor of the Republic." This pregnant admission by one of the most influential Bonapartists of the period suggests not only the important political role attributed to celebrations by the administration but also that at least certain individuals actively sought to use them to influence public opinion. Persigny, however, was apparently forced to back down before the argument presented by Minister of Justice Abbattucci and supported by Louis-Napoleon that public opinion should be left free to express itself without official influence.

But Persigny, at least in his version of events, did not rest content with this decision. He secretly summoned the prefects of the Cher, the Nièvre, and the Allier and instructed them to have the president greeted upon his arrival with "Vive l'Empereur!" and "Vive Napoléon III!," both in cheers and written on banners and triumphal arches. He took no such action concerning Orléans, the president's first stop, he says, because the prefect of the Loiret was a close friend of Abbattucci and might have given the game away before it began. The strategy, according to Persigny, worked wonderfully. At the president's arrival in Orléans, he was met only with the usual slogans. But when the official train reached the Cher, "from the first moment the Prince-president set foot in the department, he was acclaimed as emperor by a population drunk with enthusiasm. Cries of *Vive Napoléon III! Vive l'Empereur!* did not stop sounding in his ears." And that, of course, marked but the beginning of a very long trip.[44]

Granier de Cassagnac has a different, more amusing, version of what happened. He says that far from providing specific instructions to begin the imperial campaign, Persigny simply told the prefect of the Cher to "do his best" *(faites pour le mieux)*. Upon returning to his department with these rather cryptic instructions, the prefect addressed a proclamation to his mayors in which he instructed them to "let the Prince know well that in all the Berry there is but one name and one cheer to which all hearts rally. That cheer which we will all make heard before the nephew of the *Great Emperor* is: 'VIVE NAPOLEON!' " But instead of putting just one exclamation point after the cheer, the prefect thought it best to give his message more emphasis by using three of them. When printed up this led to some confusion: "Either because the typographical characters of the official printer at Bourges were not very correctly designed, or because the mayors of the Berry were not accustomed to punctuation, they took the three exclamation points to be the Roman numeral III, and came to Bourges interpreting the cry which had been assigned them by the prefect as: *Vive Napoléon III!*" [45]

Where exactly the truth lies in all of this is not entirely clear, but something does seem to have changed from the Cher onward. When the president's train passed through Orlèans, only a small contingent was on hand to greet it and the station remained undecorated.[46] At Vierzon, however, the first large town in the Cher, a large crowd that included both officials and nonofficials met the train with cries of "Vive le Président!," "Vive Louis-Napoléon!," and "Vive l'Empereur!"[47] Then, at Bourges, the *chef-lieux* of the Cher, things really began to pick up. The archbishop greeted the president as "Your Imperial Highness." According to the local newspaper:

> From the time he got off the train until he reached the archbishop's palace, the prince was everywhere and unceasingly welcomed with an immense, energetic, and continuous acclamation. Cries of *Vive l'Empereur* and *Vive Napoléon* dominated this acclamation of almost a hundred thousand voices; those of *Vive le president* were rare, and not one mouth opened to cry *Vive la République.*[48]

The following day, the president moved on to Nevers, where the name "Napoleon III" first appeared, and from that point on, the theme of the tour was the constantly articulated demand that Louis-Napoleon restore the Empire. The press reports made it appear as if the enthusiasm of the French populace for such a move was boundless. Daily accounts in almost all of the newspapers and the weekly pictorials in *L'Illustration* chronicled what seemed to be ever larger and more enthusiastic crowds demanding a return to the Empire. Nor were such impressions limited to the press. The Maréchal de Saint-Arnaud, for example, who accompanied Louis-Napoleon throughout the voyage, wrote from Grenoble:

> My words cannot describe this *crescendo*. I will only say that it grows louder and louder. All of the department of the Isère descended on the road, and

from Lyons to Grenoble—twenty-six leagues—we traveled beneath triumphal arches with garlands of flowers, bouquets, emblems, imperial relics, old uniforms, ancient eagles, crutches and cheers; cheers to wake the dead and to replace the trumpet of Judgment Day. I fall asleep, I dream, and I awake crying *Vive l'Empereur.*[49]

The cries also reached the ears of Louis-Napoleon himself, although it took awhile for him to believe that a restoration of the Empire was in the immediate offing. Speaking at the inauguration of a statue of his uncle in Lyons, he was still hesitant about declaring himself openly for restoration. The cries of "Vive l'Empereur!" were, he said, "much more a memory that touches my heart than a hope that flatters my pride."[50] But by the time he arrived in Bordeaux, less than three weeks later, Louis-Napoleon was clearly ready to assume the imperial mantle. The famous "Empire means peace" speech that he gave at a banquet given by the Bordeaux Chamber of Commerce was a declaration that he now looked favorably on such a move. The restoration of the Empire was henceforth a virtual certainty.

The tour ended with a spectacular ceremonial entry into Paris. Master of Ceremonies Feuillet de Conches had prepared two reception rooms at the Gare d'Orlèans (Austerlitz).[51] Both were elaborately decorated and hung with red velvet, but the first was reserved for very high officials and dignitaries and included a small stage with a throne placed upon it. This was perhaps a little premature, for Louis-Napoleon passed it up without stopping. After greeting some of the assembled guests, including Prince Jerome, Archbishop Sibour, and the Duc de Morny, the president entered the second room, where more officials were waiting. After about twenty minutes, he mounted a horse and left the station, accompanied by a large group of his ministers and high military officials. The group proceeded to the Place Walhubert, just in front of the Pont d'Austerlitz, where he was received by an official delegation from the City of Paris (figure 2.5). In front of a large triumphal arch dedicated to "Louis-Napoleon, Emperor," the prefect of the Department of the Seine, Jean-Jacques Berger, read a short speech in which he called upon the president to "cede to the voice of the whole people; Providence has borrowed that voice to tell you to complete the mission that has been entrusted to you by taking up once again the crown of the immortal founder of your dynasty."

From the Place Walhubert, the cortege crossed the Seine and made its way to the Tuileries Palace. The grand boulevards, decorated with a multitude of triumphal arches, held an enormous crowd. Schools had been let out by order of the prefect,[52] and organized delegations of workers, including the *dames de la halle* and many groups from outside Paris, met the

Figure 2.5. Louis-Napoleon entering Paris after his triumphal tour through the provinces, Place Walhubert, 16 October 1852. (Bibliothèque Nationale, Paris)

president with cheers and banners. According to the description in *Le Moniteur universel* (which went on in the same vein for six long columns), "The reception given the Prince in the capital of France cannot be described. Nothing is comparable to the great city on its days of ceremony. Today Paris has surpassed herself. Those who were not witnesses will never be able to get an idea of the celebration, in which the enthusiasm of the crowd surpassed even the magnificence of the spectacle."[53] The return to Paris, then, was a fitting conclusion to the voyage—but was the trip all it seemed?

Despite the fact that the overwhelming majority of sources seem to agree that the trip was "a triumphal voyage" and "one long ovation," it would be rash to accept this at face value. In his private journal, Romain Bouquet, former secretary to the mayor of La-Tour-du-Pin, described the visit of the president to Bourgouin, one of the cities on the route from Lyons to Grenoble, where the reception was so ecstatically recounted by Saint-Arnaud. His very different account, one that underscores the theatricality of the visits, is worth quoting at length:

> The official bulletins praise the reception to the skies and cannot find strong enough words to paint the enthusiasm and the delirium with which [the president] has been received and acclaimed; but if we go behind the scenes of this new sort of theater and see the strings that the stagehands pull behind the curtain, we will have to recognize that, with perhaps a few exceptions, it was pure comedy.
>
> The crowd was, in fact, numerous, but composed in large part of people who were there *by order,* and for the most part of curious spectators.
>
> Cheers of "Vive l'Empereur!" were rare . . . despite the incitements and prayers of M. the subprefect of La-Tour-de-Pin and M. the prefect of the Isère, who, in uniform and on foot in the mud ran before the Prince's carriage crying, "Vive l'Empereur!," inviting the simple citizens and requiring the functionaries to do likewise. We saw the president's lackeys who, hoisted up on the seats of the carriages, were crying, *"Vive l'Empereur!,"* as loud as they could and trying to get the crowd to do so too.
>
> The most numerous cheers came from the groups of mayors and municipal counselors and from the *old* brigade. The functionaries were, in general, sober in their acclamations.[54]

Another observer, a naval officer who saw the president's reception at Toulon, described the crowd as somewhat less enthusiastic than it had appeared to be in the newspaper reports: "To sum up, the enthusiasm can be classed as follows: that of the troops, *enormous;* that of the population, *moderate;* that of the navy, *correct.*"[55]

Alternative versions of the return to Paris can also be found. According to the Austrian ambassador, for example, the public was "rather indifferent." [56] Another witness, an American who was quite hostile to Louis-Napoleon, categorically stated that he "saw no enthusiasm" and "did not hear a single shout of *Vive l'Empereur.*" [57] And according to a local doctor who later voted for the re-establishment of the Empire, "The crowd of curious spectators on the boulevard, in the windows, and on the platforms, along with the National Guard battalions, kept silent. The cheers came, then, almost exclusively from the corporations. They were cheers by order, triumphal arches by order, inscriptions by order." [58]

We have, then, two very different versions of the tour of 1852, one describing ecstatic crowds spontaneously cheering for a new Empire and the other describing silent or only moderately enthusiastic crowds and organized cheers. One suspects that there is some truth to both evaluations. Clearly support for an imperial restoration existed, but it was not as unanimous or as enthusiastic as the press reports of the time pretended. As with the plebiscites, a combination of manipulation, repression, and censorship managed to transform what was certainly a degree of popularity into what seemed to be an astounding outpouring of support from the entire nation.

Almost a century and a half of further experience with mass politics has taught us that it is not difficult to bring out a large excited crowd when any important and controversial issue is at stake. In an open system, both sides can have rallies and then dispute which crowd was larger, more enthusiastic, and more representative of the general population. But in a system such as that in France in 1852, in which open political opposition is suppressed, official sentiments are the only ones allowed and can, thus, easily seem to be truly representative. To yell "Vive la République!" at one of the president's receptions was a dangerous action, one that might bring arrest and a prison term. Thus, it should not be surprising that the voyage of 1852 could seem such a call for imperial restoration. What is more surprising is that a few brave souls still cared enough to risk such challenges.

The Decennial Republic ended as it had begun: by plebiscite. On 20 and 21 November, the French electorate went to the polls to vote on whether or not the Empire should be officially resurrected. The conditions were similar to what they had been a year before. The result was overwhelming approval for the change: 7,824,189 voted "oui," and a mere 253,145 voted "non."

The timing of the vote was ideal; it allowed the official proclamation of the Empire in Paris to take place on one of the most Bonapartist days of the year, the second of December, anniversary of the coronation of Napoleon I, the battle of Austerlitz, and the coup d'état of 1851. At the Palace of Saint-Cloud the night before, Louis-Napoleon had been officially informed by a delegation headed by Adolphe Billault, president of the legislature, that the "national will" had restored the Napoleonic dynasty to the throne of France.[59] So, at a bit after midday on 2 December 1852, the new emperor made a ceremonial entrance into his capital.[60] The route took the official cortege through the Porte Maillot and along the entire length of the Champs-Elysées. At one o'clock, accompanied by the rousing sounds of firing cannons and beating drums, the group reached the Arc de Triomphe, where, if the official newspaper is to be believed, even the heavens paid tribute to the new sovereign—the moment he arrived, "the sky cleared and a ray of sunlight pierced the clouds."[61] Perhaps this sign of divine approval made up for the poor popular reception. According to an English observer, the emperor "cannot have been pleased with his reception to-day. I never witnessed anything colder or more uninteresting."[62]

The emperor and his entourage continued up the Champs-Elysées to the Tuileries. After reviewing several army regiments on the Place du Carrousel, the group entered the palace. Saint-Arnaud went out onto the balcony overlooking the Place du Carrousel, while Persigny went out onto the balcony overlooking the Place de la Concorde. They then each read the official proclamation of Empire, the same one that had been read that morning at the Hôtel-de-Ville. The next day, the new emperor visited the hospitals of Paris. He did not attempt to cure scrofula by touching those afflicted with the disease, as the Old Regime monarchs had done after their coronations in the heyday of mystical kingship. Nonetheless, the timing of the visit indicates that the miraculous ritual may have retained some residual meaning, aided of course by the fact that visiting a hospital presented Louis-Napoleon as a person who cared for those less fortunate than himself.[63]

The celebration in the provinces was held a few days later, the convenience of a Sunday celebration apparently outweighing the urge to commemorate 2 December.[64] At gatherings in central squares all over France, local officials read the proclamation to the assembled citizens from either a balcony or a specially constructed stage decorated with whatever imperial symbols were available. Troop reviews, gun salutes, fireworks, and other, sometimes more creative, public entertainments generally followed the ceremony. In one commune in the Oise, for example, a bust of the emperor was paraded about town by girls in white dresses carrying tricolor flags.

Besides the reading of the proclamation, the one element common to all of the celebrations was the *Te Deum*. But once again the words had been changed. Henceforth, all references to the Republic were purged, and the clergy was requested to sing *Domine salvum fac imperatorum nostrum Napoleonem* (God save our Emperor Napoleon), exactly the same form that had been used under the First Empire.[65]

THREE

Celebrating the Past

On the afternoon of 14 August 1857, the emperor, the empress, several members of the imperial family, and a clutch of notables left the Tuileries Palace and boarded six ornate court carriages to go a distance they might easily have walked in less than five minutes without leaving the building. In other circumstances, this would have been ludicrously excessive, even at court, but ceremony has its own logic, a logic that places display above simplicity, and the procession was making its way to ceremonially inaugurate one of the regime's proudest achievements: the newly completed Louvre.[1]

French sovereigns had been tinkering with the Louvre from the time of Philip Augustus on, but it was Napoleon III who brought the work to its fullest state of completion.[2] In 1848, the complex had included the Louvre itself, the Tuileries Palace, and the long wing along the Seine connecting those two buildings. Each of the individual pieces was aesthetically satisfactory, but as a whole they lacked the unity and coherence of a fully realized palace. In addition, much of the existing structure was in a dilapidated state. By 1857, however, the Louvre-Tuileries complex had been transformed into a palace worthy of a great nation. Louis-Napoleon's most striking contribution was the long wing connecting the Louvre and the Tuileries along the

Rue de Rivoli. This matched the gallery along the Seine and enclosed the Place du Carrousel, thus giving the palace a far more unified character than it had had previously.

The work actually began during the Second Republic. In 1848, the Republic had decreed the completion of the palace and the restoration of three of the most important galleries. By 1851, the ground had been cleared of the old buildings that had encumbered the area and in March 1852, the plans of Louis Visconti, an architect of exceptional talent, were officially accepted for the new construction. Four months later the first stone of the new work was set by the minister of state.[3] As with Second Empire architecture generally, Visconti's design spurned innovation to follow the lines set out in the classical tradition.[4] Visconti died before the project was completed, but his plans were carried out (in rather more florid style) by his successor, Hector-Martin Lefuel. The emperor made the completion of the palace a priority, and work progressed so rapidly that the construction site became a major attraction for visitors to Paris in the 1850s.[5] By mid-1857, the completed palace was ready for inauguration.

After crossing the Place du Carrousel on that sunny August afternoon, the procession stopped before the newly completed Denon Pavilion, where the imperial party entered. A large gallery next to the Salle des Etats had been prepared for the ceremony with two thrones on a raised dais surrounded by seats for the state dignitaries. Facing these elites sat various workers and artists who had been involved in the new construction, many of whom received awards from the hand of the emperor as part of the ceremony. The inauguration's high point was a speech by the emperor setting out a remarkable overview of French history through a discussion of the Louvre. The emperor attributed the final completion of the palace to himself and to the improved political and economic situation his rule had created. It was, he said, "order, reestablished stability, and the continually growing prosperity of the country that permitted me to finish this national undertaking." By extension, this completion made Napoleon III the heir to a long monarchical tradition. France, the emperor stressed, was a country that had been "monarchical for so many centuries" and that "continually saw in the central power the representative of its grandeur and its nationality." But the Louvre was also the product, the emperor added, of the Second Republic, and as such it demonstrated the continuity of French history:

> Just as it is remarkable that under the first Revolution the Committee of Public Safety continued unknowingly the work of Louis XI, Richelieu, and Louis XIV, both in striking the final blow against feudalism and in following

a system of unity and centralization, the constant goal of the monarchy; so too is there not something to be learned in seeing in the Louvre the thought of Henry IV, Louis XIII, Louis XIV, Louis XV, Louis XVI, and Napoleon adopted by the ephemeral power of 1848?[6]

Just as the French Revolution continued the monarchical tradition of centralization, so even the Second Republic had continued the monarchical tradition of building the Louvre. It was unnecessary to state, of course, that this made the Second Empire the fullest expression of a central strand of French history that brought together both monarchy and revolution.

In arriving at this argument, the emperor may well have borrowed (and somewhat distorted) the central thesis of Alexis de Tocqueville's *The Old Regime and the French Revolution*, published the year before. Tocqueville had reintegrated the Revolution into French history by showing how it grew out of the Old Regime and how it perpetuated certain aspects of that period, especially centralization. This idea, as one historian has noted, might have been damaging to the left since "its continuity thesis denied the concept of the new, and would have deprived the left of an idea of tremendous psychological power."[7] In other words, it undermined an important component of radical legitimacy: the essential newness and regenerative capacity of the Revolution. The same thesis that threatened the left, however, potentially helped the Bonapartists by giving them a strategy for coopting both the monarchical past and the revolutionary/republican past of 1789 and 1848. By completing the work of both the monarchy and the republics, the Napoleonic dynasty bridged the central political chasm of French history. This was the message of the Louvre inauguration.

To be sure, Bonapartists were themselves deeply divided over which side of their heritage to emphasize. Conservative Bonapartists such as Adolphe Granier de Cassagnac came down on the monarchical side and derided the French Revolution as "a stupid and bloody piece of uselessness,"[8] while liberal Bonapartists did the opposite. At the inauguration of a statue of Napoleon I in 1865, for example, Prince Napoleon, a cousin of Louis-Napoleon and the most prominent liberal Bonapartist of the age, presented the First Emperor as the savior of the Revolution from the royalists and reactionaries, the founder of a government based on the principles of 1789, and the spreader of the Revolution throughout Europe.[9] What might be called official Bonapartism tried to steer a selective course between these two extremes. Official orators, including the emperor himself, often waxed eloquent about the "principles of 1789," even while leaving the contents of those principles fairly vague. But they were even more likely to reach back into the monarchical past than they were to evoke the Revolution, especially when it came to large spectacles.

Whatever their differences on the dual heritage of the Old Regime and Revolution, Bonapartists of all political persuasions looked to the First Empire as a source of legitimacy. This disposition took the form not only of specific historical interpretations but also of the new symbols and institutions of government introduced in 1852. The very restoration of the Empire and the assumption of the title Napoleon III, after all, proclaimed the government of France to be the direct continuation of the First Empire, a regime that had passed into history almost forty years before. Along with the name and title, the Bonapartists of 1852 resurrected a ceremonial code, a host of symbols, an imperial court, and an annual holiday. They saw themselves not as creating a new Empire but as, to use their word, "reestablishing" the Empire of Napoleon I.

Beneath its historical veneer, however, their construction differed markedly from its progenitor. The first Napoleon had been a military leader cum monarch, ruling over a nation almost constantly at war with its neighbors. He effected a certain amount of economic rationalization, but economic considerations generally played second fiddle to international conquest—as with the economically disastrous Continental System. And although Napoleon I did claim at times to represent the "nation" and the ideals of the Revolution, these claims came rather late in his career and were never fully developed. Throughout most of his reign, the First Emperor styled his direct and personal rule on the Old Regime monarchs, a rule most fully symbolized by the seriousness with which he had himself crowned in the mystico-monarchical ceremony of the *sacre*.

By contrast, Napoleon III openly based his legitimacy on universal (male) suffrage and concentrated the nation's energies more on economic battles than on those of foreign wars (with a few notable exceptions). Moreover, although there was much talk of a *sacre* at the beginning of the regime, in the end it was one spectacle the Second Empire opted against. The years between the two empires had transformed France from an overwhelmingly rural and economically backward country into one beginning what David Landes has called an industrial "coming-of-age." [10] As Maurice Agulhon, Ted Margadant, and others have shown, by mid-century even most peasants had a consciousness of national politics they had not possessed forty years before. [11] All this is not to say that there were no similarities between the two regimes; the First Empire did presage much that bore fruit during the Second. But for people at mid-century, the First Empire had passed into history. It had become part of a different, earlier era.

In the Louvre inauguration, then, the emperor made the completion of the palace into a metaphor for the continuity of the history of France. The "something to be learned" from the constant building was clearly that French history had a long-term logic of development, a coherent narrative structure that culminated, like the building of the Louvre Palace, in Napoleon III himself. "The completion of the Louvre," the emperor concluded in his speech, "is not the caprice of a moment but the realization of a plan conceived for glory and upheld by the instinct of the country through more than 300 years."

The Louvre inauguration was one of the clearest articulations of the regime's desire to root itself in the national past. But the theme runs through many other celebrations as well and was often more spectacularly—if less explicitly—stated. The imperial marriage and the baptism of the Prince Imperial, in particular, tried hard to emulate the pomp and symbolism of the dynastic ceremonies of the Old Regime and the First Empire. These two self-consciously historical spectacles, both held in the Cathedral of Notre-Dame, vividly re-created the splendor of the Middle Ages and focused the country's attention on the monarchical and hereditary aspects of the new regime.

The Empire was only a few weeks old when Napoleon III announced to the great bodies of state his upcoming marriage to Eugénie de Guzman, a young woman of minor Spanish nobility. Her modest family background made Eugénie a surprising choice for the emperor, who might have been expected to bring prestige to the newly reestablished throne by marrying a foreign princess. But Louis-Napoleon had explored the possibility of making a more royal match and found himself rebuffed by the legitimate dynasties. His keen political instinct, however, allowed him to turn the potential liability of a nonroyal marriage to his advantage. In announcing his nuptials, the emperor boldly portrayed them as a love match and as "not in accordance with the old political traditions":

> When . . . one is raised through the force of a new principle to the level of the old dynasties, it is not by antiquing one's coat of arms and seeking to introduce oneself at any price into the family of kings that one makes oneself accepted. It is far more by always remembering one's origin, by keeping one's own character, and by taking frankly vis-à-vis Europe the position of parvenu, a glorious title when one arrives in power through the free suffrage of a great people. . . .
>
> I come, then, Messieurs, to say to France that I have preferred a woman that I love and that I respect to an unknown woman whose alliance would have had advantages mixed with sacrifices. . . . By placing independence, the qualities of the heart, and the happiness of the family above dynastic prejudices and ambitious calculations, I will not be less strong since I will be more free.[12]

It was a strange speech. Its evocation of universal suffrage, national independence, and family happiness in the context of a marriage whose primary function would be to provide an heir to the throne keenly reflects the intertwined archaism and modernity of Second Empire Bonapartism. It also demonstrates the emperor's political savvy. According to the Austrian ambassador, the speech "had the goal of reconciling the masses with the marriage. From that comes the democratic note that predominates in it." [13] And it seems to have worked. Although some of the prefects' reports on the public reaction to the emperor's announcement complained that legitimists were trying to use the marriage as political fodder, virtually all maintained that the common people had received the news well because they believed the emperor had the right to marry for love and that foreign princesses would lead to international complications. [14]

The wedding consisted of two ceremonies: a relatively modest civil ceremony on the evening of 29 January, followed by a spectacular religious one the next day. [15] The civil ceremony took place in the Salle des Marechaux of the Tuileries Palace with Minister of State Achille Fould officiating. About a thousand guests, including ministers, cardinals, diplomats, and members of the Bonaparte family, attended the extremely brief ceremony. Fould read the requisite questions, received the requisite answers, and declared the couple united in marriage. [16] The newlyweds and their witnesses then signed the imperial family register, in which the last entry had been the birth of Napoleon I's short-lived son in 1811. After that, the guests filed past the emperor and empress in pairs. Eugénie, according to one observer, looked "pale and fatigued," while her husband seemed "gay and high-spirited." [17]

The next day's much more spectacular religious ceremony was held in Notre-Dame, once again decorated by Viollet-le-Duc and Lassus. Extravagant decorations for Notre-Dame had long been a common element of major French celebrations, but this had usually meant hiding the cathedral beneath temporary constructions of whatever architectural style was then in vogue. For the coronation of Napoleon I, for example, architects Percier and Fontaine completely covered most of the interior of the medieval cathedral with a pastiche of classical architecture. Even when a gothic style of decoration was used, the attempt had usually been to create a completely new decor rather than to focus on Notre-Dame itself. [18] In their decoration for the *Te Deum* of 1852, however, Viollet-le-Duc and Lassus had allowed the cathedral itself to be the centerpiece of the decoration, and they went even further in this direction for the imperial marriage. As one historian noted, their intention was "to adapt a system of medieval decoration, in accordance with the style of the building and their personal taste, to the demands of the ceremony." [19]

On the exterior, the architects erected a large medieval-style portico in front of the entrance, with equestrian statues of Charlemagne and Napoleon I flanking it on either side.[20] The medieval theme was also carried through in the seeming restoration of the statues of the early kings of France, which had been toppled from their niches during the Revolution, to their places on the façade; in reality, however, the architects had merely papered over the revolutionary destruction with painted representations of the statues. Frescoes of Charlemagne, Saint-Louis, Louis XIV, and Napoleon I, whom a Bonapartist newspaper tellingly called "the four greatest figures of the French monarchy,"[21] decorated the towers of the cathedral, as did four eagles and two long tricolor banners.

The interior (see figure 3.1) was no less striking than the exterior. Velvet and brocade hung everywhere, much of it lined with ermine and adorned with "N"s, the arms of the Empire, and the arms of Eugénie's family.[22] "As you passed through the portico," said a British paper, "four or five series of draperies, of various colours, drawn up in the form of curtains, and depending from a great height, led to the interior. The first feeling of the spectator on entering was one of unmixed admiration."[23] On a platform covered with an ermine carpet in the transept, two chairs and two prie-dieux embroidered with the imperial arms had been prepared. Above the platform hung an enormous red velvet canopy decorated with imperial bees and topped by a large gilded eagle, its wings outstretched. Tribunes around the sides of the cathedral held places for invited dignitaries. All of this had been accomplished in just eight days—but barely. Workers had toiled through the night of the 29 January and finished the job just two hours before the guests arrived.[24]

The historical impulse was as obvious in other aspects of the ceremony as in the decoration of the cathedral. According to General Fleury, who organized the procession, "It was agreed that the traditional ceremonial would be observed and that the composition of the cortege should resemble as closely as possible that used for [the marriage of] Napoleon I and Marie-Louise."[25] All seven of the large and elaborate carriages were clearly relics from the past. As the London *Times* noted: "Their state and construction denoted them to be not of the present day. They were, in fact, the same carriages which had figured on all public occasions in which Royal or Imperial personages had taken part, since the beginning of the century, or perhaps longer."[26] Indeed, Napoleon III and Eugénie's carriage, on the roof of which had been placed a large gilded crown, had been used for the marriage of Napoleon I.[27]

An immense crowd gathered to watch the procession from behind the double row of troops and the decorations that lined the entire route. "I

Figure 3.1. The decoration of the interior of Notre-Dame Cathedral for the imperial marriage, 30 January 1853, from the *Illustrated London News*, 5 February 1853. (Doe Library, University of California, Berkeley)

think I have never seen a more dense mass of people than was collected along the line," said an American visitor.[28] According to Bonapartist accounts, the crowd enthusiastically welcomed Louis-Napoleon and his new bride, resplendent in diamonds and white velvet. Cries of "Vive l'Empereur!" and "Vive l'Impératrice!" exploded along the whole route, said the official newspaper, and the populace showed, in the words of the emperor's American dentist, "unbounded enthusiasm."[29] As usual, however, other accounts differ sharply. The correspondent for the *Illustrated London News,* for example, found that the spectacle "failed signally to waken any demonstration of heartfelt welcome or applause."[30] The American observer quoted above found the silence "painful,"[31] and the Austrian ambassador heard "almost no acclamations, but also no insults. The people were indifferent and impassive. One would have said they were people at a play they did not understand and the name of which they did not find worth asking."[32]

The church ceremony itself paled next to the spectacle surrounding it. The poorly heated cathedral was cold, and the words must have been difficult to hear for most of the audience. "A vast deal of mummery, with wax tapers and Paters, holy water and censers," as our American described it. The music for the ceremony, like so much else about it, resonated historically. Rejecting Hector Berlioz's newly written *Te Deum,* Persigny and his men—Louis-Napoleon seems to have had little interest in music himself—opted for a hodgepodge of older pieces, including music from the coronation of Napoleon I. "*Les vieux* triomphaient sur toute la ligne," commented the disappointed Berlioz.[33]

Three years later the union contracted in 1853 bore fruit and gave rise to yet another spectacular ceremony—the baptism of the heir apparent to the imperial throne. On 16 March 1856, the empress gave birth to Eugène-Louis-Jean-Joseph Bonaparte, more commonly called the Prince Imperial.[34] The emperor presented the new baby to the official witnesses,[35] and cannons, first at the Tuileries, and then throughout France as the word spread, sounded 101 times to mark the birth of a boy. (It would have been only twenty-one times for a girl.) The government ordered masses of thanksgiving, illuminations, and popular festivities.[36] The *Te Deum* in Notre-Dame in Paris on 23 March drew an especially large crowd, though one hardly in the mood for solemn devotion. Indeed, the group, which consisted primarily of various dignitaries, was so unruly that Archbishop Sibour complained: "It was not a religious and national solemnity that we just saw; it was a noisy spectacle in which there was neither silence, nor manners, nor respect."[37] At any rate, the major part of the official rejoicing was reserved for the day of the prince's baptism in Notre-Dame. As had been customary under the monarchy, the child had received a provisional baptism *(ondoie-ment)* soon after his birth but only went through the full ceremony later. That ceremony, with its implications of a future heir, was clearly one of the high points of the Second Empire. In later life, Eugènie would remember 14 June 1856 as the Empire's most splendid moment.[38]

It was the fourth and last such ceremony of the nineteenth century. The infant heirs to the First Empire, the Restoration, and the July Monarchy had all preceded the little Prince Imperial up the aisle of Notre-Dame, though not one of the three ever ruled. But hope springs eternal in the monarch's breast, for despite this dismal record, Napoleon III mounted a baptismal ceremony for his son that was every bit as lavish and expensive as those earlier ceremonies.[39] And to a greater degree than in any previous ceremony, perhaps because they finally had the time to do the job right, the architects Viollet-le-Duc and Lassus attempted to restore Notre-Dame to its full medieval glory. They made a concerted effort to take Notre-Dame back to what their friend Prosper Mérimée called "a true church of the thirteenth century."[40]

The most striking new/old element was paint.[41] Viollet-le-Duc and Lassus believed that medieval cathedrals were never intended to be left drab stone on the interior but were intended to be colorfully painted, and they attempted to put this theory into practice at the baptism. They painted the vaults blue with gold stars, and other architectural elements green, red ocher, white, and yellow ocher, with gold used sparingly for decoration and to bring out some of the raised elements. Additionally, they placed "stained glass windows" of transparent paper before the white glass windows, and they temporarily removed the more modern paintings and statues that usually adorned the cathedral. They also used a variety of imperial symbols and coats of arms as decoration—but quite sparingly in comparison with other Second Empire celebrations—and they brilliantly illuminated the whole cathedral with some 10,000 candles.

Seats were squeezed into every corner of the cathedral. By using not only the ground floor but the upper galleries as well, Viollet-le-Duc and Lassus managed to make room for some 5,600 guests, not including clergy or orchestra.[42] The most desirable seats were in the nave, where the architects erected large banks of raised seats for the various bodies of officials and dignitaries. A special bank of seats was placed behind the altar for the French bishops, all of whom had been invited to attend the ceremony. The presence of the bishops—a formidable mountain of red drapery once they had taken their places—both underscored the ties between throne and altar, a key theme of the day, and served as a reminder that the period conjured up by the medieval decoration was supposed to have been an age of faith.

The focal point of the ceremony was a raised platform in the transept where the altar, the baptismal font, tables for the "honors,"[43] armchair "thrones" and prie-dieux for the emperor and empress, and another slightly lower armchair for Cardinal-Legate Patrizzi were located. Patrizzi participated in the ceremony as the representative of the Prince Imperial's nominal godfather, the Pope, who had disappointed the regime by declining to come in person.[44] Over the platform hung an enormous canopy of red velvet lined with ermine.

The regime closely modeled the ceremony on the baptism of the King of Rome and on other royal baptisms.[45] Following the traditional pattern, the celebration began with a procession to the cathedral. First came the carriages of the cardinal-legate, then those of the Prince Imperial, and finally those of the emperor and empress. The same anachronistic and ornate court carriages were used as for the marriage, and once again a large number of military units accompanied the procession and lined both sides of the route. Masts bearing banners with the imperial arms had been erected in front of the cathedral, and the square had been covered with sand (to keep down noise) and strewn with flowers. The carriages pulled up outside the cathedral beneath a large porch constructed in front of the entrance. The archbishop of Paris met first the cardinal-legate and escorted him processionally to his throne. The archbishop then returned to the entrance to meet the emperor and empress, who were preceded up the aisle by a long procession of ceremonial aides, high officials of the emperor's household, ladies bearing the *"honors,"* the Grand Duchess of Baden representing the Queen of Sweden (the baby's godmother), and the prince in the arms of his governess. More officials and various members of the imperial family followed, all in their best court finery. "I saw the emperor and the empress enter," said one witness, "to the sound of the cannon and fanfares from the organ, under a canopy of fringed gold cloth floating on clouds of incense and preceded and followed by a human river shimmering with silk and gold."[46]

The emperor and empress took places at prie-dieux in the nave of the cathedral, while the other participants formed two lines on either side of them. The cardinal-legate then descended from his throne and, standing before the altar, chanted the *Veni Creator*, which was continued by the orchestra while the ladies bearing the honors placed them on the waiting tables. After this, the cardinal-legate performed the ceremony of the Catechumens at the sanctuary entrance and conducted the prince to the baptismal font, where the Grand Duchess of Baden joined them. The group to either side of the emperor and empress mounted the stage and took places around the thrones and on the steps of the stage. The emperor and empress then mounted the stage and seated themselves on their thrones. The cardinal-legate then completed the religious ceremony at the baptismal font, a quickly completed ritual given that the child had already received the baptismal water. The governess handed the baby to the empress, and a ceremonial aide advanced to the center of the choir and cried out three times, "Vive le Prince Impérial!" The emperor then took the prince from the empress and held him up to the assembly, which broke out in enthusiastic cheers, the emotional moment heightened when the orchestra and chorus broke into a grand and stirring *vivat*. The emperor then returned the baby prince to his governess, who returned with him to the Tuileries Palace. As soon as they left, the cardinal-legate sang the *Te Deum*, while the archbishop brought out the baptismal register for signing. It had been, said one witness, the "most beautiful religious ceremony that one could see."[47]

After being reescorted to the entrance of the cathedral by Archbishop Sibour, the emperor and empress boarded their carriage and the cortege reformed. Instead of returning to the Tuileries, however, they proceeded to the Hôtel-de-Ville for a lavish and expensive banquet hosted by the City of Paris, "the most brilliant festival the Hôtel-de-Ville has ever seen," boasted—rather excessively—the large commemorative album produced after the occasion.[48] A notable attraction of the celebration was the decoration of the square in front of the Hôtel-de-Ville. City architect Victor Baltard hid the ongoing construction on the square by erecting false building façades on the lots to either side of the Avenue Victoria and joining them with a triumphal arch at the entrance to the square; this work alone cost the city over 35,000 francs.[49] There were also other decorations and amusements that evening and the following day when the celebration continued both in Paris and in the provinces.[50] Fittingly, the celebratory fireworks in Paris that night represented a gothic baptistery.

Except for the decorations and the processions, the grand public did not actually get to witness very much of these ceremonies first-hand. Lengthy descriptions in the newspapers and images in the illustrated press, however, went a long way in bringing to the people what they could not see for themselves. The celebrations were also commonly depicted in the more or less popular woodcuts and lithographs of the kind sold by peddlers during this period. Since the artists responsible for these often rough images did not usually have access to the events they depicted, the illustrations contained many inaccuracies. Some of the mistakes, however, are illuminating. Thus, although an eyewitness to the marriage found that the relatively short emperor "looked insignificant, and seemed overtopped by his wife, who is not *petite* as she has sometimes been represented,"[51] the illustrations of the ceremonies almost invariably depicted the emperor as the taller of the two. The Prince Imperial fared no better. One image of the presentation of the newborn prince to official witnesses, for example, shows him already sitting up and bearing a marked resemblance to Napoleon I.[52]

The regime also intended to memorialize the baptism in more lasting and customary pictorial form by commissioning a painting of it from the artist Thomas Couture.[53] Couture's unfinished canvas depicts the ceremony at the moment the cardinal-legate reaches out to bless the infant prince. The empress kneels at a prie-dieu in the center of the composition, while the emperor stands near her—thus neatly avoiding having to deal with their disparity in height. Most strikingly, a figure of Napoleon I descending to earth with his arm outstretched in blessing dominates the entire painting, a theme often found in popular prints as well. If finished, Couture's canvas would have hung as a pendant to David's *Coronation of Napoleon I* in a special imperial museum.[54]

More than happenstance underlay the regime's artistic association of the baptism with the first Napoleon's *sacre*. It is possible to see either the marriage or the baptism as stand-ins for the *sacre* that Napoleon III, despite much talk and even some desultory negotiations with the Pope, never had.[55] Coming so fast on the heels of the declaration of Empire, the marriage ceremony, for example, clearly stood as the new regime's spectacular inauguration. And the baptism, like the coronation of the First Emperor, was an elaborate ceremony held in Notre-Dame, patterned after an Old Regime model, and administered by the Pope (or at least his legate). But the ceremonies were not *sacres*. They did not officially crown the new emperor, nor did they proclaim that he ruled by divine right, as a *sacre* would have. In this case, the will to archaic emulation was evidently outweighed by the eminent ludicrousness of such a ritual for the man who had been crowned by popular suffrage.[56] The marriage and baptism substituted for the spectacle of the *sacre*, but they were not substitutes for its underlying meaning. France had moved beyond the days of Napoleon I, when claims to rule by divine right could still be taken seriously, even when mixed with more modern claims to legitimacy. Napoleon III's legitimacy rested on his ability to represent the nation, and these ceremonies evoked a particularly important dimension of the nation as it was conceived in the nineteenth century: its continuity with the past.

The Napoleonic regime visibly linked itself to the past not only in its grandiose occasional spectacles but also in its day-to-day activities, especially those of the reestablished court. "One of the first duties of a sovereign," Napoleon III once said, "is to amuse his subjects of all ranks in the social scale.

He has no more right to have a dull court than he has to have a weak army or a poor navy." [57]

Of all the features of that odd amalgam called the Second Empire, the court is perhaps the oddest. Traditionally, the royal court had been, as Norbert Elias put it in his classic study of the court of Louis XIV, "both the first household of the extended royal family, and the central organ of the entire state administration, the government." [58] And although the court of Napoleon I differed significantly from the Old Regime model (principally because admission was based on official position rather than birth and because the focus on the body of the monarch had shifted to his office), the court remained, first and foremost, an instrument of administration; as Philip Mansel has remarked apropos of Napoleon I: "Politics under the Empire were essentially court politics." [59] The same cannot be said of politics under the Second Empire, for Napoleon III ruled not primarily through court officials but through ministers and prefects.[60] While directly modeled on the court of the First Empire, the court of the Second Empire functioned differently. As Napoleon III himself so tellingly indicated, the court had become more an instrument of amusement than of administration—which is not to say that it lacked political importance. Although the court was no longer the means of ruling the country, it more than ever provided an ongoing spectacle of state power that kept public attention focused on the emperor and his entourage.

The overall organization of the emperor's household precisely replicated that of Napoleon I.[61] Both were composed of six services: the Grand Chambellan, charged with the regulation of the day-to-day activities of the emperor; the Grand Marechal du Palais, in charge of the royal palaces; the Grand Ecuyer, charged with the administration of the stables and provincial excursions; the Grand Aumonier, responsible for religious administration; the Grand Veneur, in charge of the imperial hunts; and the Grand Maître des Cérémonies, who regulated court ceremony. The emperor also had a separate military household consisting of officers attached to the court, and both the empress and the Prince Imperial had their own households, similar to that of the emperor but smaller. Some of these services filled important needs—someone, after all, had to take charge of the administration of the imperial palaces and stables. Nonetheless, the antiquated formal structure of the household and the inclusion of such outdated positions as the Grand Veneur and the Grand Aumonier (essentially a sinecure for the archbishop of Paris) clearly owed more to historical precedent than to function.

To be received at court was a mark of social distinction. The Bonapartes, the Murats, the Taschers, and others related to the imperial family made up the elite of court society, and many of them received pensions and official positions in order to be able to pay for the honor. Beyond this, the court mirrored the good society of the grand bourgeoisie: financiers, industrialists, upper-level functionaries, foreign diplomats, high-ranking military officers, and so forth. Successful musicians, artists, and writers might also receive invitations to court. Prosper Mérimée, who had been a friend of the empress prior to her marriage, was almost a permanent fixture there. The lack of blue blood in the couloirs of the Tuileries Palace was sometimes commented on by those who felt themselves to be the true aristocracy. One of the most acerbic of these critics was the hapless Archduke of Austria, Maximilian, later emperor of Mexico. "In general there appears to be the most excellent intention of giving a proper setting to the Court," he commented after a brief visit to Paris,

> but the whole machinery does not as yet work smoothly. In spite of the unconstrained manner which they try to affect at Court, the parvenu etiquette keeps coming through everything. . . . One can see, moreover, that [the emperor's] suite has formerly been that of the president of a republic: it is often hard for them to maintain themselves on a fitting level. The bearing of the Court ladies towards the Empress, too, their shaking hands with her, their hearty friendliness, are a little shocking to our conceptions of imperial etiquette. The whole impression is, so to speak, that of a make-believe Court, the various offices of which are occupied by amateurs who are not very sure of their parts. There can be no question of a good or bad tone here, for this Court is absolutely lacking in tone.[62]

Even so, life at court hardly seems to have been an enjoyable experience. In her private letters, the empress herself complained of the demands placed on her. In 1856, eight months pregnant, she wrote to her sister that it was "truly annoying to be always in public and never to have the right to be sick when unfortunately one is subject to the same illnesses as everyone else."[63] And although court etiquette was relaxed in comparison to earlier regimes, it was still tiresome. According to Princess Metternich, for example, the evenings at Compiègne were long and stilted until the guests were allowed to retire to their rooms, where they could relax and smoke cigarettes.[64] An officer in the elite Cent-Gardes similarly noted of the evenings in the Tuileries that as soon as the imperial couple had gone to bed, "everyone else let out an *Ah!* of discreet relief, succeeded quickly by a general exit that looked exactly like the hurry of schoolboys to fly from class when recreation time arrived."[65]

Of course, life at court consisted of much more than just dull evenings. Each year, for example, between New Year's Day and Mardi Gras, up to 5,000 guests were invited to a number of official balls. Frenchmen and foreigners alike clamored for invitations to these lavish affairs, especially to those held in the Tuileries—though ministries, embassies, and the Hôtel-de-Ville also held balls, including costume balls during carnival season. But no matter how prestigious going to a court ball at the Tuileries may have been, it was not necessarily fun. The wait in the line of carriages alone could take several hours, and, inside, the food was said to be insufficient for the number of guests. Balls were essentially a chance to see and be seen, especially (it was believed) for women, who vied for notice in expensive décolleté gowns from designers like Charles-Frédéric Worth.[66] Comparing balls to a more general tendency of the age, Emile Ollivier sarcastically commented in his private journal in 1855 that "we have public expositions of flowers, paintings, and so forth. Balls are public expositions of women."[67]

But fancy dress was not solely for women. In contrast to the July Monarchy, when the basic bourgeois *frac* had been standard attire, the Second Empire revived established court dress for men.[68] This usually meant the old-fashioned silk stockings with knee breeches *(culottes)*, which had been out of fashion since the Restoration. The emperor, said a disdainful British visitor, "reverts sometimes to the costume of the last century, and shames his court into magnificence by wearing fine frills and pendant wristbands of Malines lace."[69] Indeed, at court, those with official positions were required to wear special uniforms with embroidered coats, braided sleeves, two-cornered hats, and even swords. There were sometimes complaints about the uniforms, but these generally had to do with particular uniforms rather than the idea of wearing uniforms. The architects of the imperial palaces, for example, complained in 1853 that their uniform was "ugly" and too similar to that of the Academy of Medicine.[70] And in 1860, the professors at the Ecole des Beaux-Arts themselves requested a uniform in order "to make the Ecole recognized in the public ceremonies in which it figures as a teaching body."[71]

A few court activities required even more specialized attire. For the annual New Year's reception, an arduous two-day marathon throughout most of the period, Eugénie revived the women's *manteau de cour*, a long train worn behind the dress.[72] Though quite costly, the manteau was worn only for the annual "ladies' reception," at which the women filed by the imperial couple and curtseyed. At the first such reception in 1854, Ambassador Hübner found that even though "the current generation in France has never seen a *manteau de cour*," nonetheless "these 400 women, of whom very few bore aristocratic names, managed fairly well."[73]

Hunting also required a special uniform. Here, the court revived a version of the hunting costume worn under Louis XV.[74] According to General

Fleury, the uniform "was composed of a French-cut green coat, with wide collar and trimming in crimson velvet and hunting braids of gold and silver. The braided waistcoat was crimson velvet also, and the knickerbockers were of white kid, while the three-cornered hat . . . was set off with black feathers. The necktie and gloves were white."[75] The hunts themselves, it might be noted, were butcheries in the best royal tradition. On a typical day in Compiègne, a party of nine killed 43 deer, 20 hares, 498 rabbits, 316 pheasants, 20 partridges, and a woodcock.[76] After the hunt came the *curée*, or dividing of the spoils, another carryover from the monarchy. This ceremony, at which the hungry pack of dogs devoured the offal of the day's hunt in a torchlit courtyard of the chateau, came to symbolize for Emile Zola, in his novel *La Curée*, the rapaciousness of the imperial regime.

Life at court was regulated by a seemingly rigid code of etiquette derived from that of the First Empire and, through it, from the monarchy. All of the old formulas were trotted out, including the *lever*, the ceremony in which, under the Old Regime, the various nobles associated with the royal household helped the monarch to rise and dress each morning. This ritual had been an important element of court life in Louis XIV's day, establishing privileges based on proximity to the person of the monarch.[77] Under the Second Empire, however, the *lever* simply became the emperor's first audience of the day and bore little or no resemblance to the original ceremony.[78] Nonetheless, the lingering use of such an archaic term demonstrates the residual value of symbolic links to the past even when real ties had been severed.

Making sure that the court etiquette was properly carried out was the task of the Grand Maître des Cérémonies and his assistants. Weeks before a ceremony was to take place, they drew up plans—often based on historical research—regulating the timing, music, seating arrangements, order of processions, and all of the other details that went into one of these productions. They also arranged for rehearsals when necessary and were on hand during the ceremony itself to ensure that all went according to schedule. Fittingly, throughout most of the Empire, the post of Grand Maître des Cérémonies was filled by a man with a historic name: the Duc de Cambacérès. Nephew of Napoleon I's famous arch-chancellor of the same name, Cambacérès had served in his youth as a page in the court of the First Empire. Tall, gaunt, and clean-shaven, he had an aristocratic bearing that made him at least look the part.

One of the most important aspects of court life that Cambacérès and his assistants regulated were visits of foreign heads of state and their emissaries. Such visits underscored the legitimacy of the emperor by depicting him as France's representative in dealing with other countries. When those countries were minor powers, ceremonial staging could be used to heighten the grandeur of the emperor, as Jean-Léon Gérôme's state-commissioned painting of the reception of the Siamese ambassadors at Fontainebleau in 1861 demonstrates. The painting shows Napoleon III and Eugénie seated on thrones at one end of the sumptuously appointed (and quite clearly Old Regime) Salon d'Hercule. The Siamese ambassadors, prostrate before them in oriental manner, present the imperial couple with gifts while much of the court, in uniform, looks on.[79] Although the actual ceremony lacked the impact Gérôme gave it,[80] the painting was destined to be seen by a far larger audience than the ceremony. Or, more precisely, the ceremony was destined to be seen by a large number of people through the painting. Thus, such ceremonies were not for the court alone.

Visits of European sovereigns enhanced the prestige of the Empire, while at the same time they flattered the socially insecure French. Not only did the authentic legitimacy of the visiting sovereigns seem to confer more than parvenu status on the Bonapartes, but the frequency of such events contrasted with their relative dearth during the July Monarchy. Napoleon III and Eugénie fêted royal guests in the highest and most historical style, with elaborate entries, military reviews, gala opera performances, fêtes at Versailles, hunting at Fontainebleau, and lavish balls, all aspects of which were discussed in the press at great length, illustrated in journals, and sometimes painted by state-commissioned artists. The year of the second Universal Exposition, 1867, was especially popular with royals, with the Tsar of Russia, the Emperor of Austria, the King of Prussia, the Sultan of Turkey, the King of Portugal, and a number of others almost stumbling over each other to get to Paris.

Of all the royal visits during the Empire, however, the most memorable was that of Queen Victoria and Albert at the time of the Universal Exposition of 1855.[81] This first official visit of British royalty to France in some 400 years cemented the Anglo-French alliance then being forged on the battlefields of the Crimea. The emperor met his guests at Boulogne on 18 August and returned with them to Paris, where a gala public welcome had been planned. The streets had been decorated and triumphal arches constructed along the route from the train station to Saint-Cloud by way of the grand boulevards. Unfortunately, they were later than expected and night had fallen when the twenty-one-gun salute sounded their arrival at 7:20. The Parisians were not amused. Despite this inauspicious beginning, the visit as a whole was successful. There was a fancy ball at the Hôtel-de-Ville, an extraordinarily lavish festival and fireworks show at Versailles (based on one that had taken place under Louis XIV), and visits to many of the monuments of Paris, including the tomb of the First Emperor in the

Invalides. The irony of the nephew of that great foe of England ushering Victoria about Paris was lost on no one; in allying France with Great Britain, Napoleon III had clearly broken not only with tradition but also with a cornerstone of First Empire policy. The visit, then, reminds us that Louis-Napoleon was not locked into blindly following the paths laid out by his uncle. He was an imitator when imitation was useful—as in the reestablishment of the court—but he was also capable of discarding and altering whatever parts of his uncle's heritage did not serve his needs.

Whether it was a royal visit, the reception of an ambassador, or an imperial birthday, court life during the Second Empire drew an enormous amount of public attention. Newspapers carried long accounts of court festivities, and journals like *L'Illustration* published lively engravings not only of the big celebrations like the baptism but also of the hunts and balls and daily life of the emperor and empress. These texts and images allowed a mass audience to vicariously experience the resplendent spectacle of court life and endowed Napoleon III and everything around him with an attractive aura of opulence and luxury. Men, like the minor functionary in Guy de Maupassant's short story, "Les Dimanches d'un bourgeois de Paris," imitated the cut of the emperor's hair and beard.[82] People loitered near the Tuileries hoping to salute the emperor or his wife as they went out for a drive, or they wrote away for tickets to attend a mass in the Tuileries chapel, where along with several hundred others they would crane their necks for a glimpse of royalty.[83] For the even more fortunate who managed to get an invitation to a ball or reception, guidebooks explained what to wear and how to address the sovereigns if one was lucky enough to get that close.

The imperial court, as Louis Girard has noted, "resuscitated a dazzling model of aristocratic life."[84] At first glance, the court of the Second Empire, with its monarchical rituals and old-fashioned distinctions, would seem out of touch with the "bourgeois century" and a society Tocqueville had already characterized as "democratic" in 1835. But as Ambassador Hübner's reference to the paucity of aristocratic names at the 1854 New Year's reception reminds us, these epithets are not incorrect. Despite its aristocratic playacting, the court of Napoleon III remained a court of parvenus; in it, we see a new elite adopting the archaic ritual conventions of a previous generation. As Eric Hobsbawm has noted, "Rising classes naturally tend to see the symbols of their wealth and power in terms of what their former superior groups have established as the standards of comfort, luxury, or pomp."[85]

But a purely social explanation is not sufficient. After all, "rising classes" had formed the social basis for the government of the July Monarchy as well, yet Louis-Philippe had not established a court on a par with that of the Second Empire. The difference between the July Monarchy and the Second Empire was primarily political, not social. The advent of universal male suffrage taught Napoleon III to appeal to the masses and not just to the *pays legal*. In doing so, he discovered something that later history would sadly bear out: an image of grandeur often goes further than one of soundness and modesty. And a lavishly appointed court with all its historical richness, Napoleon III realized, was an essential component of grandeur in nineteenth-century France. The court of the Second Empire was not just for those who were "received" there but also for those who read newspapers or looked at paintings and published illustrations—in short, everyone. Perhaps better than any other French sovereign, Napoleon III fulfilled that duty "to amuse his subjects of all ranks in the social scale;" it was a "duty" that served him well . . . for a while.

O f all of the references to the French past in Second Empire spectacle, those to the period of Napoleon I clearly predominated. Every regime in French history, at least since 1789, has had its heroes. The revolutionaries looked to the Romans, to Rousseau, and to their own martyrs. The Restoration, defining itself in opposition to the Revolution, gave pride of place to Louis XVI, Marie-Antoinette, Charlotte Corday, and others, and the July Monarchy, with its unerring will to political suicide, actively promoted the cult of Napoleon I, thus opening, as Jean Tulard noted, "the Pandora's box from which came Napoleon III." [86]

The official cult of the First Emperor reached new heights after Louis-Napoleon came to power. By 1856, the state had supplied every prefecture with the First Emperor's bust,[87] and full-size statues of him had been erected in twelve cities: Lyons, Bastia, Napoléon-Vendée (now La Roche-sur-Yon), Lille, Auxonne, Cherbourg, Brienne, Paris, Ajaccio, Rouen, Montreau-faut-Yonne (Seine-et-Marne), and Saint-Vallier (Alpes-Maritimes). Louis-Napoleon personally inaugurated two of these statues, even though, perhaps because such ceremonies subtly placed him in a position inferior to the person memorialized, he rarely inaugurated statues.[88] It should also be noted that fully 27 percent of the public statues erected in France between 1849 and 1870 (50 of 182) were of figures associated primarily with the First Empire.[89]

A number of other celebrations also kept the memory of the First Emperor alive. Each year on 5 May, for example, the anniversary of the death of Napoleon I, wreaths were placed at the foot of the Vendôme Column, and a mass, attended by many of the ex-soldiers of the Empire, was said in the chapel of the Invalides.[90] Also, in April 1861, when the elaborate sarcophagus in the Invalides was finally completed and the body of Napoleon I placed inside, Napoleon III made it the occasion of a special ceremony. Less important but still notable, the house the emperor had occupied on Saint-Helena was purchased and made into a sort of shrine, and when the British government presented his funeral cart to France in 1858, that too was cause for a ceremony.

Napoleon III also used the ex-soldiers from the wars of the First Empire to perpetuate the memory of that period. In 1857, for instance, he created a special medal, the Médaille de Sainte-Hélène, for these veterans, and had it distributed in cities, arrondissements, and communes all over France. The official newspaper described the medal as the "last wish of the Emperor Napoleon I accomplished by the Emperor Napoleon III" and interpreted the ceremonies as important lessons: "Those who witnessed these distributions, imposing in their simplicity, certainly seized all of the importance of these lessons, even more striking because they emerge without effort from the simple bringing together of names and deeds." But in order for the First Empire to have wide appeal, it was important that its memory not be construed solely as military conquest. "It was not only a question of recalling a military past of which France has a very good right to be proud," the article continued, "but also of renewing a national and dynastic tradition, a tradition entirely liberal—to take that word in a truer sense than that which is sometimes attached to it." [91]

Important as these various occasional celebrations were, the most significant ongoing homage to the First Emperor remained the annual "fête nationale" on his birthday, 15 August.[92] The 15 August celebrations generally followed the same pattern throughout the country: in the morning, there were *Te Deum* masses in the churches and troop reviews wherever there were garrisons; in the afternoon, popular amusements such as concerts, military pantomimes, free theater, rope dancers, and clowns; after dark, illuminations and fireworks. The most magnificent celebrations took place in Paris, where the regime and the City of Paris collaborated to produce fantastic decorations and illuminations. On occasion the emperor himself took a direct interest in the arrangements. After the 1862 celebration, for example, he specifically requested several changes, and the following year's program submitted by the architects bears the marginal note, "read by the Emperor, 5 August 1863." [93]

The state-Paris collaboration sometimes worked far from smoothly, in part because of the regime's high-handedness and in part because Prefect of the Seine Haussmann was uncommonly prickly about his city. In 1855, the emperor canceled the celebration altogether, ostensibly so that the money could be given to widows and orphans of troops who died in the Crimean War but in reality, at least according to one source, because of a disagreement between city and state architects over whether the celebration should be heavily concentrated on the Champ-de-Mars or dispersed more evenly throughout the city.[94] In 1860 further problems arose when the enlargement of Paris in that year meant that more monies were needed, especially for the charity distributions, which were in the city's part of the budget. Haussmann complained that the city was being forced to spend more than the state, but to no avail. Haussmann complained again in 1861, this time because the plans had not been submitted to him before the state architects began obstructing streets with their constructions.[95] But at some point in the mid-1860s a simple solution seems to have been found; rather than having the plans unilaterally decreed by the state, they were hammered out at a meeting that included both Haussmann and the responsible government minister, as well as both city and state architects.[96]

The architects assigned to the 15 August decorations were men of the highest distinction. In 1853, Louis Visconti, chief architect of the new Louvre and an innovative festival architect under Louis-Philippe, was in charge.[97] Visconti died later that year, and his place as 15 August architect was taken by the same man who succeeded him at the Louvre, Hector Lefuel. Lefuel, assisted by the decorative painter Pierre-Victor Galand, remained in charge of the 15 August celebrations for the rest of the Empire. The city architects were equally illustrious. The task generally fell to either Victor Baltard, architect of Les Halles and of the ornate ceremonial starcase at the Hôtel-de-Ville, or to another Haussmann protégé, Adolphe Alphand, the brilliant landscape architect who designed the Bois de Boulogne and a number of other Parisian parks.

For the 15 August celebrations, as for all imperial celebrations, the architects were assisted by a number of *entrepreneurs des fêtes*, private contractors who translated the architects' plans into the actual decorations.[98] Although the contracts were open to bidding, a few large enterprises tended to dominate the industry: Adolphe Belloir and Alexis Godillot for constructions and decorations, for example, and Ruggieri for fireworks. These companies had the knowledge and materials necessary to carry through elaborate plans on short notice. In at least one case (Belloir), the company still exists and still works on state functions.

Together, the architects and the entrepreneurs created elaborate, exotic, and often distinctly political decorations. The centerpiece was usually a large structure on the Place de la Concorde illuminated either by gas or by thousands of colored jars of oil, or *lampions*. In 1858, they adopted a Chinese decor intended to represent Peking by night, a theme they repeated in 1861 in order to "recall the recent actions of the French army,"[99] by which they meant the Anglo-French invasion of China and burning of the Summer Palace in Peking the year before. Similarly, in 1864, while the army was in Mexico with Maximilian, the Place de la Concorde was decorated "in a style half Mexican and half Moorish."[100] Bonapartist symbols also provided political content. Eagles, bees, imperial coats of arms, and so forth were always present, and at times they were made the centerpiece of the celebration. In 1865, for example, Alphand turned the obelisk into a "needle of fire, on the four faces of which appear[ed] glittering palm leaves supporting the imperial letter and formed from almost 50,000 jets of gas."[101]

Immense crowds packed the public spaces of Paris for the 15 August festivities. For the free admission to the theaters, a tradition dating back to the Old Regime, one had to arrive early and wait in a long line—sometimes as long as four or five hours.[102] In addition to the regular play, the 15 August showings included special short musical numbers appropriate to the occasion. These were usually didactic poems set to music, sometimes by well-known composers.[103] A cantata sung at the Opera in 1860, for example, included the following lyrics:

> *Napoléon, c'est la sainte espérance*
> *Des opprimés, des pauvres, des petits!*
> *C'est l'union, c'est l'ordre qui s'avance,*
> *C'est la retraite et la mort des partis!*
> *C'est le drapeau qui marche à la victoire*
> *Et du bon droit ne s'écarte jamais!*
> *C'est pour la France un avenir de gloire*
> *C'est pour l'Europe un avenir de paix!*[104]

Paternalism, union, order, glory—all watchwords of Bonapartism. In the absence of the public speeches that would later be a hallmark of Bastille Day, poems like these provided one of the fullest official articulations of the meaning of the 15 August celebrations.

If the theaters were crowded, the fireworks were mobbed. Usually two shows took place simultaneously: a larger one by Ruggieri in central Paris (the precise location varied) and a somewhat smaller one at the Barrière du Trône (now the Place de la Nation). These were long, spectacular affairs that usually included set pieces such as the giant "N" with the words "Puebla" and "Mexico" on either side of it in 1865. "From ten o'clock to midnight," as one observer later described the shows, "one heard the noise of a torrent which flowed, resonant and regular, for whole hours."[105] The crowds, however, were monstrous. One author (no friend of the Empire) described a woman so tightly squeezed that she fainted and later died.[106] And at the end of the show in 1866, nine people were crushed to death in a crowd attempting to cross the Pont de la Concorde when the other side was closed by troops. Nor were these the only mishaps. Burning fireworks sometimes landed in the crowd, causing injuries, and on at least one occasion a house caught fire in Passy.[107]

The government paid very close attention to the popular response to the 15 August celebrations. Officials sometimes systematically went through the newspaper reports, and prosecutors and prefects both reported on how the celebrations had been received in their districts, after receiving reports from their subordinates.[108] There were sometimes problems. Priests occasionally refused to sing the *Te Deum*, for example, and the uncertain August weather often made things difficult. For the most part, however, the reports were extremely positive. "Perhaps never has the population of Grenoble shown itself more sympathetic to the emperor," reported the prefect of the Isère in 1856.[109] And according to the Paris prosecutor in 1863, "The festival of 15 August, through the sincere and spontaneous manifestations that it everywhere aroused, has once again proven that the confidence of France in the emperor is unbreakable."[110]

In an influential book, historian Arno Mayer has traced what he calls the "persistence of the Old Regime" through 1914.[111] On the surface, the evidence presented in this chapter would seem to bear out Mayer's thesis. In the latter half of the "bourgeois century," throwbacks to the Old Regime and to the First Empire had a centrality most traditional accounts would not lead us to expect. But Mayer, perhaps due to his assumptions about economic development (for example, that manufacturing is essentially "Old Regime"), insufficiently recognizes that the cultural predominance of the past in the nineteenth century indicates not the "persistence" of old elites in positions of power but a *new* valorization of the past by *new* social and political groups.

In British historian Eric Hobsbawm's view, social changes in nineteenth-century Europe had undermined the old hierarchical structures of power and necessitated new strategies for maintaining social cohesion. One of most important of those strategies was the "invention of tradition," which Hobsbawm defines as "a set of practices, normally governed by overtly or tacitly accepted rules and of a ritual or symbolic nature, which seek to inculcate certain values and norms of behaviour by repetition, which automatically implies continuity with the past. In fact, where possible, they normally attempt to establish continuity with a suitable historic past."[112] Invented traditions, then, used emotionally charged symbols taken from the past to rally the masses to new "all-embracing pseudo-communities,"[113] like the nation.

The ceremonial aspects of the Second Empire examined here both support Hobsbawm's thesis and extend it. In the ritualistic use of history and historically sanctioned symbols to legitimate a sovereign who no longer even pretended to rule by divine right, we have the essence of invented tradition. At the same time, the fact that these ceremonies and symbols embodied a particularly Bonapartist view of history reminds us that there were, at least in France, competing visions of what those traditions should be. Through these visions, the various groups that claimed a right to rule defined both themselves and each other. The historical bent in Bonapartist ceremonies, in other words, was not only a new device to solidify social cohesion in a changing world but also a political tool to be used against republican and legitimist rivals. Through its version of French history, Bonapartism, sometimes in a vague and amorphous manner and sometimes with pellucid clarity, staked its particular claim to represent the nation.

Why, however, was it the past that became so important in defining the new social identities and political legitimacies of the nineteenth century? At one level, the past, at least in the sense of a continuity with past ages of national greatness that pervaded these ceremonies, provided a semblance of certainty in a world undergoing rapid social and political change. Just as the myth of an ideal rural England examined by Martin Wiener emerged during the period of rapid industrialization precisely because it provided an alternative to that process,[114] so a manufactured linkage with previous regimes loomed largest in France during the period of her greatest political transformations. The silk stockings and knee breeches, the medievalism of the ceremonies in Notre-Dame, the statues of great men of the past, then, gave the French an illusion of continuity and rootedness that belied the very real and very disturbing changes taking place around them.

But deeper currents may also be running here. In one of his last major works, Lionel Trilling suggested that the great narrative national histories of the late eighteenth and nineteenth centuries may have helped fill the place religion had occupied in an older world:

> When God died, as by common consent he did, however slowly the explicit news of the demise reached us, history undertook to provide the beginnings which men once thought necessary to the authenticity of the world and themselves. Nietzsche says that the realization of the death of God had the effect of making all things, and man himself, seem "weightless": the great narrative historians in some considerable degree maintained the weightiness of things by thickening the past, making it exigent, imperative, a sanction of

authority, an assurance of destiny. The tale they told interpreted the sound and fury of events, made them signify *something*, a direction taken, an end in view.[115]

Did not the focus on the past in the public life of the Second Empire provide the same kind of grounding in a more amorphous but also more distinctly public and political manner? Did not Louis-Napoleon seem the "weightier" for standing in the place of his uncle and of so many monarchs of the past? And while it is difficult to demonstrate the precise role or even the fact of the "death of God" in these ceremonies, it is nonetheless clear that the God of the past, the God who sacralized the authority of the kings of the Old Regime, of Napoleon, and perhaps even of Charles X, was no longer present. As in the figure of Napoleon I descending from heaven to bless the new heir to the throne in Couture's unfinished painting of the baptism and in some popular engravings, it was not divine authority that sacralized the regime in these ceremonies, it was history.

FOUR

Spectacles of Prosperity

Although allusions to the past can be found throughout virtually all Second Empire spectacle, the heart of those references remained the activities and celebrations that were already a part of the monarchical and imperial traditions. More modern allusions were never entirely absent even from these events, as we saw in the emperor's announcement of his marriage, but they were generally peripheral to the imitation and commemoration of past regimes.

This balance was reversed, however, in two of the Empire's most common types of celebration: inaugurations and ceremonies honoring the setting of the first stone. Virtually every new public building, bridge, statue, school, and other material addition was fêted with one or both of these ceremonies, more or less lavish depending on the object's importance. At a social level, the mania for this kind of celebration—which was by no means limited to France—can be seen as the bourgeoisie patting itself on the back for the material progress it had brought. Their frequency—rarely did a month go by without some inauguration important enough to be mentioned in the major newspapers—seemed to make the progress and prosperity of the new age palpably evident.

Politically these celebrations played a similar role, although here it was often more explicitly stated. The new additions, according to innumerable orators, were made possible only by the leadership of Louis-Napoleon Bonaparte. Economic progress and prosperity had been a crucial part of Louis-Napoleon's appeal from the beginning. As he said in his most famous speech, the Bordeaux address of 2 September 1852 heralding the reestablishment of the Empire,

> We have immense uncultivated territories to clear, roads to open, ports to dig, rivers to render navigable, canals to finish, our network of railways to complete. . . . That is how I understand the Empire, if the Empire is to be restored. Such are the conquests I contemplate, and you, all of you who surround me, you who desire, as I do, our country's good, you are my soldiers.[1]

These were not empty words. Although the ultimate results of imperial economic policies would be mixed, the regime did make a real effort to foster prosperity. It modernized the credit and banking laws, promoted free trade, underwrote a massive expansion of the railroads, and pursued public works programs designed to reduce unemployment at the same time that they provided the necessary infrastructure for further commercial and industrial development. But the rhetoric was even louder than the reality. In Louis-Napoleon's hands, even wasteful expenditures on court luxuries became a fostering of prosperity through economic stimulation. And a central theme running through many of Louis-Napoleon's speeches was his claim to bring jobs, markets, hospitals, housing, and other amenities to the working classes. Bonapartism, as Theodore Zeldin has remarked, "in its most simple interpretation, meant prosperity."[2] There was, as Zeldin well understood, more than this to Bonapartism, but his remark justly suggests that many Frenchmen supported the Second Empire not because they were convinced that the Bonapartes had a valid hereditary claim to be rulers of France but because they saw in the Empire the best guarantor of prosperity and economic progress.

Inaugurations and stone-setting ceremonies allowed Louis-Napoleon to identify and to forcefully underscore the positive benefits bought by his good government. The new railroad lines, boulevards, ports, hospitals, and other objects of these ceremonies seemed tangible demonstrations of the truth of his claims to bring prosperity and to provide for the future. At the same time, the newness and the importance of the objects, as well as the various attractions of the celebrations, made it easy to draw large crowds of curious spectators. These crowds, especially as described and interpreted in the Bonapartist press, became evidence for Louis-Napoleon's ongoing popularity.

In many ways, inaugurations and stone-setting ceremonies were very similar. In the stone-setting ceremonies, an official or other dignitary, sometimes the emperor or empress, set the first stone of a new hospital, marketplace, school, or other edifice using a special ceremonial trowel.[3] Frequently the stone in question had been hollowed out so that a box containing various mementos could be placed inside it, rather like a time capsule. When Minister of the Interior Billault set the first stone of the home for convalescent workers at Vincennes in 1855, for example, he placed inside it a box containing coins from that year, as well as a commemorative medal bearing the portrait of the emperor that had been struck for the occasion.[4] Like inaugurations, these ritual acts of construction linked the regime to material objects of benefit to the community and provided the occasion for speeches and newspaper articles praising the enlightened leadership of Louis-Napoleon. Without an actual building to excite curiosity, however, the ceremonies lacked much of the punch of inaugurations. Moreover, while inaugurations seemed to demonstrate what the regime had actually done, stone-setting ceremonies were merely promises of what it would do, and those promises were not always kept. The first stone of the new Sorbonne, for example, was ceremonially placed in 1855, but, as Louis Girard noted, it was "still waiting for the second stone in 1871."[5]

Stone-setting ceremonies were also generally reserved for buildings, while almost anything might be inaugurated. Statues received inaugural celebrations, as did churches, schools, fountains, bridges, roads, and virtually every other addition of general public utility or beautification. The emperor even "inaugurated" the man-made lake in the Bois de Boulogne, starting the flow of water into it. The majority of inaugurations were predominantly local affairs, though reports and illustrations of them often appeared in the national press. A local official, usually the mayor, prefect, or subprefect, presided over such ceremonies, which normally included speeches, decorations, spectators, and a banquet. Inaugurations of more important objects—major railroad lines and statues of well-known figures, for example—usually included the presence of one or more national officials and more lavish preparations. These could sometimes be rather long affairs. At the 1861 inauguration of the statue of Louis Jacques Thénard in Sens, for example, a crowd of 10,000 stood through a number of cantatas sung by local musical associations in honor of the great chemist and two hours of speeches by eleven different orators.[6]

The principal act in an inauguration often consisted of a sort of ritualized first use of the new object. Thus statues, which functioned as visual embellishment, were unveiled and opened to public view. New streets, bridges, and railroad lines, on the other hand, were "used" in their own ways. In these inaugurations, official processions rode through the streets and crossed the bridges, and trains bearing inaugural parties rode over the new routes. Sometimes the authorities went to great lengths to reserve this first use for the inaugurations, but in other cases it was purely formal. A statue of the eighteenth-century naturalist Georges Louis Leclerc, Comte de Buffon, in his native Montbard, for example, had actually been in place for several years before it was finally inaugurated in 1865.[7]

Like other Second Empire celebrations, inaugurations and stone-setting ceremonies often underscored ongoing ties between regime and Church. In these ceremonies, this usually took the form of a blessing bestowed upon the new or soon-to-be-built object by the local religious authorities. Catholic priests happily blessed all sorts of buildings, canals, bridges, fountains, and a variety of other objects. Statues of nonreligious figures, however, were somewhat problematic. In 1853, the archbishop of Paris refused the emperor's request, transmitted through the minister of state, to bestow the official blessing in the inauguration of Rude's statue of Marshal Ney on the spot where he was executed in Paris. "The inauguration of a statue, however great the man honored," Archbishop Sibour wrote, "is a purely civil festival, and the Church has in her rituals neither prayer nor benediction for such a ceremony."[8] But other members of the clergy were sometimes more obliging. At Montereau-faut-Yonne in 1867, for example, the bishop of Meaux blessed a statue of Napoleon I, though not everyone was pleased with his action.[9]

If the clergy often participated in ceremonies that were not essentially religious in nature, regime officials returned the favor by attending religious celebrations such as inaugurations and stone-setting ceremonies for new churches. A striking example of this took place in September 1852, shortly before the restoration of the Empire, when Louis-Napoleon set the first stone of the new cathedral in Marseille. The ceremony, as his speech on the occasion made clear, was calculated to reassure the Church of his support. His government, he said, was one of the few that supported religion "not as a political instrument, nor in order to please a party, but solely through conviction and through love of the good [religion] inspires and the truths it teaches." But his very next words seemed to belie this selfless support and to approach more closely the real intent of such ceremonies. "When you enter this temple to call the protection of heaven onto those dear to you or onto the enterprises that you have begun," he said, "remember the one who posed the first stone of this edifice and believe that, identifying himself with the future of this great city, he shares the spirit of your prayers and your hopes."[10] The stone-posing ceremony, then, was supposed to make the new cathedral into a lasting reminder of Louis-Napoleon and a demonstration of his concern for the welfare of the people of Marseille.

Over the course of Louis-Napoleon's reign, the close Church-state relations exemplified in the Marseille cathedral stone-posing ceremony deteriorated significantly. The Italian campaign of 1859, in particular, led to a rift between the regime and the Church that never completely healed, though by 1868 Roman intransigence and the necessity of dealing with social problems had forced some of the regime's erstwhile clerical opponents back into the Bonapartist fold.[11] This rift, however, cannot easily be traced in the ceremonies of the period, since both regime and Church had too much at stake in mutual participation for the tensions to lead to such an open and public break. To be sure, certain individual clerics and officials with particularly extreme views did sometimes openly refuse to participate in each other's celebrations, but such incidents were rare.

Nonetheless, we can see a cooling of Church-state ceremonial relations during these years, more discernible in a general change of attitude than in open clashes. In this respect, the Marseille stone posing was a striking affirmation of the closeness of Church and regime in the early 1850s, but it was not the only such affirmation. Soon after the reestablishment of the Empire, for example, the inauguration of the Church of Saint-Geneviève (formerly the Panthéon) sent the same message. Much of this important ceremony consisted of moving the relics of the saint back to the church in the first major religious procession in Paris since the Restoration. Archbishop Sibour personally asked the emperor to attend,[12] and although the emperor declined the invitation, several of his ministers and a number of other officials did participate.[13]

The 1860s, on the other hand, while they saw no sudden change in the normal ritual relations of Church and regime, also saw none of the exuberance that marked the ceremonies of the 1850s. The emperor did not, for example, attend the 1864 inauguration of the Marseille cathedral whose stone he had so devoutly and publicly set in 1852. And officials in some parts of the provinces may have allowed their participation in religious rituals to gradually slip. For example, in 1853 the *cour impériale* at Agen decided to take part each year in the Corpus Christi procession, but by 1858 so few magistrates attended that they canceled the resolution.[14]

The religious element in inaugurations and stone-setting ceremonies did not hinder the emphasis on the modern. This can be seen clearly in the inaugurations of railroad lines. Railroads generated enormous excitement in the nineteenth century; they were symbols of industrial modernity, emblems of the new age of iron and steam.[15] Moreover, these new links between Paris and the provinces seemed to many to be uniting the country in a way that went beyond more rapid and efficient travel. France seemed to be becoming an integrated unit rather than a miscellaneous collection of provinces. Railroad inaugurations took on a particular fascination because every new line seemed to mark another step in these important transformations. "What, after all, can we say of the opening of a new line?," asked *L'Illustration* apropos of the inauguration of the Tours to Angers line in 1849:

> It is a new channel opened to the ever rising waters of civilization; it is a breach through which rush the ideas of progress and amelioration; it is the bringing together of all the parts of this great whole we call France; it is the most cordial and intimate harmony of the members of the social body: through these new arteries, blood flows more warmly and quickly from the heart to the extremities and returns to the heart richer by all it has collected on its route.[16]

Railroads, then, symbolized much more than just material progress. They were the geographical equivalent of the social unity that was such an important part of Louis-Napoleon's Bonapartism.

As president of the Second Republic, Louis-Napoleon had made a concerted effort to associate himself with the new lines uniting the nation by personally inaugurating no fewer than twelve of them. These ceremonies almost invariably had the same form. A decorated official train left Paris on the morning of the ceremony bearing 200 to 300 important guests to the city at the terminus of the new line. There a large crowd, sometimes augmented by substantial numbers of people shipped in from Paris the day before,[17] greeted the group as church bells and cannons sounded. After an exchange of formal greetings came the blessing of the locomotives, usually performed before an altar erected at the station. Prelates did not generally object to this odd benediction, though they may not always have understood exactly what was going on. One Breton archbishop, apparently surprised when the imposing locomotive in front of him began to move, commanded it to "get back, Satanic thing!" instead of bestowing the traditional blessing.[18]

Such incidents were unusual. More typical was the 1851 Nantes inauguration in which the bishop, accompanied by all of his clergy, his cross, his banners, and several military units, made an elaborate procession from the cathedral to the train station while singing religious hymns. Once there, he approached the altar and waited in silence while the locomotives moved forward. After more hymns, the bishop, preceded by his acolytes, sprinkled holy water over the tracks and the engines. Then came a *Te Deum*, a processional return to the cathedral, and an orison and pontifical benediction to close the ceremony.[19] After the religious blessings at these celebrations, the remainder of the day and evening were usually taken up with various other entertainments, often including troop reviews, banquets, speeches, and illuminations.

By the mid-1850s, however, a surfeit of such ceremonies, combined with a general tapering off of popular enthusiasm for railroads, meant that railway line inaugurations lost some of their luster.[20] *L'Illustration*, once the celebrations' most enthusiastic chronicler, now began to belittle them as "hardly festivals at all any more" and to complain that they all "looked alike," and that "the same decorations serve in the north, the south, the east, and the west."[21] As a result, railroad inaugurations became less frequent in the mid-1850s and 1860s. Sometimes railroad companies neglected to inaugurate new lines at all, preferring a public donation to charity of the money that they would have spent on a ceremony.[22] And although most lines—especially the larger ones—continued to receive festive welcomes, Louis-Napoleon now attended them much less frequently, though he did often send important dignitaries whose speeches attributed the new lines— and sometimes much else as well—to his progressive leadership. In a toast at the inaugural dinner for the line from Nantes to Lorient, for example, the prefect of the Morbihan underscored all the emperor was doing for Brittany:

> It is to the Emperor, to his generous and patriotic plans, to his ardent love for all which can be useful to the country, that we owe this complete network crossing Brittany in every direction. It is to him that we owe the amelioration of our ports, the development of our roads, the encouragement given to our agriculture and our industry. It is through him that our churches have been restored and that others will open for your faith.[23]

If new railroad lines seemed a bit passé by the mid-1850s, the same cannot be said for the new streets of Napoleon III's transformation of Paris, a project then just beginning to come into its own. In rebuilding Paris, Napoleon III and Baron Haussmann carried out a vast and multifaceted project. The prolonged demolition and construction provided employment for thousands, made Paris a cleaner, healthier city, and provided the necessary infrastructure for continued urban expansion and for greater commercial prosperity. By the same token, however, the rebuilding also destroyed much that was of historical and emotional value to Parisians, extended the state's ability to quell insurrection by providing a means of military access to poorer areas, and brought higher rents that forced many of the less affluent out of the center of the city.

Along with these social and economic mutations, Haussmannization also brought a new dimension to the visual experience of the city—the city as spectacle. In art historian T. J. Clark's view, for example, the streets of the new Paris provided a permanent spectacle of modernity that functioned as the setting for the visual display necessary to a modern consumption economy.[24] But the visual transformation of the city also had a more explicitly political component. As Philip Nord has remarked, "Just as the baroque of the seventeenth century celebrated the power of the absolutist state, so the pseudo-baroque of Imperial France enshrined the neoabsolutism of the Bonapartist state."[25] Like other urban projects before it, then, the rebuilding of Paris under Napoleon III made the city itself into a permanent reminder of the greatness of the regime. Through it, Napoleon III left his mark indelibly inscribed in the very stone of the buildings and the structure of the streets.

But if the idea of the city as a spectacle of power is an enduring part of urban building projects, the nature of that spectacle in the new Paris differed markedly from previous projects. The central monument of the typical project of the past had been a representation of the monarch himself, as in the equestrian statues of the kings placed in the center of the public squares they constructed—Louis XIV on the Place des Victoires, for example, or Louis XIII on the Place des Vosges. By contrast, the equivalent monuments for Napoleon III were objects designed to be of public utility: railroad stations, parks, the Opera, the stock exchange, the new streets themselves. This change reflects a fundamental shift in the nature of political legitimacy in the nineteenth century, a shift from emphasizing the physical person of the leader to emphasizing what the leader had accomplished.

That Louis-Napoleon's monuments were also his accomplishments did not make them any less permanent visual symbols of power than the statues and triumphal arches of his predecessors. In this respect, the new monuments did, however, function very differently from the old ones. They were no longer the centers around which everything else rotated but the culminations of broad, straight avenues, drawing the spectator's attention through the contrast between their distinctiveness and the regularized monotony of the buildings on the approaching avenues—what François Loyer terms a "rigorous antithesis of unity and plurality."[26] Nor should the paucity of direct representations of the sovereign lead us to think he was absent. Indeed, one of the strengths of Louis-Napoleon's urbanization is that he made it far more difficult to efface his presence than would have been the case had he memorialized himself in the more traditional manner. It is easier to pull down a statue than to rip out a boulevard, which helps to explain the particular French penchant for renaming streets.

The new permanent spectacle of the city and the regime's predilection for ostentatious celebration came together in three showy inaugurations of new boulevards.[27] The opening of a new street in any city normally provides the occasion for a municipal ceremony. In what has become a standard ritual of urban life, the mayor, or some other local official, gives a short speech and cuts a ribbon tied across the street, after which the thoroughfare is considered open to public use. In form, the three major inaugurations of new boulevards in Second Empire Paris (Sébastopol, Malesherbes, and Prince Eugène) were really just very elaborate versions of this basic ceremony. But these were not ordinary new streets, especially for a regime that, as one of Paris's best historians put it, considered "the city's grandeur as inseparable from its own."[28] As a result, the chief inaugurations were not mere ribbon-cutting ceremonies but major extravaganzas of national importance that focused attention on the transformation of the city and that carried the message that the new boulevards were important accomplishments of the imperial regime.

The inaugural ceremony for the Boulevard de Sébastopol set the standard for the boulevard inaugurations. Napoleon III and Haussmann had divided their proposed transformations of Paris into three "networks" of streets to be successively undertaken. The finished Boulevard de Sébastopol marked the completion of the first of these, but the second was still unfunded. The Municipal Council of the city of Paris had approved the new plans in March but had found the 180 million-franc price tag too high for the city alone to manage, so a law to be presented to the legislature called for the state to provide one-third of the money. Such spending, however, was controversial since, as David Pinkney has noted, "Provincial deputies objected to spending so many millions in Paris when construction of railroads and highways was held up by lack of funds, and they raised the old specter of revolution led by workers the construction would attract to Paris."[29]

Persuading these deputies that the work in Paris was of truly national importance and reassuring them of the loyalty of the Parisian populace to the emperor were major considerations at the inauguration. The deputies received excellent seats at the ceremony, and the emperor directly addressed their concerns in his speech. Moreover, the regime chose to send its proposed law on the second network to the legislature just one day after the inauguration.[30] The inauguration, then, was at least in part an attempt to "publicly spur on the legislative body," as Emile Ollivier put it.[31]

Named for the French victory at Sébastopol in the Crimean War several years earlier, the boulevard was completed in the spring of 1858. For over four years, workers had blasted and burrowed their way through one of the most densely populated and rebellious sections of Paris. The thirty-three-yard-wide, one-and-a-quarter-mile-long boulevard they built extended the Boulevard de Strasbourg to the Seine, creating the right-bank section of what has remained Paris's main north-south thoroughfare. The new boulevard was especially important because it connected Paris's eastern train station, the Gare de l'Est, with the center of the city by way of the Boulevard de Strasbourg. The ceremony underscored the boulevard's function of providing access to the station by extending the area inaugurated all the way to that station, that is, by including the Boulevard de Strasbourg as well, even though that boulevard had actually been inaugurated in a less important and very badly botched ceremony a few years before.[32] The new street modernized transportation within Paris at least as much and perhaps more than any other single addition until the construction of the Metro began in 1900. But that was not the limit of its utility. It also helped provide Parisians with another convenience people have grown used to in the past century or so: a modern sewage system. Beneath the boulevard, an enormous sewage collector drain had been constructed. The importance of this drain in the inauguration of the new boulevard serves to recall the significance of the Paris sewers for the men of the Second Empire, a significance that, as Donald Reid has shown, had as much to do with the symbolic association of the old sewers with crime and sedition as it did with genuinely hygienic concerns.[33] In visiting the clean new sewer, Napoleon III symbolically affirmed that the new Paris would be not only cleaner and more sanitary physically but also morally superior.

City architect Victor Baltard, who had designed Les Halles, was in charge of the decorations for the inaugural ceremony.[34] Assisted by one of the largest of the *entrepreneurs des fêtes,* Adolphe Belloir, and a team that included the decorative painters Nolau and Rubé, he erected hundreds of flagpoles on both sides of the boulevard from the Place du Châtelet to the Gare de l'Est. Atop them, he alternated tricolor banners with green banners bearing Napoleonic bees and "N"s and, at the base of each pole, trophies of flags and shields bearing the imperial arms and those of the City of Paris. At each end of the boulevard were two masts thirty meters tall, bearing twenty-meter-long tricolor banners, and along the way, many of the buildings and street crossings had been decorated by the residents. The decorative centerpiece, however, was the enormous gold lamé curtain stretched across the boulevard just before the point where it meets the Boulevard Saint-Denis and turns into the Boulevard de Strasbourg (see figure 4.1). The curtain was suspended from two tall minarets and decorated with gold stars and green diamonds; above it floated a row of tricolor banners.

In addition to exotic garniture and Napoleonic emblems, the decoration included prominent reminders of the progressive nature of the new con-

Figure 4.1. The inauguration of the Boulevard de Sébastopol, 5 April 1858, from *L'Illustration*, 10 April 1858. (Doe Library, University of California, Berkeley)

struction. Painted allegorical figures of Commerce, Industry, Art, and Science placed at the base of each of the minarets, for example, evoked the values supposedly served by the new addition to the Parisian landscape, and in a special enclosure near the minarets, many of the machines and tools used in the construction of both the boulevard and the new sewer were prominently displayed. In front of these "veritables trophées du travail," as one journalist called them,[35] stood a number of workers who had taken part in the construction.

It was Monday, 5 April 1858. Long before noon the workers had put the finishing touches on the decorations, and the crowd, brought out in force by the excellent weather, had begun to gather. During construction, the boulevard had been fenced off to keep out unauthorized visitors, and at least part of this fence had been left in place until after the curtain was hung so that the panoramic view would remain hidden until the curtain was opened. At a few minutes after two o'clock, the emperor, preceded by an escort of his elite Cent-Gardes, left the Tuileries Palace. Following twenty paces behind him came his military staff, which included many of the most illustrious figures of the regime. The empress and the Princess Mathilde, the emperor's cousin, followed the military staff in an open carriage, and an escort of Lancers of the Guard brought up the rear. As he often did on such occasions, the emperor rode horseback and wore the uniform of a divisional general. By riding at a distance from his escorts, the emperor drew attention to himself more forcefully than usual, a move that in the aftermath of the Orsini assassination attempt less than three months earlier was interpreted as an act of bravery.[36]

The procession followed the quais along the river to the Place du Châtelet, where Haussmann and Prefect of Police Boittelle welcomed the emperor. As the emperor turned onto the new boulevard, a tricolor flag was raised, giving the signal to draw back the curtain at the Boulevard Saint-Denis to present the long perspective to view for the first time. The curtain opened in the center, and the two halves fell back upon the minarets. From one end of the boulevard, the imperial cortege advanced. At the other, the various guests assembled for the inauguration, including the members of the legislature, watched and admired from banks of seats constructed in front of the Gare de l'Est. Behind the lines of troops along the way, thousands of spectators peered at the imperial procession as it made its way to the station.

The drawing back of the curtain was the most spectacular element of the celebration. Described by one viewer as something "out of a magical play,"[37] it had an undeniably theatrical quality. It unveiled the new street as if the street itself were a monument, which indeed it was; a monument that by its very nature symbolized modernity and progress. It was, as Walter Benjamin noted, part of the nineteenth-century inclination to "ennoble technical necessities by artistic aims."[38] By giving such an elaborate "unveiling" to a new street, the emperor underscored the idea that the transformation of Paris was not merely utilitarian but also aesthetic; that it was visually appealing as well as useful. This is not to say that unadorned utilitarianism was slighted. Indeed, part way up the boulevard, the cortege actually halted so that the emperor could descend into the new sewage drain installed beneath the boulevard to examine the displayed tools, which workmen operated in his honor.[39]

While the emperor visited the sewer, the two prefects continued on to the train station. Accompanied by the Municipal Council of Paris, they greeted the emperor when he arrived and escorted him into the train station, where a large salon had been formed with hangings of green silk. Many of the high functionaries of the regime occupied banks of seats erected around a platform, on which seats for the emperor and empress had been placed. After they had taken their places, the emperor read a prepared address to the Municipal Council of the City of Paris. As usual with such speeches, the emperor's words were heard only by those very near him. Most people did not learn what was said until later, through newspapers and public posters, put up by the authorities, which contained the text of the speech. Nonetheless, the speech was an important part of the spectacle, for it verbally expressed the major themes of the inauguration and provided a more complete overview of the significance of the new boulevard.

The emperor emphasized the value of the boulevard to the capital and to France as a whole and argued that the nation needed to continue with such improvements in order to meet the challenges of the modern world. Urban amelioration of this nature was necessary, the emperor said, because railroads were dramatically altering the economic and social conditions of life in the city. They contributed to a large and rapid increase in population and were becoming the main channel for goods coming into the city. But the Municipal Council had risen to the task, he continued. It had supported new constructions to lodge the influx of population and had torn down some "unhealthy districts" in order both to let "light and health" in and to build large "arteries" that connected the center of the city with its periphery. In addition, the emperor praised the council's charitable efforts and its construction of new churches, hospitals, schools, sewers, and markets. But the value of its efforts went beyond immediate practical utility, he believed, since the aesthetic worthiness and the names of the new constructions made them "inspire high sentiments" not only in the present but into the future as well: "When the generations who follow traverse our great city, not only will they acquire a taste for the beautiful through the spectacle of these works of art, but in reading the names inscribed on our bridges and on our streets they will remember the glory of our arms from Rivoli to Sébastopol." Against a backdrop of preparation for the future, then, the emperor linked his regime's modernization of Paris to both of the military victories of the two empires and explicitly stated his will to remake the city as spectacle. Just as the visual aspects of the ceremony had combined the utilitarian and the aesthetic, so too were they woven together in the emperor's speech.

The emperor went on to praise those responsible for these accomplishments. He complimented the legislature for not having let "provincial egotism" get in the way of support and said that they had "understood that a country like France needed a capital worthy of her." He continued with similar praise for the Municipal Council and Haussmann and concluded with a plea that went to the heart of the immediate political objectives of the ceremony:

> But our task, Messieurs, is far from being finished; you have approved a general plan that should continue what you have so well begun. The legislature, I hope, will soon vote for it, and we will thus see each year great arteries opening, the populous quarters cleaned up, rents coming down through numerous constructions, the working class enriching itself through work, misery diminishing through better organized philanthropy, and Paris thus answering more and more its high destination.

Simply put, more funds were needed to continue the work that had begun.

After his address, the emperor presented awards to four of the engineers most closely involved in the project. Haussmann's protégé Eugène Belgrand, who headed the city's water and sewer service and who had been responsible for overseeing the construction of the sewage drain beneath the boulevard, was promoted to the top of his grade. In addition, one roadway engineer was made an officer of the Legion of Honor, and two lesser engineers received chevalier's crosses in the same order. Such awards were typical of many Second Empire celebrations; they were frequently presented at celebrations of this nature and often given to engineers.

The procession returned in the same order as it had arrived but by a different route, turning right at the Boulevard Saint-Denis and following the grand boulevards around to return to the Tuileries Palace. That evening the festivities continued. The emperor and empress attended a costume ball at the Ministry of Foreign Affairs that one witness described as "splendid and cold," [40] while the rest of the population was allowed access to the new thoroughfare. The boulevard was lit up both with its permanently installed gas lights and with special decorative illuminations, and long into the night, people strolled along the wide swath that had been cut through their city.

During the next few days, the press discussed the new boulevard and its inauguration at length. As with all celebrations, no matter how large the actual crowd of spectators might have been, it is clear that a far larger number experienced the event vicariously through these press reports. They therefore constitute an important aspect of the celebration. Moreover, by looking specifically at the enthusiastic accounts in the newspapers that supported the regime, we can see what the Bonapartists believed—or at least professed to believe—the ceremony demonstrated. Unfortunately, we cannot explore what the regime's opponents thought in the same manner. Even in the nonaligned press, it is hard to find anything that is actually critical of the inauguration. Although the accounts vary somewhat in enthusiasm, there is no mention, for example, of the frivolity of spending so much

money for a celebration or of any dissident voices in the crowd of spectators, though there must have been at least a few. This seeming unanimity,
however, surely stems from censorship rather than from consensus. After
Orsini's attempt to assassinate the emperor in February, the frightened regime had brought in a more hard-line minister of the interior and added
to its already formidable arsenal of restrictive laws one of the most repressive pieces of legislation in French history, the National Security Law.[41] By
the time of the inauguration, the country was in the midst of a new wave
of arrests and deportations of radicals to Algeria. In this climate, the fact
that the nonaligned press used standard accounts of the ceremony or limited
it to a short review in the *faits divers* section almost seems like criticism.[42]

When they discussed the merits of the street itself, the press accounts
generally followed the lines mapped out by the emperor's speech. Many
papers emphasized the benefits to the community: the cleaning up of the
"fetid miasmas," more efficient transportation, and beautification of the city.
Some also went further and argued that the new street would have an
advantageous moral and political impact on the traditionally rebellious area
it passed through. One journalist, for example, maintained that "Paris
cleaned up, Paris inundated with air and light all the way down into the
depths of those quarters where, previously, misery, ignorance, and physical
degradation had been packed in together, means a pacified Paris and a
tranquil France."[43]

The Bonapartist papers showered praise on everything about the inaugural ceremony and tried to make it seem an event of historic proportions.
The official government organ, *Le Moniteur universel*, crowed that "never
has a new street been inaugurated in Paris with so much solemnity,"[44] and
Le Pays rhapsodized about "an *éclat* that will remain engraved in the memory of the Parisian population."[45]

The Bonapartist papers also claimed, as they always did when reporting
on such celebrations, that the emperor received an overwhelmingly enthusiastic welcome from the spectators. A. L. Ravergie maintained in *La Patrie*,
for example, that "in no other epoch have we seen the acclamations explode
with such enthusiasm" and that "the inauguration of the Boulevard de
Sébastopol will remain in the memory of those who witnessed it as the
souvenir of an event that was at the same time both useful and glorious
for the reign and for the nation."[46] Henry Cauvin, writing in *Le Constitutionnel*, took this barrage the furthest by turning the inauguration into a
sort of miniplebiscite that proved the continuing legitimacy of the emperor.
Contrasting the rebelliousness of the population of the area in 1848 to its
seeming unification behind and enthusiasm for Napoleon III in 1858, Cauvin claimed that "the inauguration of the Boulevard de Sébastopol has great

significance and far-reaching consequences. The fifth of April has proved once again that despite the efforts of factions, nation and emperor think and act with the same confidence and the same sympathy. The nation still recognizes in him its elected." [47]

Because of press censorship, it is difficult to know how the crowds really reacted, but one would guess that they probably gave the emperor—or at least the new boulevard—a generally warm welcome. The continuing expenditures and disruptions of Haussmannization had not yet soured the taste for new streets, and, if voting results are any indication of popularity, the Empire still had the allegiance of most Parisians. In the legislative elections the year before, the government had retained a majority of the votes in Paris, although that majority was significantly smaller than it had been in 1852 and several opponents of the regime were elected. Also, according to at least one independent and sometimes critical observer, the Austrian ambassador, a numerous and largely working-class crowd "applauded a lot." [48]

But for Cauvin to move from even the wild enthusiasm he perceived to the nation's continuing recognition of its "elected" is patently specious—and very telling. It reminds us that while the spectators did not have an active role to play at such celebrations in the same way that the emperor or Haussmann did, they constituted, along with the emperor and the boulevard itself, one of its most crucial elements. The decorations, the troops, the emperor's presence, the paid cheerers who were almost certainly present were all in large part designed to mobilize popular enthusiasm both for the new boulevard and, in the long term, for the Empire itself. Furthermore, as we see with the Cauvin argument—and it is typical of Bonapartist reporting on such celebrations—that enthusiasm itself became grist for the mill of the imperial publicists as further evidence for the ongoing popularity, and thus legitimacy, of the Empire. In this way, the spectacle fed the myth of a nation unified (and hence pacified) by Louis-Napoleon Bonaparte.

Despite the impression of overpowering success that comes through in the Bonapartist papers, the inauguration of the Boulevard de Sébastopol clearly failed, at least in its immediate objective of influencing the legislature to provide further funds for Haussmannization. Although the legislature finally did agree to provide 50 million francs from state funds, this still fell 10 million francs short of the original demand, and it took such an effort to obtain it that Haussmann afterward sought other ways of raising money for his projects—some of which would eventually get him into hot water.[49] Nonetheless, new streets continued to open, and two of them received inaugurations similar to that of the Boulevard de Sébastopol.

For the first of these, the August 1861 inauguration of the Boulevard de Malesherbes, the city had erected a large circular pavilion and a triumphal arch at the point where the new boulevard met the ring of exterior boulevards. The words emblazoned on the arch summarized the day's message like an advertising billboard: "PARIS," shouted one side of the arch, "CLEANED UP-BEAUTIFIED-ENLARGED." The other side was more subtle. "URBS RENOVATA," it proclaimed, the Latin formulation recalling Napoleon III's pretension to do for Paris what Augustus had done for Rome. The inaugural ceremony itself followed the same pattern as that for Sébastopol. The emperor—this time riding in a carriage instead of on horseback—made his way from the Tuileries to the inaugural site, where he gave a speech calling for a reduction in consumption taxes on necessities. He then followed the new boulevard, decorated with venetian mast and lined with spectators, to the new and luxurious Parc de Monceau before returning to the Tuileries by the same route.

For the inauguration of the Boulevard du Prince Eugène in 1862, the regime tried a slightly different approach, while at the same time going back to what had made the Sébastopol inauguration so striking. The emperor was once again on horseback, and the boulevard was once again hidden by a large curtain that was pulled back at his approach. The novelty of the ceremony was that the decorations on the Place du Trône (now the Place de la Nation) were supposed to be full-scale models of permanent constructions. These consisted of an elaborate colonnade with places for some 10,000 spectators encircling the entire Place, a monumental fountain, and a triumphal arch, which Victor Baltard had modeled on the Arc de Triomphe du Carrousel (see figure 4.2).

The theme of the decoration, in keeping with the idea of naming the new boulevard after Josephine's warrior son, was military glory. The fountain included a huge globe, topped with a statue of Glory holding a figure representing Victory in one hand and a crown of laurels in the other. And Baltard's arch was decorated with statues of soldiers and an inscription dedicated to the victories of Napoleon III's army. Had it been completed, this militaristic project would have been a Second Empire version of the First Empire's Place de l'Etoile, but located in the heart of popular Paris rather than in the wealthier western quarter of the city. The decoration, however, was not a success. As individual pieces, both fountain and triumphal arch were overdecorated, and the colonnade, while gracefully curved and tastefully ornamented, probably would have obstructed traffic unnecessarily. Taken together, these three elements got even worse marks, for they showed neither unity of conception nor concern for the harmony of the space as a whole.[50] The failure of the design was so apparent that Hauss-

Figure 4.2. The decoration of the Place de la Nation for the inauguration of the Boulevard du Prince Eugène, 7 December 1862, from the *Illustrated London News*, 13 December 1862. (Doe Library, University of California, Berkeley)

mann himself noted in his address to the emperor that the project had not resolved some "very complicated artistic questions."[51] Happily, the regime never went forward with the permanent constructions.

In the various inaugurations and first stone-setting ceremonies of the Empire, we can see the regime depicting itself as bringing France material benefits. These ceremonies distinctly smack of the sort of "gifts to the community" that Paul Veyne has seen as the essence of the "bread and circuses" political economy of the ancient world.[52] Clearly, when the emperor inaugurated a new railroad line or boulevard, when he opened something to view and to use for the first time, he symbolically took credit for the addition. But the new objects were not personal gifts from the emperor and were not portrayed as such in the actions or speeches of these ceremonies. The message that the new Caesar sent in these ceremonies was something both broader and more modern than that of the Roman emperors. It was that the new object and the general prosperity implied by that object were the results of his sound government.

But this symbolic play was not acted out in a vacuum. As with other Second Empire spectacles, a crowd of cheering spectators was an integral part of the picture, even if it had to be made up or (more probably) exaggerated by the imperial press. We can see something similar in a slightly different kind of inauguration from those examined here. When the new Paix department store opened in the spring of 1869, the store put out so many flags and trophies in the surrounding streets and attracted such a crowd that one journalist (who was probably in the employ of the store) compared it to a 15 August celebration and described it in terms very similar to those the Bonapartists used for the spectacles of the *fête impériale*. "All Paris responded to the call," he wrote. "What a crowd, what an avalanche, what a tumultuous flood! People lined up for hours before being able to get in. . . . Never has the opening of a store produced such a sensation."[53]

Spectacle, in the Paix opening, was used as advertisement. By making the opening seem a major event, a dazzling spectacle on a par with the national holiday, the Paix inauguration heightened the importance of the new store and, by extension, the desirability of the products sold there. Moreover, in both the department store inauguration and in the *fête impériale* generally, a key element of the spectacle was the crowd of supposedly enthusiastic spectators. The crowd's recognition, at least in the eyes of those who wished to see it, of the desirability of the new store on the one hand and Louis-Napoleon on the other functioned to give them a sort of "aura of popularity," a particular appeal stemming from the idolization of large numbers of people. The power of such an appeal, which we still feel strongly today, is probably rooted in the democratic egalitarianism of modern society. As Alexis de Tocqueville, the nineteenth century's most insightful commentator on that phenomenon, put it:

> The nearer men are to a common level of uniformity, the less are they inclined to believe blindly in any man or any class. But they are readier to trust the mass, and public opinion becomes more and more mistress of the world.
>
> Not only is public opinion the only guide left to aid private judgment, but its power is infinitely greater in democracies than elsewhere. In times of equality men, being so like each other, have no confidence in others, but this same likeness leads them to place almost unlimited confidence in the judgment of the public. For they think it not unreasonable that, all having the same means of knowledge, truth will be found on the side of the majority.[54]

The problem with Tocqueville's otherwise brilliant analysis is that it stops short of asking how the "side of the majority" can be determined. In fact, public opinion is a fuzzy and fungible creature, which may include many different opinions. One of the functions of Second Empire spectacle was to hide these nuances and to present public opinion as unified and unanimous in its support for the emperor and all he was doing. In this respect, the crowds at the spectacles served as powerful representations of popularity, representations that were relatively easy to manipulate for a government that banned most political opposition, stifled criticism in the press, and had men like Henry Cauvin ready to do its bidding. Inaugurations held particular allure in this universe because they brought together not only people and emperor but also a tangible benefit, an apparent proof that the emperor was worthy of the popular acclaim because of the prosperity his rule guaranteed.

FIVE

The Limited Universe of
Nineteenth-Century France

The *Expositions Universelles*
of 1855 and 1867

O f all of the many and various state spectacles put on by the regime of
Napoleon III, none drew larger audiences than the two so-called Universal Expositions.[1] In 1855, over 5 million people paid to see the vast display
of objects assembled in the Palace of Industry, a permanent exhibition hall
constructed for the exposition on the Champs-Elysées in the space now occupied by the Petit Palais and the Grand Palais. And in 1867, some 7 million
came to see the huge exposition housed in a large temporary structure on the
Champ-de-Mars. But these visitors saw (and sought) more than just a collection of objects; they came to visit the world. As one visitor in 1867 put it:

> Without undertaking long and perilous journeys, without running the risk
> of being frozen in the North, or melted in the South; we have seen the
> Russian drive his *troïka* drawn by Tartar steeds, the Arab smoke the *narghilé*
> or play the *darbouka* under his gilt cupolas, the fair daughters of the Celestial Empire sip their tea in their quaint painted houses; we have walked in a
> few minutes from the Temple of the Caciques to the Bardo of Tunis, from
> the American log-hut to the Kirghiz tent.[2]

Such descriptions, so reminiscent of the perceived "annihilation of space
and time" by another invention of the industrial revolution—the railroad—

evoke both the image of a world reduced to the dimensions of the exposition and that of an exposition expanded to the dimensions of the world.[3]

In this transformation lies an effort to understand, and thereby to assert a certain power over, the world, or even the "universe" if the French term is taken seriously. As Claude Lévi-Strauss said of reductions generally, "Being smaller, the object as a whole seems less formidable. By being quantitatively diminished, it seems to us qualitatively simplified. More exactly, this quantitative transposition extends and diversifies our power over a homologue of the thing, and by means of it the latter can be grasped, assessed and apprehended at a glance."[4] But this apprehension "at a glance" (an interesting phrase given the importance of vision at expositions generally)[5] was made possible only through systematic orderings somewhat akin to those traced in primitive cultures by Lévi-Strauss and other anthropologists.

Systems of classification, spatial arrangements of the displays, and allegorical decorative elements all gave structure to the "worldview" of the expositions. They created organized and ordered worlds that bore a striking resemblance to an idealized and perfected liberal capitalism. But if they successfully functioned, as Richard Terdiman put it, "to consecrate the triumphs of the dominant mechanism," they did not do so solely, as Terdiman would have it, because of a lack of alternatives to capitalism.[6] Like many rituals and beliefs of other cultures, they provided a positive vision of harmonious wholeness. They were a radiant dream of an enchanted capitalist isle, spectral and stirring.

But the utopia of the expositions was far from truly ideal. As Pierre Bourdieu has shown, no matter what their cognitive functions, what he calls "mythico-ritual systems" function socially to legitimate domination.[7] So too the expositions. As the product of a specific time, place, and social milieu, the expositions, whatever universal needs they may have met or pretensions they may have had, shared the limitations of their origins. Although they envisaged unlimited production and greater prosperity for all, at the same time they marginalized women and considered workers primarily as adjuncts to owners. At the same time, they also provided an opportunity for Napoleon III to link politics and culture by integrating images of his regime into powerful representations of the world of production.

Pared down to their essentials, the Paris Expositions of 1855 and 1867 were giant prize competitions for "all of the material products of human work."[8] Industrial machinery, clothing, musical instruments, agricultural products, food, furniture, fine arts, and almost all of the other material goods produced by humans were placed on display and evaluated by special juries of experts. Products judged sufficiently meritorious earned their producers medals and honorable mentions that the emperor distributed in the lavish ceremonies that capped the expositions. Out of this competition was to come "progress," one of the key watchwords of exposition rhetoric.

Recurrent metaphors of competition and rivalry characterized discussions of the expositions. Words like "struggle," "contest," and "conquest," usually modified by the adjective "peaceful" or some variant thereof, crop up almost everywhere, though sometimes the formulations are quite elaborate. According to the emperor, for example, the expositions were "Olympic games of the entire world, in which all peoples, vying with each other in intellect, seem to rush together into the infinite course of progress."[9] The "grand result" of this rivalry, said the British *Art Journal*, "is a system of combined action growing out of individual effort."[10] Or, as an amateur poet put it in a "Cantate à l'Exposition":

> *Luttons tous par les arts*
> *Luttons par l'industrie*
> *Le progrès marchera par la rivalité*
> *Et nous enricherons chacun notre patrie*
> *En travaillant toujours à sa prosperité*
> *En travaillant toujours à sa prosperité.*[11]

This vision of universal prosperity stems, at least in part, from the influence of the followers of Henri de Saint-Simon, the "utopian socialist" from the beginning of the century.[12] Many of the central organizers of the expositions, including Michel Chevalier, Frédéric Le Play, Jean Barthélemy Arlès-Dufour, Emile Pereire, and others, had links to the Saint-Simonian movement, and Chevalier had even been the personal secretary of Prosper Enfantin, chief Saint-Simonian leader after Saint-Simon's death.[13] But for Chevalier and many others, the "utopian socialism" of the 1830s had evolved by the 1850s into a sort of "utopian capitalism." Indeed, Chevalier was co-author of the free-trade Cobden-Chevalier Treaty with Great Britain in 1860, and much of his introduction to the published reports of the international juries of 1867 is a paean to freemarkets as the motor of progress. He now seemed closer to Adam Smith (whom he cited in the introduction) than to Saint-Simon (whom he did not).[14] The Saint-Simonians did, however, retain a certain idealism, which often comes out clearly in the rhetoric of the expositions. As Siegfried Kracauer has noted of the Saint-Simonians during these years, though they focused on practical matters like railroad building and industrial development, they "went on believing themselves to be the leaders of a movement that would result in world peace and universal prosperity. Never for one moment did they suspect that they were introducing the age of class struggles."[15]

The essential identity of the expositions' ethos and that of liberal capitalism should be apparent. In this respect, the expositions can be viewed as representations of an idealized capitalist marketplace, a sort of freemarket utopia in which progress emerged from the unimpeded competition of producers. The imperfections of the real market had been banished from this wonderland; there were no transport costs, no import or export duties, no truculent workers to hinder the competition for medals as they sometimes hindered the competition for profits in the real world.[16] In the fantasy world of the expositions, even fickle consumers had been replaced by bodies of informed experts, the international juries that decided which producers would receive medals.

Critics of the expositions sometimes undercut their pretensions to be more than glorified markets by denigrating them as "bazaars" or "fairs." The most able of these critics, men like Charles Baudelaire and Ernest Renan, focused their attentions on the materialism of the expositions and argued that this materialism led to a neglect of the moral side of life. As Baudelaire put it apropos the exposition of 1855, the average Frenchman "has become so Americanized by zöocratic and industrial philosophers that he has lost all notion of the differences which characterize the phenomena of the physical and the moral world—of the natural and the supernatural."[17] Or in Renan's formulation of the same year: "Blinding spectacle for the eyes, instructive study for the practical and peculiar man, it says little to thought. Where in all this is the sentiment of the superior destiny of humanity?"[18] The Catholic Victor Fournel was similarly dismayed by the materialism of the exposition in 1867 and used it as a lesson to remind his readers that "beyond material progress there is moral progress, of which the first is only the visible sign and the humble auxiliary."[19] Another critic of 1867 was less sanguine: "The rivalry of interests and the excitation of desires cannot lead either to peace or to wisdom," said a Swiss periodical.[20]

That these criticisms hit home can be seen in the fact that proponents of expositions, including the emperor himself, often responded to them more or less directly. In presenting Legion of Honor medals to some of the French exhibitors who had participated in the London Exhibition of 1862, for example, the emperor stated that "Universal Expositions are not just bazaars, but striking manifestations of the force and genius of peoples."[21] And at the prize distribution ceremony for the 1867 Exposition he told the audience:

In these great reunions, that seem to have only material interests for their object, there is always a moral thought that is liberated through the competition of intelligence, a thought of peace and civilization. Nations, in coming together, learn to know each other and to esteem each other; hatreds die out and it is more and more realized that the prosperity of each country contributes to the prosperity of all countries.[22]

So whereas the critics of the expositions saw the crass materialism of the common bazaar, the emperor and other defenders saw civilization, social harmony, and world peace.

On the international plane, the optimism of those who favored expositions was often rooted in a utopian vision of an integrated world economy. In his report on the 1855 Exposition, for example, Prince Napoléon, titular head of the exposition and cousin of the emperor, wrote:

> A nation does not at all form an isolated unit. . . . From an industrial point of view, all people tend to be united by a bond of solidarity. Each country is gifted with a natural or special production which assigns it a particular place in human work and makes it useful to the others. [Expositions aid] . . . in the march toward the true industrial and commercial organization of the world, which comes to us from Providence and which consists of allowing each group of the great human family to develop the branch of work to which it is destined by its climate, soil, mineral riches, means of communication, temperament, and national genius.[23]

In Prince Napoleon's view, then, there existed an ideal industrial order in which each nation would produce what best suited its particular material and moral position in the world. Although Prince Napoleon put a heavier accent on the providentially ordained nature of the ultimate order than did most of his contemporaries, his belief in what historian Whitney Walton has termed "specialized industrialization"[24] was quite typical of the age. Walton, in her study of French participation in the Great Exhibition of 1851, shows that specialized industrialization—in particular the supposed French bent toward artisanal production of tasteful consumer goods—was seen by political economists as an antidote to the problems of poverty and social unrest in the wake of 1848 and used by them to advocate free trade.[25] But as the quote above makes clear, it was not merely social problems at home that underlay the belief in specialized industrialization but also a vision of a harmonious world order constructed out of separate nations, each with its own national genius.

The belief that each nation had its own particular genius was by no means limited, at least in 1855 and 1867, to political economists or to industry. It permeated virtually all of the commentary—both pro and con—concerning the expositions and extended to the realm of culture. The 1855 Exposition, for example, included a retrospective art exhibition that one art historian has called the "major art event of the 1850s."[26] In 1867, the fine arts component was somewhat less important than in 1855, but the later exposition emphasized even more strongly than the earlier one the presentation of nations not only as producers of goods but also as distinct cultural and historical units. Traditional national costumes, for example, were a popular and frequently illustrated display in 1867, as were national architectural forms. The 1867 Exposition also included a retrospective display of objets d'art from different nations and even had restaurants where national foods were served. The men of the expositions, then, saw nations as, in Prince Napoleon's words, "essential elements of human organization."[27] They not only ordered the displays at both expositions by nation-state but also grouped together the separate states of what they recognized as individual nations—Germany and Italy. They did not, however, intend the expositions to be only for industrial or European countries. Indeed, they made a point of bringing in "exotic" countries and far-flung parts of colonial empires.[28]

Still, France remained the single most important state at both expositions. Napoleon III's government oversaw virtually all aspects of the expositions. Imperial decrees announced most major decisions concerning them, and men closely associated with the regime were placed in all positions of real authority. Even when the government allowed private entrepreneurs a role, such as in funding the exposition palace in 1855, the state still took charge of the important architectural decisions. Moreover, Napoleon III was on more prominent public display at the expositions than any product of modern manufacturing. The emperor's bust, for example, graced the façade of the 1855 exposition building (see figure 5.1), just as his profile appeared on the exposition medals that he personally handed out to winners in elaborate ceremonies, ceremonies that allowed him to pose, in Emile Zola's words, "as the master of Europe, speaking with calm and with force and promising peace."[29]

Not only were the expositions designed to appeal to industrialists and bourgeois consumers, but they constituted part of what historian Madeleine Réberioux has called "a global politics of social seduction."[30] The working class especially was targeted for special treatment by the government, though with only partial success. The efforts to include workers took a number of different forms. In 1855, for example, in order to get workers simply to come see the expositions, bargain trains, free or reduced entries, and inexpensive meals were arranged. But a mere 10,000 took advantage of these efforts, deeply disappointing Prince Napoléon.[31] He was equally dismayed by the results of another innovation, the effort to give prizes to individual industrial workers as "cooperators" with the owners. The measure, as Prince Napoléon admitted, "ruffled too many prejudices and interests." Most industrialists simply did not see any reason to share their glory

Figure 5.1. Sculptures on the façade of the Palace of Industry, Universal Exposition of 1855, from *L'Illustration*, 19 May 1855. (Doe Library, University of California, Berkeley)

with their workers. Others, perhaps understanding the problem better than the prince, put forward their entire work forces for the award, a suggestion rejected by the prince as "exaggerating the sentiment of justice" underlying the measure.[32] Clearly, the individualist nature of the exposition was difficult to square with the conditions of modern industry.

The regime redoubled its efforts to include workers in 1867 but with similarly disappointing results. As part of a special section (Group X) for objects intended to "ameliorate the physical and moral condition of populations," *independent* workers were invited to display both products (class 94) and procedures (class 95), which meant actually performing their labors at the exposition. Laborers employed by others (i.e., most industrial workers), however, were not included unless they also produced at home on their own time. Furthermore, even with respect to the independent artisanal workers toward whom it was aimed, the measure had only moderate success. The display of products did demonstrate that many of the artisans produced high-quality work, and it did allow at least a few women and workers' cooperatives to exhibit.[33] However, the display as a whole was trivialized by the inclusion in the class of such items as a large paper mosaic portrait of the emperor by an army captain and tapestries made by the Princess de Beauvau, who won a silver medal.[34]

The display of procedures did not enjoy even this modicum of success. A number of independent producers applied for admission in this class—one that turned out to be very popular with the crowds—but the administration decided that the financial demands placed on exhibitors would overstretch the resources of the independents and opted to have owners of larger workshops bring in their employees instead.[35] Thus, even in the special section designed for workers, they effectively became the exhibits rather than the exhibitors. Given the strength of luxury craftsmanship at the expositions, they may have been, as Jeanne Gaillard put it, "the glory of the Parisian artisans."[36] But the expositions failed with respect to workers generally, primarily because there was no easy way to fit wage laborers into the symbolic matrix of the exposition except by subordinating them to their employers.

Another promising new innovation in 1867 from the perspective of workers was a so-called "History of Work." This was touted as "not an abstract history, inaccessible to the illiterate, but a living and palpable history, addressed to everyone, intelligible to everyone, and linking by an uninterrupted chain the rudimentary engines of primitive man with the complicated machines which the industrial genius of the nineteenth century invents every day."[37] But as a glance at the catalog demonstrates, the display had little to do with actual labor and consisted instead of various artifacts and objets d'art from ancient times through the eighteenth century that functioned primarily, as Burton Benedict has remarked, to allow each country to "project its national identity back to the Stone Age."[38] Swords, shields, ciboriums, reliquaries, mirrors, candelabra, and a large variety of other museum pieces were placed on display in this "retrospective museum," as it quickly came to be called, by the eleven countries, all European, who participated in it.

Of greater significance for most workers than actual participation in the expositions was the formation of workers' delegations under the auspices of the Commission d'Encouragement aux Études des Ouvriers in 1867. Elected worker delegates from all of the major industries visited the exposition, studied the exhibitions pertaining to their particular areas of expertise, and wrote up detailed reports.[39] These reports provide a remarkable counterpoise to the reports of the official juries both in form (cheaply produced pamphlets instead of expensive leather-bound volumes) and in content. In the official reports, for example, workers are often strangely absent from the descriptions of the procedures; the machines are at the center of the operations and sometimes seem to work themselves.[40] The workers' reports, in contrast, placed the worker at the center of production, even highly mechanized production, and often criticized machines as a tool by which owners kept wages down and workers weak.[41] The workers also undercut many of the utopian ideals of the exposition. In contrast to the exposition's ideology of progress, many of the reports complained that workers' positions had actually deteriorated, and some had long, critical discussions of the economic system.[42] A few even specifically criticized the fact that the exposition gave recognition not to the real producers—workers—but to nonproducers—capitalists—who merely purchased the labor of workers.[43]

The true social policy of the expositions, then, did not lie in the inclusion of workers in this arena in which they did not easily fit and did not really perceive themselves as fitting; instead, it was expressed in two of the central tenets of the utopian capitalist vision. The first was the idea that everyone benefited from competitive industrial production, which turned out more and better goods at lower cost than ever before. As Michel Chevalier put it in 1867: "The development of productive strength, then, makes objects which had originally been reserved for a small number of privileged people accessible to a constantly growing number of individuals and families."[44] At the suggestion of Thomas Twining of the Society of Arts in London, this idea found expression in 1855 in a special exposition of "objects of general utility," meaning high-quality products at a low price.[45] As part of a display of objects tending to develop the physical and moral conditions of the population, the 1867 Exposition broadened the scope of products aimed at the lower classes to include a variety of objects ranging from low-priced corsets ("indispensable from a hygienic point of view")[46] to cheap worker housing, a category that allowed the emperor to demonstrate his commitment to bettering the conditions of workers' lives by entering and "winning" a gold medal.

To this vision of universal progress the 1867 Exposition also added philanthropic paternalism, an idea that took the form both of displays of products destined for use in various charitable and scholarly institutions (classes 89 and 90) and of a special award destined for "persons, establishments, or localities which through organization or special institutions have developed good harmony between all those who cooperate in the same labors and have assured material, moral, and intellectual well-being to workers."[47] The jury distributed 12 awards and 24 honorable mentions among the 600 dossiers submitted, mostly to paternalistic industrialists and to private institutions of charity.[48] The expositions demonstrated, then, a sympathetic attitude to the problems of workers. But what emerged most strongly was support for a paternalistic capitalism in which responsibility for social problems was left to the private sector rather than assumed by society as a whole.

Peasants fared even worse than workers at the expositions. In contrast to the problematic place of industrial labor at the expositions, agricultural labor had almost no place at all—this despite the fact that France remained a predominantly agricultural and rural country throughout this period. To be sure, agriculture itself did receive a good deal of attention. Special displays of model agricultural buildings, equipment, products, and even live animals were erected at special agricultural display areas. But these areas were located outside of Paris, at Trappes in 1855 and on the Ile de Billancourt in 1867. Furthermore, no effort comparable to that made to bring workers to the expositions was made for agricultural laborers. Given their importance to the economy, peasants were the expositions' most inadequately represented group.

Women at the expositions have yet a different story. With few exceptions (almost all either in traditional women's trades such as dressmaking or in the fine arts), women did not participate as independent exhibitors. They did, however, have certain specific roles. They worked as waitresses, for example, in the international restaurants, and groups of women workers sewed and made items such as shoes, flowers, and fans as part of the displays of the procedures of production (see figure 5.2). Despite the fact that this moderate presence far underrepresented the real role of women in the industrial economy,[49] however, it was resented by men of all social classes. The workers' delegations, for example, used their reports to inveigh against women workers,[50] and Maxime du Camp saw the international waitresses as little better than prostitutes: "Under pretext of local color, girls in low-cut dresses, made up, impudent, and provocative, dressed as Austrians, as Bavarians, as Spaniards, pour drinks for passers-by, spar verbally with the bolder, and defend the approaches to science, industry, work, and study with a circle of debauchery and luxury."[51]

Women were slightly better represented in the fine arts than they were in industry. In 1867 they made up some 5 percent of the exhibiting French painters.[52] Rosa Bonheur, one of the most popular artists of the period, even won two major prizes, a first-class medal in 1855 and a second-class medal in 1867. Yet even this small female presence could still raise a frightening specter for men: "There are no laws, no barriers, that can preserve the holy family hearth," one 1855 art reviewer declared, "from that disease, that plague, that infection, which takes a daughter from her mother, a wife from her husband, a mother from her children." And as if that were not strong enough, he continued by proclaiming that "any woman who, through a silly

Figure 5.2. Display of work at the Universal Exposition of 1867, from *L'Exposition universelle de 1867 illustrée,* 2 September 1867. (Doe Library, University of California, Berkeley)

pride, a mad vanity, does not remain in her sphere, in the purest, most noble attributions of her sex, overthrows nature and botches her providential mission."[53]

Very few women were in a position to overthrow nature by exhibiting, but a great number did at least come to the expositions in the usual way.

Virtually every image of spectators at the expositions includes one or more women, usually bourgeois women, judging from their dress. Women, as Whitney Walton has admirably shown, were perceived to have a particular role to play in consumption, a role that helped to break down gender-specific spheres by bringing them into contact with the supposedly male world of production, especially in a forum such as an exposition.[54] However, the already arguably passive role of spectator and consumer was sometimes depicted as being doubly so for women, who supposedly spent inordinate amounts of time near the displays of elegant clothing, jewels, and fine fabrics, those "irresistible traps for feminine coquetry."[55] Women's passivity was further underscored by the wheelchairs from which, pushed along by male companions, they were sometimes portrayed viewing the expositions (see figure 5.3). Originally installed for the sick and disabled, the chairs became fashionable for women after the Empress Eugénie used one during the 1855 Exposition.[56] Despite the popularity of the image of the woman in the wheelchair, most women clearly did not use the chairs, and the image better reflects the ideals and prejudices of the male journalists and illustrators who propagated it than actual practice.

Turning from real men and women at the expositions to more abstract

Figure 5.3. The entrance to the Danish section at the Universal Exposition of 1867, from *L'Exposition universelle de 1867 illustrée*, 2 September 1867. (Doe Library, University of California, Berkeley)

concepts, we find a somewhat different situation. One of the central preoccupations of the organizers of the expositions was the representation of an "ordered world,"[57] a world they expressed and reified in classification systems, architecture, and building decor. Frédéric Le Play, a well-connected engineer and sociologist, drew up the general classification systems for the products to be displayed in both 1855 and 1867. Outwardly the two classifications differ greatly, in large part because in 1855 Le Play relied heavily on the English classification of 1851, while in 1867 he attempted to come up with a more integrated system.[58] The 1855 classification, for example, had two divisions (Fine Arts and Industry) and eight groups, while the 1867 version had no general divisions and ten groups.[59] This change was by no means merely cosmetic but signaled a demotion of art with respect to the much larger category of industry. In 1855 the distinctiveness of the two groups was made quite explicit by the two general divisions and was given concrete form by housing the art exhibition in an entirely separate building from the rest of the exposition. In 1867, however, though the fine arts were still given a high place in the schema (they made up Group I), they were no longer an entirely separate category from industrial production. The 1867 organizers reinforced this change by scaling down the size of the art exposition and by housing it in the same building with everything else, a development that did not please artists.[60]

The organizing principles behind the groups in the two systems also differed. The 1855 groups attempted to bring together particular *industries,* while those in 1867 brought together particular kinds of *products.* In other words, each group in 1855 tried to assemble the whole process of production for a certain type of good (i.e., "textile manufacturing"), while 1867 focused on types of products (i.e., "clothing [textiles included] and other objects borne on the person"). The reason for the change was that the 1855 system had broken down when it came to placing such things as machinery, which were products of one industry yet used in another. The actual machinery used in textile production, for example, ended up going not in the "textile manufacturing" group but in that designated as "industries having for particular object the use of mechanical forces," that is, machinery. The 1867 categorization by products got around this difficulty, although at the cost of adding a certain confusion of its own. Portable arms, for example, ended up being classified with clothing as another "object borne on the person."

Above and beyond these differences, however, both classification systems attempted to mirror a very similar hierarchy of values. Thus, both systems placed agriculture and horticulture at one end of the classification, industrial production in the middle, and fine arts at the other. Clearly, dealing with raw materials, and especially agricultural work, was regarded as lower than painting and sculpture on the totem pole of production. And although industry was somewhere in between the two, the constant concern of the expositions was to bring industry closer to the fine arts. Hence the continual discussions at the expositions of "art applied to industry."

The meaning of the expositions was not expressed only in classification; allegorical decoration and spatial arrangements reinforced and expanded those systems. In 1855 this was primarily a question of decoration. The main building, the Palace of Industry, was originally designed only for national expositions and was already under construction when the British commissioners arrived to find that their products alone would fill it.[61] As a result, separate buildings had to be constructed not only for the fine arts but also for machinery, a development that meant that "one did not immediately perceive the link between machine and product."[62] Unlike the fine arts building, however, which had both a separate entrance and a separate admission fee, the machinery gallery did connect directly to the main building by means of a passageway. Le Play also made it clear in the introduction to his classification system that the division was an unintentional product of circumstances.[63]

What it lacked in spatial arrangements, the Palace of Industry more than made up for in decoration. Although the roof of the building was of the type of iron and glass architecture pioneered by Joseph Paxton at the Great Exhibition of 1851,[64] the exterior was stone, thus allowing a traditional, decorated façade (figure 5.1) and two colorful stained glass windows (figure 5.4), all of which used allegorical figures to symbolize the exposition.[65] The principal sculptural group (by Elias Robert) translated the exposition to stone by portraying France distributing laurels to Art and Industry. Directly below this group, a frieze by Desboeufs depicted "the primitive industries marching progressively toward Science and Fine Arts."[66] The twenty-two human figures and three animals of the frieze were arranged on either side of a bust of Napoleon III, with Painting and Sculpture at the center and the most "primitive" industries (Carpentry and Agriculture) to the outside. Sculpture, in the frieze, puts the finishing touches on the emperor's bust. Finally, below the frieze and around the central archway of the entrance to the building were two angels blowing trumpets and several allegorical figures offering laurel crowns to an imperial eagle.[67]

On the interior of the building, decoration was provided primarily by two large stained glass windows, the work of Laurent-Charles Maréchal.[68] The eastern window showed France, seated on a throne supported by Art and Science, inviting the nations to the exposition. To her right, the side of Art, the "industry of the Orient" was represented by a male shepherd

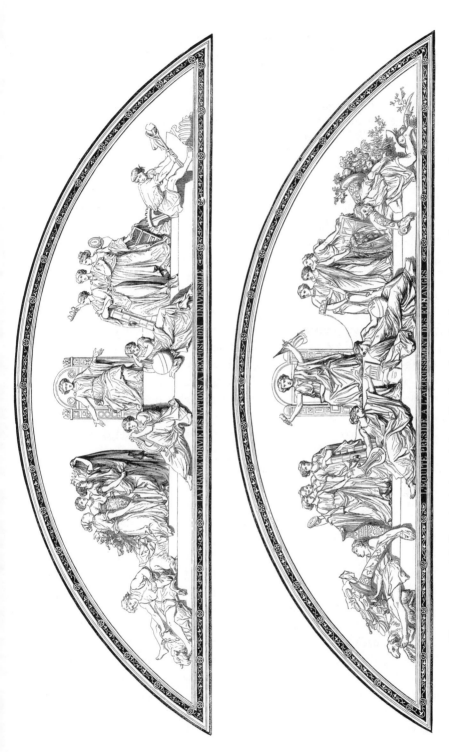

Figure 5.4. Maréchal's stained glass windows for the Palace of Industry, Universal Exposition of 1855, from *L'Illustration*, 19 May 1855. (Doe Library, University of California, Berkeley)

and by three women carrying a shawl from India, a Chinese vase, and jewels and arms from Arabia. On her left, the side of Science, were a male blacksmith and three more female figures representing European nations and holding the more advanced tokens of western industry. On the other side of the palace, Maréchal's western window, which depicted Equity presiding over the growth of exchange, continued the allegory. All of the same figures reappeared, though now the figure in the throne was Equity rather than France, and the nations had exchanged their emblems, as had Science and Art.

The decoration of the Palace of Industry, then, directly reflected Le Play's classification. Art and Industry were separate but equal in Robert's sculptural group, as they had been in Le Play's system. And just as Le Play had placed them at either end of an axis running from industries involved in the extraction of raw materials to the fine arts, so Desboeuf's frieze depicted the progress of industry from its primitive state to the fine arts.

There was, however, one very important element present in the façade that had not been present in the classification: the state. Indeed, Robert's France, the central figure of the upper sculptural group, stood on a pedestal bearing an imperial eagle. Directly beneath, in the center of Desboeuf's frieze, was the bust of Napoleon III, and beneath that and directly over the entrance to the building was an eagle, the symbol of the Bonapartist dynasty. Maréchal's eastern window, the one depicting France inviting the nations to the exposition, clearly also gave the state a central position. The state, then, played an important role in these compositions and, by extension, in the symbolic order of the exposition. Significantly, however, the role was not so much that of an active, interventionist state but that of an overarching, protective state that stood above the figures of the exposition.

In contrast to the exposition of 1855, that of 1867 eschewed allegory; instead, the meaning of the exposition was embedded in the physical layout of the exposition palace itself: "It is important that the public follow the transformation of matter step by step, that it see the unfinished state and the finished state, and that it judge the difficulties conquered. A living encyclopedia, so to speak, the exposition should reveal all the secrets of the work of man to the public who is avid to learn."[69] Thus, following a suggestion made by Prince Napoléon after 1855 (and perhaps stealing the idea from a British architect), Le Play designed a single-story oval building that used a gridlike arrangement in order to place products both according to their place in his classification system and according to country (see figure 5.5).[70] He divided the building into seven concentric oval galleries arranged around an open, central garden. Each gallery housed a separate

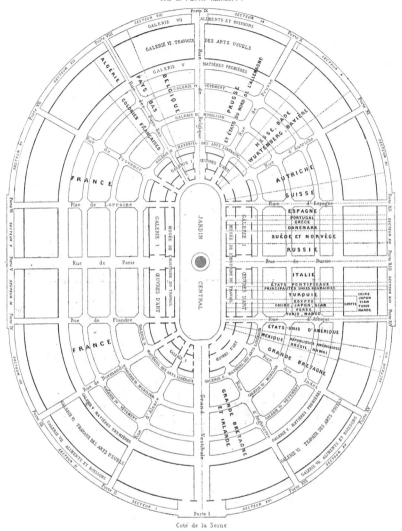

Figure 5.5. Plan of the building layout for the Universal Exposition of 1867, from *L'Exposition universelle de 1867 illustrée*, 29 September 1867. (Doe Library, University of California, Berkeley)

group from Le Play's classification.[71] National exhibitions, separated by "streets," radiated out from the garden, traversing each of these galleries and enabling visitors to follow either the exhibition of a single nation through all of the categories or that of a single category through all of the individual nations.

The very outermost gallery and the patio running around the palace consisted of food displays and restaurants from around the world. Though Maxime du Camp saw this section of the exposition as little more than a den of vice, others had a more favorable impression. According to one American: "Here you can listen to the different kinds of national music, see the different national types and costumes, and eat the different national foods. We go almost every day, and it is always a delight."[72] Or, as Ludovic Halévy put it, "One eats and drinks in all the languages."[73] Moving in toward the central garden, gallery by gallery, the visitor could "see the complete panorama of universal production, with its most grandiose perspectives, successively unrolling before him,"[74] until he got to the innermost circles, which housed Fine Arts and the History of Work.

One of the most popular galleries was that displaying machinery and procedures of work, found just inside the building. In this first and largest of the main galleries, both machine production and human labor became spectacle; it even included a raised walkway to provide visitors with a "panorama of human work." It was here that the spectator could see not only working machinery, as in 1855, but also the machinists and craftspeople performing the procedures they performed in the factories and workshops that employed them. Sociologist Dean MacCannell, who has studied modern tourists' interest in seeing displays of work, has argued that "it is only by making a fetish of the work of others, by transforming it into an 'amusement' . . . , a spectacle . . . , or an attraction . . . , that modern workers on vacation, can apprehend work as part of a meaningful totality."[75] Although MacCannell errs by placing the development of this interest rather late and by seeming to limit it to workers, his analysis as a whole is fruitful. It reminds us that the Universal Expositions attempted to replicate in microcosm the *totality* of production. They reunited the product with the raw materials and the work, both machine and human, that constituted it and thus made the whole of production immanent within that product. This, I think, is why the expositions became what Walter Benjamin has termed "places of pilgrimage to the fetish Commodity."[76]

The 1867 exposition palace attempted not only to make visible the whole productive process but to do so globally. "To make the circuit of this palace, circular like the equator, is literally to go around the world," said one official publication.[77] This small-scale world lacked geographical features, of course. There were no mountains or valleys, no rivers or seas. Nonetheless, Le Play tried to establish an ordering that approximated the locations of countries on the globe in relation to France. Thus, moving away from the French section in one direction, one came to Belgium, and in the other direction, to Great Britain. The further one moved, the more distant and exotic the country, until one arrived in Asia, on the opposite side of the building from the French displays—though colonies were tellingly included with the European country to which they belonged. To mark their territory from that of their neighbors, countries erected entryways to their sections and decorated them with national symbols such as flags and busts of eminent national figures (see figure 5.3). Despite the internationalist rhetoric that accompanied it, then, the exposition clearly divided the world into separate states and colonial empires.

Additional space for such display was provided in one of the 1867 exposition's most important innovations. The exposition grounds, or "park," were designed by Adolphe Alphand, architect of a number of Paris's permanent parks. On the four large corners of the Champ-de-Mars not occupied by the palace, countries and some individuals were for the first time allowed to construct the pavilions that would henceforth be a standard part of all Universal Expositions. The result was a combination of popular novelties and displays of national styles of architecture. Among the other attractions located here were an elaborate Chinese teahouse constructed by the French after the Chinese government refused to cooperate, an underwater aquarium, an American log cabin, a ruined "feudal" tower, a Swiss chalet, an Egyptian palace, a "gothic" church, and the emperor's pavilion, a gaudy combination of Moorish architecture and imperial kitsch.

In addition to providing greater scope for national display, the park generally played nature to the palace's culture. In contrast to the organization and order that reigned inside the building, the park seemed confusing and disordered. "We become here somewhat bewildered," remarked one visitor, "for it is impossible to follow anything like a regular plan in the intricate maze of alleys."[78] "This indefinable jumble," said a more serious critic, "places almost simultaneously before our eyes that which is most serious in industry and most charming in art, side by side with the most futile and even most ridiculous part of the search for amusement."[79] But despite such criticisms, the park was popular. For most people, its gently curving paths, haphazardly distributed attractions, and proliferation of "natural" features such as trees, grass, streams, and lakes offered a welcome respite from the rigid order of the palace. An "Eden-Exposition," one visitor termed it; "a marvelous garden that is a rest for the eyes and for the spirit."[80] But might we not see here, even more forcefully than in the overly ordered interior of the building, the culmination of the ordering impulse of the expositions? For as with the other parks of Paris, the seeming disorder was specious, the creation of man. It was nothing less than, as François Laisney astutely put it, "the means of ordering disorder in conferring upon it the apparent irregularity of nature."[81]

"Meaning, not raw facts," literary critic Alvin Kernan has noted, "is what humanity seeks, and society is a collection of kits or codes for processing raw facts into meaning. Ordering is one of the simplest and most durable methods for finding or making meaning."[82] The Universal Expositions are a superb demonstration of this truism. By reducing the world to the exposition and by ordering and systematizing it, the expositions made it more easily understood, more easily "grasped, assessed, and apprehended at a glance." In so doing, they brought order and meaning to a chaotic world.

But there is another side to the story as well. As Pierre Bourdieu reminds us, "forms of classification are forms of domination."[83] The concepts and categories reified in the expositions helped to empower certain groups at the expense of others. Their organization of production, for example, made bourgeois domination of the economy seem part of the natural order of things, just as their relegation of women to certain roles perpetuated male domination. This is not to say that this organization was nothing more than a means of hiding real power relations. The whole system was credible precisely because it reflected much that seemed self-evidently true to so many at the time. As Michael Mann has noted: "Powerful ideologies are at least highly plausible in the conditions of the time, and they are genuinely adhered to."[84]

The important place given Napoleon III at the expositions was an attempt to graft political power onto this overarching vision of economic and social organization. His profile on the exposition medals, his presence at the inaugurations and prize distributions, and his image and that of other symbols of his regime on the façade of the Palace of Industry did much more than honor the expositions with an official stamp of approval; they closely associated the regime with everything the expositions stood for. Just as the regime's historically oriented spectacles linked it to a powerful vision of French history, so the expositions linked it to ideals of industrial progress and economic prosperity.

SIX

The Politics of Sincerity

The Charitable Work of
the Empress Eugénie

At a bit before ten on a brisk October morning in Paris in 1865, a dark unmarked coach drawn by two horses clattered up to the entrance of the Hôpital Beaujon in the Faubourg Saint-Honoré in Paris. A handsome woman in her late thirties, elegantly but soberly attired in a black silk dress and grey bonnet, stepped out of the coach and was respectfully greeted by a small group of doctors and nurses. At the woman's request, the doctors escorted her to the wards reserved for the victims of the cholera epidemic then ravaging Paris. There, the woman approached each of the beds and said a few words to each patient. By the end of the day, she had visited the cholera wards of two more hospitals, and for the next week, all Paris talked of little else. The woman was the Empress Eugénie, and in making these dangerous visits, she had found a particularly powerful means of conveying an image of a caring and solicitous regime.

Such visits do not fit our usual ideas of state spectacles or rites of power. There were no decorations and no speeches. Eugénie was not surrounded by gilded eagles or welcomed by large crowds of cheering onlookers. But such rituals were just as much rites of power as parades or inaugurations. In them, however, the objective was the demonstration of the sovereign's sincerity and solicitude for the people rather than the ability to command troops or ensure prosperity. Such rituals were not designed to overawe the populace with demonstrations of force or popularity but to seduce it into believing in the goodness of the rulers. As such, these rituals were constructed very differently from most other political rituals and even in opposition to them. It was precisely through the lack of pomp and the seemingly direct contact between sovereign and subject that Eugénie's visits expressed the sincerity of her concern. Here, then, were rites of power that worked by conspicuously eschewing the usual trappings of imperial spectacle. Not all of Eugénie's charitable work was of this nature, of course, but the best publicized and most effective of it was. And throughout all of her charitable endeavors—the titular presidencies and the court receptions for prominent charities, as well as the less formal visits to hospitals and schools—the emphasis was always on her personal devotion to the best interests of her subjects.

The association between French sovereigns and charity was a long-standing one. As one of the highest of the Christian virtues, charity had traditionally demonstrated a sovereign's piety and, especially from the eighteenth century forward, his or her general goodness and humanity.[1] Kings and queens both practiced charity, but queens were often supposed to have a special affinity for it. According to one popular historian, all of the queens of France "have exercised the divine ministry of charity: founders of abbeys and convents . . . generous almoners, great matchmakers, born protectors of orphans and the underprivileged, one sees them in every calamity, one invokes them in every disastrous circumstance."[2] Some French queens were better known for their charity than others, of course, and it is perhaps significant that Eugénie held two of these, Blanche de Castille and Anne of Austria, in particular esteem.[3] The long tradition of the solicitous *souveraine* was by no means dead during the nineteenth century. After the revolution so unsuccessfully tried to do away with both sovereigns and royal charity, the successive empresses and queens from Josephine to Marie-Amélie had taken up the charitable mantle and had at least gone through the motions of fulfilling the time-honored role. Charity, then, was an integral and ancient part of Eugénie's *métier*, and it would have been inconceivable for her not to have practiced it.

And yet there was also something distinctly modern about Eugénie's charitable works. Compared with her Old Regime models, Eugénie's charity was more secular in orientation, more directed at social problems and less at the propagation of religious faith. To some degree this can be attributed to the fact that many of the main Catholic charities were dominated by legitimists such as Armand de Melun and thus had a different political agenda than did Eugénie. In 1861 one of these organizations, the Société de Saint-Vincent de Paul, refused to accept a lottery prize donated by the Empress and displayed a bust of the Bourbon pretender to the throne, the Comte de Chambord, at a meeting. Such overt political action was rare, however, in part because of the consequences it might entail. After the incidents mentioned above, the regime gave the Société de Saint-Vincent de Paul the choice of either accepting a president appointed by the government or disbanding. The society chose to disband.[4] Not all of the Catholic charities were as openly legitimist as the Société de Saint-Vincent de Paul, but most still distrusted the regime, suspecting it of acting solely on political motives.[5] They, of course, wanted the credit for good works to go to the Church rather than the regime, and they were fearful not only of the regime's intervention in their organizations but also of the growth of public assistance generally and any encroachment on what they called the "freedom of charity."[6]

All this is not to say that the efforts of the various public and private groups to aid the less fortunate merely acted as a front for politics or religion. Indeed, just as striking as the tensions between these groups was their ability sometimes to set aside their differences and work together. Armand de Melun, for example, a legitimist and the chief "social Catholic" of the period, was the main architect of the regime's policy toward mutual assistance societies,[7] and various orders of charitable nuns staffed hospitals, orphanages, schools, prisons, nursing homes, and other public institutions, in addition to visiting the sick and distributing medicine for the *bureaux de bienfaisance.*[8] Nonetheless, the different underlying goals of the regime and the Catholic charities led to mutual distrust and to a division among charities according to political orientation. The Société de Saint-Vincent de Paul and the Oeuvre de la Miséricord, for example, were Catholic and legitimist, while others such as the Société de la Charité Maternelle and the Société du Prince Impérial were Bonapartist. As one would expect, Eugénie paid far more attention to the second type of charities than to the first.

Eugénie's charitable involvement was shaped not only by politics but also by the increasing importance of charitable activity in the lives of nineteenth-century women. The process seems to have begun in the latter part of the eighteenth century and culminated in the mid-nineteenth century. One historian has pointed to a distinct "feminization" of charitable bequests in wills over the period between the 1740s and the 1810s,[9] and the term "dame de charité" would seem to have only become current during approximately the same period.[10] By mid-century, charity had become a basic social duty for upper-class women, as well as the most important and widespread arena of feminine action outside the home. For a cynical observer such as Edmond de Goncourt, these women learned charity only "through obedience to the program of duties and occupations of a well brought up young woman," [11] but clearly much more than social convention was at stake for many. After all, bourgeois families during the early Third Republic devoted no less than 3 to 7 percent of their budgets to charity, as much as they spent on taxes and insurance and almost as much as they spent on wages.[12]

One of charitable work's most important functions was to provide an outlet for rich women who found the safe and cosseted environment of the home too limiting. In contrast to almost all other areas of public life in the nineteenth century, women took important and active roles in organizing and running charities, many of which were sizable organizations. Joining a religious order was an alternative for some women, and Claude Langlois has attributed the great success of such orders in the nineteenth century to the fact that they offered women the possibility of varied work and important responsibility.[13] But the necessary devotion to God and the sacrifice of home and family and the pleasures of life eliminated joining a religious order as an option for many women. For wealthy women, secular charity offered one way to lead a more active life without those sacrifices.

Women were perceived as having a special role to play in charitable work, a role rooted in their particular virtues as seen by nineteenth-century society.[14] In the first place, they were supposed to be more sincerely religious. "It is woman," declared the liberal Catholic Comte de Montalambert in accepting the Montyon prize in 1862, "who is our chief guardian of the priceless treasure of Christian virtues and truths." [15] Secondly, women's place was supposed to be the home. In most circumstances, this limited the role women played in public, but in the case of charity, the domestic orientation of women's lives actually gave them a way to get out of the home. More precisely, nineteenth-century charity did not allow women to break out of the private sphere so much as it extended that sphere by getting them involved in the domestic situations of the working classes, thus giving bourgeois women a larger arena of action, even while reinforcing highly gender-specific social roles.

The rationale for extending the "private" sphere in this manner was that so many of the problems facing the working classes stemmed from their lack of a stable domestic environment and specifically from the failure of working-class women to create a home environment on the bourgeois model. As the Baron de Watteville, an aristocrat active in social work, expressed it:

> It is rare to meet a young woman of the people who knows how to keep
> her little household with order, with cleanliness, with intelligence, and with

economy. She almost never knows how to make her own clothes, much less those of her husband and children; she does not know how to prepare with care the family meals. The result is that the husband, tired of being home and disgusted by the food that is presented to him, goes to the cabaret to look for a better meal and for distractions which he does not find at home. From there, first comes trouble, then misery. The mother of the family holds in her hands domestic happiness, her children's future, and, in consequence, the future of society.[16]

Such a formulation of woman as problem clearly called for women to be involved in the solution. Upper-class women, it was believed, would be models and mentors to their erring working-class sisters. As a result, in addition to the political division, there was a very clear sexual division of labor among the charities of nineteenth-century France. Of course, there were exceptions and areas of overlap, but generally speaking, charities run by women dealt with problems perceived to fall within the sphere of women and the home, while those dealing with more "masculine" problems were run by men. The charitable involvement of Napoleon III and the Empress Eugénie followed this pattern of sexual division. The emperor's largesse to indigent workers and old soldiers, his visits to disaster-stricken areas such as those flooded in 1856, his construction of workers' housing and convalescent homes, his support for mutual aid societies, and other such efforts are the mirror image of the empress's efforts to aid women, children, the sick, and the infirm.

Much of what passed for charitable work in Eugénie's life involved only minimal actual participation in either ceremonial or charitable activities. Highly publicized titular presidencies of important organizations, for example, served as reminders of Eugénie's attitudes while requiring very little real effort on her part. Just a few days after her marriage, she was made "President and Protectress" of the Sociétés de Charité Maternelle, begun in 1788 under the auspices of Marie-Antoinette but suppressed during the Revolution. Each of the successive *souveraines* of France from Marie-Louise to Eugénie presided over this charity, which grew larger and larger as the century progressed. By the Second Empire, most major cities had a local chapter, often dominated by the wives of men closely associated with the regime. In Paris, all of the leading positions except that of treasurer were filled by women, including two whose husbands ranked among the highest officials of the Empire, the Duchesse de Bassano and the Comtesse Walewska.[17] The purpose of the charity was to help poor married mothers by providing them with a layette, some minor financial support, and lots of good advice. The *dames patronesses* visited pregnant and nursing women in their homes and provided support and advice.[18] Eugénie herself did not actually visit the poor mothers helped by the charity, but by presiding over it, she put herself at the top of what seemed to be a great network of maternal solidarity.

Eugénie's solicitude extended to somewhat older children through her support for *crèches* and *salles d'asile*. Since their institution in 1844, Parisian *crèches* had been taking in children under two years old and providing day care for a minimal fee while mothers were at work. These institutions were controversial because, despite the requirement that mothers return to nurse their unweaned babies, many, including the emperor, felt that the separation of mother and child would lead to the weakening of familial ties, and it was not until 1862 that Eugénie was officially made their patron.[19] *Salles d'asile*, the equivalent of today's *maternelles* or public nursery schools, provided basic instruction to children between the ages of two and six. Not all children attended these institutions, but many did. In Paris in 1861, for example, almost 12,000 children were enrolled in a *salle d'asile*.[20] All of the *salles d'asile* were required by law to display Eugénie's portrait, and Catholic *salles* were also required to put up a crucifix and an image of the Virgin Mary.[21] As with the Sociétés de Charité Maternelle, Eugénie's duties vis-à-vis these institutions were not great, but her symbolic role gave the regime a moral and maternal tone that it might otherwise have lacked.

A number of Eugénie's works also underscored her willingness to sacrifice worldly pleasures in the name of helping others. One of the best examples of this was the Maison Eugène Napoléon, located in the impoverished Saint-Antoine quarter of Paris, which provided professional instruction for poor girls between eight and twenty-one years of age. The institution was founded after Eugénie declined the Municipal Council of Paris's offer of a 600,000-franc diamond necklace as a wedding present. In what might be considered her first successful "publicity stunt," she wrote to the council:

> I suffer great pain at the thought that the first public act linked to my name at the time of my marriage is a considerable expenditure by the City of Paris. . . . You will make me happier by spending the money that you had set aside for this on charitable works. I do not wish my marriage to impose any new burden on the country to which I belong from now on; my only ambition is to share with the emperor the love and esteem of the French people.[22]

The self-sacrificing new empress also gave to charity the dowry provided her by the emperor, but perhaps because it seemed to sum up the choice between luxury and charity in such a tangible object so redolent of expensive feminine frivolity, her rejection of the diamond necklace caught and held public attention much more effectively. The institution founded with the money was inaugurated on 28 December 1856 and, because of its origin, became known as the Maison du Collier.[23] As a lasting reminder of the foundation, the decoration of the school included a large fresco in the chapel by Barrias that represented the empress, surrounded by admiring young women, offering her necklace to the Virgin and child.[24]

Perhaps because the rejected wedding present brought such good publicity, the next major event in Eugénie's life, the birth of her son, was similarly observed. A "spontaneous" subscription was opened in Paris and its suburbs for the purchase of an objet d'art for the new mother and child. In order to keep the subscription popular, contributions were limited to between 5 and 25 centimes, a limitation that both permitted those without much money to feel that they were fully participating and underlined the regime's general popularity.[25] More than 600,000 people contributed a total of over 80,000 francs. Eugénie accepted the large volumes containing the names of all the subscribers[26] but, as she had done with the wedding present, requested that the money collected be put toward a good work, this time to help poor orphans and to be placed under the protection of her son. "She desires," wrote the minister of the interior to those responsible for the subscription, "to place the poor orphans under the patronage of her son; she wants the poor worker taken prematurely from his family to at least carry with him in dying the consoling thought that imperial benevolence will watch over his children."[27] The resulting institution was called, as one might expect, the Orphelinat du Prince Impérial.

A few years later, the Prince Imperial gave his name to the Empire's most politicized charity, the Société du Prince Impérial. This semipublic institution provided low-interest loans to young workers for the purchase of tools and raw materials. In founding it, the regime clearly hoped to offset the negative publicity of the closing of the central office of the Société de Saint-Vincent de Paul the year before. The charity was unusual in that the money loaned was provided by children under eighteen, who could become *associés* by contributing 10 centimes per week. Bourgeois families apparently signed their children up in droves to show their loyalty to the regime. In return, there were elaborate children's parties, such as one held in the Tuileries garden on 8 May 1864, when long tables of refreshments, two orchestras, four puppet theaters, and a circus were on hand to entertain an estimated 30,000–35,000 children and adults.[28] The familial image inherent in the charity was reinforced at these parties, which the emperor, empress, and Prince Imperial often attended together. According to a description of one party in Fontainebleau, for instance, "Fathers and mothers were there, their hearts pounding with hope in the expectation of a look or word for their dear child from the august hosts. The empress, absorbed by her role as mother and understanding the feelings of these family groups, did her utmost to respond to every desire and wish expressed in the faces of this both joyous and respectful crowd." Typically, the author also proclaimed that the event would remain "engraved in the memory" of those who had witnessed it and that it would lead to a reinforcing of the "ties of affection and devotion that link our city to the imperial family." [29]

As president of the Société du Prince Impérial, Eugénie presided over a constellation of Bonapartist luminaries including the Princesses Clotilde and Mathilde, the Comtesses Walewska and Morny, the Baronne Haussmann, and Madams Baroche and Troplong. The institution received the exaggerated praise and condemnation common to highly politicized endeavors. The mayor of Clermont-Ferrand, for example, told Eugénie that "the recent establishment of the Société du Prince Impérial is there to prove to us that you are more than the sovereign, that you are the mother of all of the French people." [30] But to an eye less enamored of the dynasty, the society was something the empress had "invented, in order to replace the Société Saint-Vincent de Paul that Persigny destroyed because Christian charity must be governmental and wear the official emblem." [31]

Several years after the creation of the Société du Prince Impérial in 1865, Eugénie was put in charge of the general institutions of charity dependent on the ministry of the interior. [32] These institutions (the insane asylum at Charenton, the imperial institution for young blind people, the three imperial homes for deaf-mutes, the two homes for convalescent workers at Vincennes and at Vesinet, and the imperial travelers' hospice on Mont Genèvre in the Alps) were among the most important national organizations concerned with temporary and permanent relief. With these institutions, as with all of the others that Eugénie nominally headed, the empress's actual input was minimal. As patron, she received an annual report on the moral and material state of each establishment and had the right to decide who would receive free admission. These various presidencies and patronages were, however, powerful symbols of imperial benevolence, of the benign and beneficent rule of the Bonapartist state as personified by Eugénie.

A variety of other activities, some of them rather pompous court ceremonies, also allowed Eugénie to demonstrate her charitable zeal. Some of the works she patronized, for example, held an annual reception at the Tuileries at which the empress was presented with a report on what the charity had accomplished during the year. These were gala affairs attended by the leading members of the charity and the court. Significantly, the first major function over which the empress presided without the aid of her husband, the presentation of the Société de Charité Maternelle to Eugénie by the archbishop of Paris in 1853, was of this nature. It was not, however, a success; the archbishop forgot his speech, and the nervous new empress was not self-possessed enough to put him at ease. Instead, unable to think of anything to say other than the now superfluous response to the archbishop's speech that her husband had written for her and that she had carefully memorized, Eugénie fled the room in tears, followed by her ladies-in-waiting.[33] Although she soon overcome her nervousness, Eugénie never seems to have cared for such occasions and rarely said more than a few words, if anything at all.

Other ceremonies gave the empress a chance to visit the works she supported. Inaugurations and stone-setting ceremonies for charitable institutions, for example, served as reminders of Eugénie's role as beneficent provider, just as those of her husband underscored his role as bringer of prosperity. Eugénie also sometimes attended fund-raising events, especially those benefiting the works over which she officially presided. Charities used a variety of strategies to raise money. Balls, sales, lotteries, sermons, concerts, and plays were all put into service, especially during the winter months, or "charitable season," when the poor were most miserable and the rich, who traditionally spent winters in the city, most available. These occasions were often as much social as charitable. The charity that benefited from the amateur society theatricals of the Princess Beauveau, for example, has been almost forgotten, while the theatricals themselves, the one fund-raising innovation of the period, are mentioned in a number of memoirs.[34] Since imperial prestige could help charities raise money, connections to the empress were at times underscored by the locations and dates of the fund-raising events. Sales to benefit the empress's orphanages, for example, were sometimes held on her fête day, 18 November.[35] She and the emperor might purchase a few items, but, more important, her patronage set the tone for others connected with the Empire. "All of the palace intimates, all of high officialdom," said Zola in describing one such sale, "were sure to attend in order to pay court."[36]

Eugénie's supposed personal kindness in the face of misery was highly publicized from the very start of her career as empress, and not only by big events such as when she gave up the diamond necklace wedding present. As the republican Henri Rochefort sarcastically commented, as soon as the imperial marriage was announced, the newspapers began "printing touching stories concerning the goodness, the magnanimity, and the intrepidity of this Diana, who with a turn of her pretty hand quieted the most fiery steed. It became impossible to number the garrets visited by this young lady of whom nobody had heard three weeks before, and how many sufferers she had saved from misery and even from suicide!"[37] Nor did the flood of publicity abate over the course of the Empire. According to one laudatory account of the empress's visit to Egypt for the opening of the Suez Canal in 1869, wherever she went, "she never forgot the poor and the sick, and if [she] sometimes neglected to visit some palace or celebrated monument, she never delayed her visit to a hospital or put off her offering to an indigence fund."[38]

Given the heavy publicity, it was probably inevitable that Eugénie would be besieged with requests for aid. She had a special secretary to deal with these demands, which often came supported by people either friendly with the empress or well-known in society.[39] Both Prosper Mérimée and George Sand, for example, successfully asked for aid for others on a number of occasions. But Eugénie also had a convenient way of refusing the demands without actually saying no. Because she was not in the regular chain of assistance, her secretary could simply inform the person that the empress sympathized with his or her problem and had forwarded the request to the proper ministry—then the ministry could turn down the request without doing too much damage to the reputation of the empress.[40]

But if the reality of Eugénie's aid to individuals was rather bloodless, the myth was not. The touching stories that circulated in newspapers and in popular biographical accounts told of her spontaneously adopting poor orphans of cholera victims or emptying her purse into the lap of a blind beggar. These stories made Eugénie into a sort of secular saint, distributing goodness (usually in the form of money to the poor and miserable) wherever she went. According to the *Almanach de l'Impératrice*, for example: "The entire life of the Comtesse de Montijo de Téba [the Empress Eugénie] has been but one long series of good works, and wherever she has gone, a sweet memory has followed her, similar to those stars, those comets crossing the deserts of the sky and leaving everywhere a luminous trail."[41] According to others, the empress also anonymously visited the poor at home on a regular basis, driving in her unmarked coach and accompanied only by a lady-in-waiting. On occasion, she is even supposed to have made the bed of a worthy unfortunate with her own hands.[42]

This stress on personal interaction also marked Eugénie's visits to charitable institutions. Both in Paris and on her frequent trips to provincial cities, she often stopped at *crèches*, *salles d'asile*, schools, hospitals, hospices, insane asylums, and even prisons (for women and children) with little fanfare. She used the same unmarked coach as for visiting individuals and kept her attendants to a minimum. During these visits, Eugénie spoke with both those who distributed charity and those who received it. In the schools and *salles d'asile*, for example, she talked to the directors and watched the students at their lessons. And on a visit to a girls' school in the Marais in

1865, "she attended all of the lessons, had the daily homework corrected in front of her, and showed herself to be very satisfied with the students and with their general behavior."[43] In a similar vein, on her prison visits she spoke with the inmates and tried to convince them to lead better lives.[44] Such visits were supposed to leave lasting and favorable memories, though the lesson sometimes needed to be reinforced. On the first anniversary of a visit to the *salles d'asile* of Bourges, for example, the 500–600 children Eugénie had seen went to church to pray, hear a mass, and listen to a sermon on "the incomparable goodness of our empress."[45]

The most eulogized of all of Eugénie's charitable visits were those to the cholera wards in Paris in 1865 and in Amiens in 1866. From time to time throughout the Empire, both sovereigns made well-publicized visits to hospitals as part of their general charitable duties, but the visits to cholera wards received more attention than the others. Cholera was the bubonic plague of the nineteenth century, the most feared disease in the pantheon of public illness. The potential danger of infection while visiting cholera victims was real and had been demonstrated during the first major epidemic in 1832. Neither Louis-Philippe nor his queen, Marie-Amelie, had dared a visit to the wards, but their eldest son, the Duc d'Orléans, and the premier, Auguste Casimir-Périer, had, and as a result, Casimir-Périer contracted the disease and promptly died.[46] During the epidemic of 1849, the worst in French history, Louis-Napoleon, then president of the Second Republic, had visited the hospitals and the most famous victim of that epidemic, Maréchal Bugeaud, all to good effect in the newspapers,[47] though neither sovereign seems to have paid such visits during the smaller outbreak of 1853–54, when the Empire was at its apogee. Perhaps because she was a woman undertaking something both unexpected and dangerous, Eugénie's 1865 and 1866 visits made even more of a splash than the earlier visits and elicited a more positive public response than anything she had done since the birth of the Prince Imperial in 1856.

Although the cholera epidemic of 1865 would ultimately turn out to be far less severe than those of 1832 and 1849, at the time there was no way of knowing how soon it would end. During October, the most devastating month, 4,536 people died of the disease in Paris, 130 of them on the day of Eugénie's visits.[48] The emperor had visited the Hôtel-Dieu on 20 October, and Eugénie followed his lead three days later, visiting the Beaujon, Lariboisiere, and Saint-Antoine hospitals. She was accompanied by two of her ladies-in-waiting, her equerry, and one of the emperor's aides de camp. Attended by the doctors and sisters who staffed the hospitals, the group entered each of the cholera wards, where Eugénie went from patient to patient, saying a few encouraging words to each of them.

The following year, when cholera broke out in Amiens, Eugénie made similar visits to the wards in that city. She arrived in Amiens by train the morning of 4 July and went immediately to the Hôtel-Dieu. After lunch she visited other charitable institutions before taking an afternoon train back to Paris. The response to the visit was enthusiastic. Medals were struck, poems were written, and Amiens named a city square and one of the hospital wards Eugénie had visited in her honor.[49] Speeches also helped to propagate the image of Eugénie's "heroic" action. Minister of the Interior Ernest Pinard said to a group gathered for the inauguration of a home for the blind: "The heroine of Amiens fears nothing but praise, and I can describe neither the perils that she confronts nor the pain that she eases. But you my children, . . . you must always remember that you are her charges and that her kind protection binds you. Her protection is your glory and your heritage."[50]

Heavy coverage of the cholera visits in the Parisian and provincial press also helped to cement in the public mind an image of the solicitous empress. The official *Moniteur universel*, for example, stressed that the empress made the visits to the Paris hospitals despite having a violent cold and "forgetting her own fatigue out of concern for the suffering and the bereavement of others."[51] There was more of the same at Amiens. One local paper there reported that at the hospital, "the empress stops at the bed of each patient. She takes the damp hand of each and, with unflagging courage, bends down to listen to the weakened voice. Two hours after her visit, the patients were calling their nurses and the hospital administrators to repeat to them the good words that, in lifting their morale, seemed at the same time to have called them back to life."[52] These cholera victims "called back to life" by the visit of the empress are, of course, distinctly reminiscent of the medieval thaumaturgic kingship, but it would be hasty to assume that a link between Eugénie's visits and the king's touch existed. Despite the high-flown rhetoric of some journalists, Eugénie was never really seen as a miracle-worker by either the regime or its publicists. Such illusions in the mid-nineteenth century would only have made the imperial regime seem even more ridiculously retrograde than it was. Eugénie's hospital visits provided an image of her as a caring, solicitous sovereign who provided hope and consolation, but not a magical one whose mere touch had the power to cure.

Popular engravings and images in the illustrated journals, the visual equivalent of newspaper accounts, depicted the same solicitude as the printed press (see figure 6.1).[53] In the illustrations, Eugénie is almost always portrayed at the head of a hospital bed, a caring hand outstretched toward a dying patient. Eugénie and the patient occupy the center of the scene, and they are surrounded by doctors, hospital sisters, and members of the

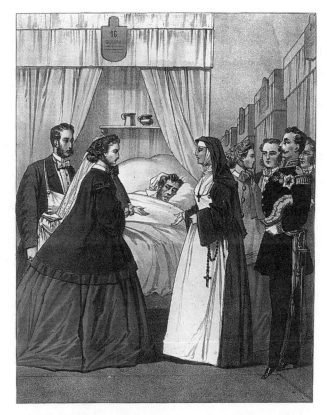

Figure 6.1. The Empress Eugénie visiting a cholera hospital.
(Bibliothèque Nationale, Paris)

imperial entourage. In almost all of the images, the patient is male, a factor
that seems to underscore Eugénie's idealized femininity, her status as a
model of bourgeois female virtue.

Beneath some of the images are short texts putting the lesson into words.
"In setting this magnificent example of courage and humanity," reads one,
"the august wife of Napoleon III has once again shown France that her
soul is as high as her elevated rank, and that there is but one voice in all
mouths to thank her and to bless her."[54] Some recognized that the emperor
undertook similar obligations. One of these, for example, recorded that the
"noble devotion of the emperor and the empress elicited everywhere a
general admiration, which shall serve as an example to those who believe
that their position or their wealth excuse them from humanity or from
contact with the unfortunate classes."[55] Popular visual images, then, supple-

mented by texts such as these, drove home the devotion of the empress and the popularity that it supposedly engendered.

Several much-repeated anecdotes also captured the spirit of the visits in a way that delighted the public. The best known of these first appeared in the *Journal des débats* two days after the visits to the Paris hospitals. According to the paper, the empress addressed a very sick patient who, in responding, mistook her for one of the nuns who staffed the hospital and called her "sister." When the attending sister started to correct the patient, Eugénie stopped her, saying that "sister" was "the most beautiful name that he could give me."[56] The Amiens visit gave rise to a similarly touching story. As the empress was leaving the hospital, "two poor children who had been made orphans by cholera were presented to her by the prefect. 'I adopt them,' she said. And tears came to everyone's eyes at these simply stated words."[57] Yet another interesting anecdote took place after the Amiens visit when a famous military figure expressed to the empress his fear that such visits might be dangerous. "Monsieur le Maréchal," the empress is supposed to have responded, "that is our way of going into battle."[58] Self-sacrifice, simple piety, touching and compassionate solicitude— these were the chief elements of Eugénie's character publicized in these visits.

Historian Simon Schama has described a long-term shift toward a more personal image of the sovereign, which he calls the "domestication of majesty." In his examination of royal portraits from the sixteenth to the nineteenth centuries, Schama found a growing tendency toward familiar, familial virtues and concluded that monarchies survived in large part because they came to be seen as "the family of families, at once dynastic and domestic, remote and accessible, magical and mundane."[59] As depicted in her charitable work, Eugénie's image was not perhaps the strongly maternal "Queen Mother" figure the English throne has used so successfully, but neither was it that of an aloof and indifferent ruler. Her charity, especially her seemingly unheralded visits to hospitals and the poor, reinforced a feminine image of personal kindness and unassuming solicitude that may ultimately have been as important a support for the imperial throne as many of the more traditional rituals of power.

Eugénie's charitable works showed her playing one of the traditional roles that French queens were expected to play, yet doing so with a particularly compassionate and self-sacrificing attitude that was closer to a nineteenth-century paragon of feminine virtue than to a traditional *souveraine*. She was, in the words of one popular image, "The First Lady of Charity of the French

Empire."[60] Like her queenly models, Eugénie's wide-ranging charitable work and the feminine and often maternal orientation of that work became evidence for her supposed personal goodness, her devotion to those in need, and her piety. But the image of Eugénie's charity went beyond that of the Old Regime queens, as it went beyond that of her husband. The imagery and texts depicting Eugénie's charity publicized and even mythologized her as an ideal woman, and often did so through her "private" actions, actions theoretically unconnected with her public position. If Eugénie's charity was politically effective, as I believe it was, it owed at least part of this success to the fact that it managed to tap into the particularly strong nineteenth-century conception of the world as ordered into separate, gendered spheres. But politics in this instance was not solely parasitic on culture; in exploiting cultural stereotypes, it also raised those stereotypes to the level of myth and thereby helped to perpetuate them. In this respect, the fact that Eugénie might be portrayed in domestic situations that would have been seen as demeaning for her husband—visiting the poor in their homes, for example, or even making some poor person's bed—reinforced gendered roles that imposed on women the "virtues" of sacrifice and humility while leaving the public side of life to men.

SEVEN

Playing Soldier

O ne of Louis-Napoleon's most common public roles was that of the
military leader, the commander of troops. Indeed, nothing was more
typical of Second Empire spectacle than the presence of large numbers of
soldiers. Even for ostensibly civilian events such as inaugurations and legislative openings, mounted troops accompanied the imperial processions, and
rows of soldiers lined both sides of the streets along the route. The emperor himself usually wore a general's uniform and was often accompanied
by his military staff. Other ceremonies gave the military an even more
central place. The emperor often held mammoth troop reviews, for example, especially during the visits of foreign sovereigns, and the return of the
troops from the Crimea and from Italy during the 1850s were occasions
for huge military display.

Military spectacles tended to draw large and enthusiastic crowds. It was
a commonplace during the Second Empire that love for military display
was a deeply ingrained French national characteristic. As one of Napoleon
III's equerries put it, "If the French person is a born spectator, he is also
a born chauvinist. When he sees a passing regiment from his window, when
he attends a moving drama from our military history, it is rare that his
heart does not beat in time with the drum."[1] "A military government,"

noted another observer, "is essentially in the talents of the French people, who love the fife, the drum, handsome uniforms, pretty colonels, *éclat*, splendor, and gala."[2] But many French people also feared the military, especially given its role in the coup d'état and the political repression. The result, according to a British observer, was that the French often greeted the army with "a ludicrous mixture of fear and affection."[3]

However militaristic its image, the Second Empire was no military dictatorship. Unlike his uncle and despite his uniform, Louis-Napoleon never served in the military. His chief advisers and ministers were almost all civilians, and no matter how much he owed the army in December 1851— and he owed it a lot—he never let generals dictate policy. In short, the military emphasis in Second Empire spectacle did not reflect military-based political power. Instead, it grew out of the particularly important place of the military for Louis-Napoleon's claim to his uncle's heritage and the emotionally resonant place of the military in the symbolic construction of the French nation in the nineteenth century.

Much of Louis-Napoleon's charm rested on his ties to the First Emperor and on his seeming ability to restore France's place as the preeminent continental power, as it unquestionably had been during the First Empire. The Second Empire underscored these themes by modeling its military celebrations on those of the First Empire, by using Napoleonic symbols, and by setting ceremonies in locations closely associated with the First Empire. It also brashly celebrated its own military adventures, adventures that may have lacked the luster of those of the First Empire but that stood in marked contrast to the relative inactivity of the Restoration and July Monarchy.

At the same time, these celebrations allowed the Second Empire to tap into and exploit the more general, popular association between nation and army. No institution more closely resembled the ideal of a unified national community or so poignantly evoked the strong, emotional commitment conjured up by the nation—especially in facing death in the service of that community—than the army. Thus, as we will see, the celebrations following the two major conflicts of the period, the Crimean War and the Italian Campaign, focused attention more on the struggles and sacrifices of the troops than on the victories themselves. In contrast to the norm for the *fête impériale*, these celebrations gave prominent place to the Place de la Bastille, the symbolic locus of the Revolution, and even seem to have tacitly condoned the singing of the "Marseillaise," an act that was not usually permitted. Beneath these surprising evocations lies the Bonapartist desire to bring together the revolutionary and monarchical traditions in French history. As we have seen, this was a common thread in many Second

Empire spectacles. If it took the specific form of using the Place de la Bastille and the singing of the "Marseillaise" in these celebrations, it was probably because of the close historical association between the national army and the French Revolution. Whatever the reality of the revolutionary armies, ideas such as the *levée en masse* and the "nation-in-arms" powerfully expressed the national community, a community that, as Benedict Anderson reminds us, "is always conceived as a deep, horizontal comradeship."[4]

Public, military festivals, especially those associated with major conflicts, brought army and people together in one emotionally charged moment. The experience of such a moment was described by Jules Michelet in 1845 as essential to the education of a young Frenchman. As the boy and his father look down upon the troops and people, the father speaks:

> Look, my son, look: there is France; there is your native land! All this is like one man—with one soul and one heart. They would all die for a single man, and each one ought also to live and to die for all. Those men passing by, who are armed and now departing, they are going away to fight for us. They are leaving their father and their aged mother who will need them. You will do the same, for you will never forget that your mother is France.[5]

Although Michelet was a republican, his description might apply equally well to the ideal military celebration of a Bonapartist. In both we see the same masculine emphasis on fraternity and bravery, the same underlying concern with national unity. But in contrast to Michelet's ideal, the Bonapartist celebrations always included one additional element: the emperor. Despite his lack of military experience, Louis-Napoleon usually took center stage in these celebrations. As he paraded about, wearing a uniform he had not earned and a sword he had never used, he assumed a role he had inherited from his uncle, the military leader. But what had come naturally to the First Emperor was playacting for his heir.

Soldiers were the most constant and conspicuous element of Second Empire spectacle. Troops accompanied all official processions, and a "hedge" of troops always lined both sides of the route taken by those processions. These hedges played both a defensive and a decorative role; the rows of troops kept spectators (and possible assassins) back from the head of state and provided reserves in case of emergency, while at the same time the elaborate military uniforms added a splash of color to the celebration. Since drab browns and greens have now replaced the bright colors and fanciful designs of these uniforms with a grim utilitarian sameness, it is difficult to grasp just how visually attractive these celebrations must have been, with the spahis and turcos in their elaborate and outlandish uniforms, others in plumed hats and on prancing horses. Certainly flashy soldiers were something of an obsession with Napoleon III, who in 1854 created a special unit of elite troops, the famous Cent-Gardes.[6] These soldiers, Napoleon III's personal guard, were chosen for their stature and prowess and were given an elaborate and impractical uniform—one that came complete with an armored breastplate that, unfortunately for the soldiers who happened to pass through Algeria, worked something like a convection oven in the hot North African sun.[7]

Another military element common to most spectacles was provided by the emperor's customary attire for such occasions—a military uniform. As noted earlier, he had begun this practice soon after his election to the presidency of the Second Republic by showing up for a troop review in the uniform of a general in the National Guard. After the coup d'état of December 1851, he continued to dress in uniform on many occasions, but he now sported that of a general in the regular army.[8] The wearing of a military uniform generally lends a political leader a certain stamp of authority, and this was especially true for Napoleon III. A short and unprepossessing man, the Emperor cut a more "manly" figure when seated on a large horse, his shoulders broadened by military epaulets. He often set himself off further by riding at a short distance from his escort and by turning to either side and touching his hat to acknowledge acclamations from the crowd. As an English observer noted on one such occasion, "even his worst enemy must have avowed that he became his place and that he looked the emperor."[9] In short, the military trappings made the Emperor seem effective, solid, and patriotic: the protector of the national interest carrying out his assigned role.

The annual 15 August celebrations were particularly fecund in military display, with troop reviews, military units in the official processions, and concerts by military bands all common elements of the holiday. Especially stirring were the military pantomimes performed every year as part of the celebrations in Paris and in some larger provincial cities (see figures 7.1 and 7.2). Like many other elements of Second Empire celebrations, the pantomimes harkened back to the traditional entertainments of the Old Regime but were put to work for the greater glory of Napoleon III. In 1854, for example, after the Crimean War had begun (but before the French had seen any action), the pantomime on the Champ-de-Mars whipped up popular enthusiasm for the war by depicting a siege at which the Turks fought the Russians. Fifteen hundred actors on a 25,000-square-meter stage, at least according to the program, participated in this exciting show.[10] Similarly, in 1861, the pantomime at the Invalides recounted the French military adventure in China the year before.[11] The pantomimes were also notable

Figure 7.1. A 15 August military pantomime as depicted in *The Illustrated London News*, 24 August 1861. (Doe Library, University of California, Berkeley)

for their populism and for their use of common stereotypes. The three shows put on in Paris in 1867 provide a good example of the range of themes used. At the Barrière du Trône was "Les Seigneurs, Paris en 1769," a populist and mildly anti-Semitic piece that pitted the Seigneurs, aided by a devious usurer named Isaac, against the Gardes Françaises and Pierrot. On the Trocadéro, two more plays showed the French army in action. The first reenacted an episode from Senegal in 1865 and portrayed the Senegalese as murderous savages beaten in the end by the brave and gallant French. The second also made the French troops the heroes, this time protecting a small mountain village from "brigands." [12]

In addition to the formidable but ancillary military presence at virtually all Second Empire celebrations, a large number of celebrations made the military their principal focus of attention. The troop review was by far the most common such event. All troops were periodically reviewed by their commanders, but these performances did not normally rate the status of public spectacle except on the most mundane level. When the emperor held a review, however, or when the ceremony was part of a larger celebration such as a 15 August celebration, these events often became state spectacles of the highest order. Announced in advance, they drew large crowds of spectators and were fully reported in the press.

Figure 7.2. A 15 August military pantomime as depicted in *L'Il-lustration*, 22 August 1857. (Doe Library, University of California, Berkeley)

These lavish and frequent reviews came to symbolize the close relationship between Napoleon III and the troops. The ceremonies invariably began with the actual review, in which the imperial party rode up and down before the assembled troops, and then ended with the file-past, in which the troops marched and rode past the now stationary reviewing party. The emperor clearly paid homage to the military through his presence at the reviews and through the publicity and the seeming importance his presence gave them. He also often distributed medals at these reviews. The institution of the new *médaille militaire* in early 1852, for example, provided the occasion for two reviews at which Louis-Napoleon, then still president of the Decennial Republic, personally handed the medals out for the first time. The medal, he said in an address, was designed to allow him to extend more rewards to valiant soldiers without watering down the Legion of Honor. Coming directly on the heels of the coup d'état as it did, the new medal clearly enabled the president to thank the army for its support in repressing the resistance to that action and to assure the soldiers that he would stand behind them. It also gave him the chance to articulate in words that special affinity for the military underlying the reviews. "[W]ear it," he concluded his address to the soldiers, "as a proof of my solicitude for your interests and of my love for this great military family whose head I am proud to be because you are its glorious children."[13]

The reviews not only allowed Louis-Napoleon to recognize his glorious children but also allowed the troops to return the favor by recognizing the emperor as their leader. Unlike modern troops, the troops at these reviews did not usually file past their commander-in-chief in disciplined silence. Instead, they yelled out slogans such as "Vive l'Empereur!" and "Vive Napoléon III!" as they passed and sometimes added other flourishes, such as galloping rather than walking their horses or vigorously waving their hats and swords while cheering. Career military men looked askance at such behavior. Even a good Bonapartist such as the Maréchal de Castellane, who claimed to understand the "political reason" for the cries, still found them "regrettable" and would have liked to see them at least made more orderly and regular.[14] But political reason prevailed over military discipline, and the reviews continued throughout the 1860s. How well they worked is difficult to evaluate, but according to at least one soldier's account of his first imperial review, his heart "beat a little faster" at the approach of the imperial couple (both the emperor and the empress were present) and the empress was "like a vision" he would "never forget." "After we had returned to the barracks," he concluded, "reviews of this nature were for a long time the subject of all conversations and contributed more than a little to maintaining the devotion of the troops."[15]

The most frequent pretext for a large review was the visit of a foreign monarch. "Decidedly, sovereigns have a singular way of exchanging courtesies," declared an amusing account of one such review. "As soon as one goes to visit another, the host, to do his guest honor, starts by parading the troops in front of him and tries to have as many of them as possible out that day."[16] Napoleon III certainly put as many as he could out on 6 June 1867, when he found that he had not one but two sovereigns visiting at the same time. Even the jaded General du Barail, who had participated in so many reviews that he felt that they "all resemble each other," found this one particularly extraordinary, though it was actually just the same old form with more troops, more sovereigns, and more spectators than usual. Some 60,000 troops arrived at Longchamps in the Bois de Boulogne at about eleven-thirty and assembled within an hour.[17] The reviewing party, which arrived at two o'clock, included not only the emperor but also the Russian Tsar, the King of Prussia, and numerous accompanying officers, including Otto von Bismarck. This group reviewed the soldiers by riding in front of the assembled columns and then took places before a tribune in which the empress and various other guests had places while the soldiers filed past them. The cavalry squadrons were the final units to pass, and having done so, they closed up, wheeled about, and galloped back toward the sovereigns, stopping just sixty meters before them and letting out enthusiastic cheers of "Vive l'Empereur!" "It was magic," du Barail later recorded. "There was in it an unforgettable minute in which actors and spectators understood the idea of an unbreakable confidence and an irresistible force that, still alive three years later, has to explain our enthusiasm, our delirium, and our illusions."[18]

But such public ceremonies, as the denouement of this one demonstrates, could also have much more immediate dangers. Returning to Paris together in a carriage, the tsar and emperor suddenly saw a young man run from the crowd and fire a pistol at them. Fortunately, the pistol misfired. Its barrel blew off, and the bullet went into the head of the horse of an equerry named Rainbeaux, who had seen the assassin at the last second and spurred his horse forward to put himself between the man and the imperial carriage. The would-be assassin turned out to be a zealous and disgruntled Pole named Berezowski who thought killing the tsar would help free his country. Happily, the only casualty, apart from the horse, was a lady from Puy de Dôme who was hit in the cheek by the pistol barrel, and the sovereigns suffered nothing worse than being a bit splattered with the horse's blood. Nonetheless, the close call served as a reminder of the possible dangers involved when sovereigns attempted to get too close to the public.

Troop reviews were not the only aspect of military life that took the form of public spectacle during the Second Empire. Maneuvers, despite their ostensible training purposes, were also often treated as festivals. The mock battles sometimes involved thousands of soldiers and were generally held on military properties outside of Paris such as the Plain of Satory, near Versailles, or, after it was completed, the base at Chalons, about seventy-five miles east of Paris. Spectators, often railroad day-trippers, crowded along the sides of the fields in which the maneuvers took place, and the press usually carried full accounts of the events, especially when the emperor was "in command." Even more than reviews, maneuvers allowed the emperor to project an image of himself as military leader. Fewer actual spectators may have seen him riding across the field at the head of a column of troops than saw him on the reviewing stand, it is true. Still, the lack was more than made up for by engravings in the illustrated press depicting him leading battlefield charges, cheered on by bourgeois and working-class spectators.[19]

The aesthetic militarism of the Second Empire—reviews, uniforms, medals, maneuvers, and so forth—both demonstrated and contributed to the close association between Louis-Napoleon and the army. But the imperial regime gave the army more than just a chance to strut about on a parade ground in fancy dress and engage in phony combat. Its numerous foreign wars and adventures provided soldiers with the opportunity to perform the tasks for which the parades and maneuvers supposedly prepared them—the killing of other human beings. But here too, spectacle played an important role, not perhaps on the battlefield but in publicizing and popularizing the Empire's aggressive foreign policies and in propagating the association of Napoleon III with the glories of Napoleon I.

In France and in the rest of Europe, one of the lessons of the period from 1789 to 1815 had been that war and revolution went hand in hand. Thus, leaders in the period following the fall of Napoleon I made a concerted and successful effort to avoid entangling themselves in major foreign conflicts. But as Eric Hobsbawm has noted, after the armies of Europe had proved themselves such able defenders of the social and political order, "this motive for diplomatic restraint was much weaker. The generation of 1848 was an age not of revolutions but of wars."[20]

The foreign activities of the French army during Louis-Napoleon's reign make up a particularly long list: the occupation of Rome throughout the period; the Crimean War of 1854–56; the expedition to Syria in 1860; the expedition to China with the British in 1860; the taking of Indochina of 1858–65; the Italian campaign of 1859; the Mexican campaign of 1863–67; and, ultimately, the disastrous Franco-Prussian War, which brought down the final curtain on the imperial stage. Even the less distinguished of these adventures usually gave rise to some form of celebration: reviews for departing troops, evocative 15 August decorations, *Te Deums,* gun salutes, illuminations for victories in particular battles, and so forth. These activities, however, paled in contrast to the grandiose spectacles associated with the two major campaigns of the 1850s—Crimea and Italy. During the conflicts, the Empire used spectacle to drum up and maintain popular enthusiasm. Afterward, elaborate parades for the returning troops paid fitting tribute to their courage and valor but at the same time turned the "victories" to the greater glory of the regime.

The Crimean War, the largest armed European conflict between 1815 and 1914, pitted Great Britain and France against Russia over dominance in Turkey and central Europe. Unlike Britain, where public opinion was instrumental in pushing the country into war, France experienced no such pressures. Indeed, public opinion seems to have been against French entry, to have resigned itself to involvement only in a halfhearted way, and ultimately to have influenced the government to end the conflict more quickly than it might have otherwise.[21] But because it had at least a modicum of appeal for both sides of the political spectrum, the Crimean War did have the advantage of not dividing the French polity into two hostile camps. To the conservatives, it could appear as a crusade to free the Holy Lands, and to the liberals as a campaign against the autocratic Russian empire.

A variety of public spectacles attempted to present the conflict in an understandable and attractive manner. Departing troops, for example, received gala reviews at which the emperor addressed them—and, through them, the country as a whole—with words calculated to appeal to their patriotism, their sense of justice, and their pride in the nation as represented by its military traditions. He wanted them, he said, to be "worthy sons of the victors of Austerlitz, of Eylau, of Friedland, and of Moscow."[22] "The army is the true nobility of our country," he remarked at another review; "it preserves intact from age to age the traditions of glory and of national honor."[23] But if the emperor could use celebrations to invoke historical glory, he could also use them to offset less desirable historical implications. In particular, the traditional hostility between England and France had to be set aside, since despite their past opposition they now found themselves fighting as allies. The newfound goodwill between these two nations was underscored by two highly publicized matched visits. In the spring of 1855, Napoleon III and Eugénie traveled to Great Britain, where they were warmly welcomed by Victoria and Albert; in August, Victoria and Albert returned the honor by coming to Paris, where they received perhaps the most enthusiastic reception of any visiting monarch of the age.

Even more popularly received, however, was the news of the fall of Sébastopol. The siege of this important Russian fortress had been long and costly for the allies, but when victory finally came on 8 September 1855, it signaled the incipient end of hostilities. Word reached Paris the next day, and after official confirmation by the booming cannon of the Tuileries, spontaneous celebrations broke out. A Swiss newspaper not known for favoring the Empire recorded:

> Noisy enthusiasm exploded everywhere. The city was covered with flags in the wink of an eye, many more than for the Queen of England. You could not find for sale either *lampions* or colored lanterns, and the illuminations of public buildings were outshone by the ensemble of the private ones. Paris was fired and frenzied despite the wind and the showers that occurred from time to time without diminishing either the ardor or the movement of the crowd.[24]

Four days later, thousands turned out again for the official *Te Deum* ceremony in Notre-Dame, which was decorated as usual by Viollet-le-Duc and Lassus. According to one witness, "The guides were in front of the emperor's carriage, the Cent-Gardes behind. It was magnificent. An immense crowd spilling over all the streets let out acclamations."[25]

However ecstatic these celebrations, the most memorable ceremony of the war was reserved for the return of the first large contingent of troops, including the Imperial Guard, to Paris on 29 December 1855.[26] In the morning, the troops massed on and around the usually avoided Place de la Bastille, and a little after eleven o'clock, the emperor, escorted by his military staff and wearing a general's uniform, rode out from the Tuileries to meet them. Rows of troops lined both sides of the *grands boulevards* between the Place de la Bastille and the Place Vendôme, and the entire route was decorated with tricolor flags, garlands, and triumphal arches. The most impressive arch, erected on the Place de la Bastille at the entrance to the Boulevard Beaumarchais, bore the names of the Crimean battles and the inscription, "A la gloire de l'Armée d'Orient," as well as eagles, statues of Victory, flags, and the imperial arms. From a spot beneath the July Column, a monument to the Revolution of 1830 surmounted by a statue of the Spirit of Liberty, the emperor read a short address of welcome to the soldiers. He told them that they represented all French troops who had fought in the Crimea, that they had been "worthy of the *patrie*," and that their courage and perseverance had "once again glorified our eagles and reconquered for France the place due her." Once he had completed this patriotic praise for the soldiers' efforts, he rode back along the *grand boulevards* to the Place Vendôme, where he positioned himself beneath the column bearing the statue of his uncle.

The long parade of troops followed the emperor to the Place Vendôme, where they filed past him in review. According to all accounts, the streets were crowded with spectators. "The people were everywhere in the lateral streets of the boulevards," wrote one witness; "the windows and balconies were crammed with spectators, and groups climbed to the very roof of the houses."[27] What they saw was not just another colorful display of strutting soldiery. Indeed, the troops marched not in their parade-ground finery but in their worn campaign uniforms, many quite ragged with wear. Their battle standards, too, were torn and tattered, and their eagles dented and scarred. Most strikingly, at the head of each unit, the walking wounded, many of them missing arms and legs, provided tangible evidence of the suffering these men had endured in their country's service. This was not, then, a ritual of exultation, but one that, as a Bonapartist journalist put it, "revealed in characters of iron and of fire, of mourning and of glory, the solemn reality of war."[28]

The return of the troops belies the common misconception of Napoleon III's regime as little more than a "carnival Empire" bent on keeping the masses quiescent with puerile entertainment. Although many aspects of the *fête impériale* did function in that manner, the troop return demonstrates that Bonapartists, no less than republicans, could deploy profoundly emotional images of personal suffering and sacrifice. Such images have played an essential role in the nineteenth and twentieth centuries in what one anthropologist has called "the symbolic construction of community"[29]—in this case, the symbolic construction of that broad, horizontal community of the nation. No better symbol exists of the nation's claim to a status higher than geographical accident than the fact that large numbers of its citizens have been willing to face violent death for it. This, I think, is why the suffering of the soldiers rather than victory itself was placed at the center of the most important public spectacle of the Crimean War.

In the troop return, the country paid genuine homage to the soldiers who had served in the Crimea. It must have been difficult not to be moved by the sight of the wounded and mutilated and by the thoughts of the many who would never return. France had lost 100,000 men in the Crimea, more than in any other conflict between the Napoleonic Wars and World War I. But the more distinctly political aspects of the celebration should not be neglected. The deployment of imperial emblems, for example, evoked the Empire everywhere along the route, and the dented and damaged eagles on the battle standards mingled the suffering of the soldiers and the Empire in a single, particularly evocative symbol. Most important, the emperor himself, by welcoming the troops and thanking them for the whole country, appeared as a sort of incarnation of the nation. At the same time, through his wearing of military uniform and by leading the troops through Paris, he managed to seem a privileged representative of the military as well.

That the emperor led the troops not through the Arc de Triomphe and up the Champs-Elysées but from the Place de la Bastille to the Place Vendôme is also important. The Place de la Bastille evoked the Revolution and, through its column, the July Monarchy. The Place Vendôme, by contrast, evoked the Old Regime in its architecture and the First Empire in its column, made from cannons captured at Austerlitz and surmounted by a statue of Napoleon I. The curiously matched use of these two sites in the celebration seemed to symbolize the bringing together of these different strands of French history and politics in common struggle and under the leadership of Napoleon III.

Other celebrations marking the end of the war continued over the next few months, though for sheer spectacle none came close to the return of the troops to Paris. As more units arrived back from the Crimea, they received similar welcomes in other cities,[30] and the peace conference, held in Paris, finalized a treaty in April to further rejoicing.[31] But the popularity of the Crimean victory ultimately had dire consequences for the young regime. Looking back on this period ten years after the fall of the Empire, Alphonse Granier de Cassagnac, a fervent but nonetheless intelligent Bonapartist, suggested that the popularity of the Crimean War presented an ideal that would lure the emperor into further adventures: "From that moment forward, the emperor dared much, perhaps too much, and . . . public opinion energetically pushed him to pursue all that the overexcited ambition of the country wanted." [32]

But as Cassagnac must have realized better than most, it was not warlike public opinion that pushed a docile emperor into foreign wars. The Crimean War stood as an encouragement to further adventures not because it demonstrated the benefits of pandering to an aggressive public opinion but because it showed that peaceful public opinion could ultimately be overwhelmed by the deep feelings attendant upon war. The sad lesson of the Crimean War was that images of national struggle, sacrifice, and victory could turn even an unpopular, needlessly bloody, and poorly understood conflict to the favor of the regime. This was something Cassagnac clearly understood, for when the next chance for a foreign war arrived a few years later, far from opposing popular aggression, he helped Napoleon III to write propaganda designed to convince the public to support the effort.[33] Nor was printed material the only means used; public spectacle also played an important role in preparing the way toward war in Italy.

The Italian campaign of 1859 resulted from the deliberate machinations of Napoleon III and Camillo di Cavour, prime minister of Piedmont. In the Plombières agreement of July 1858, the two politicians agreed that France would help Piedmont in a war against Austria "provided that the war be undertaken for a nonrevolutionary cause, which could be justified in the eyes of the diplomatic circles, and still more, of the public opinion of France and of Europe." The emperor was particularly concerned to "not stir up French Catholics" by alienating the Pope, something Cavour assured him could be easily avoided.[34] As with the Crimea, the emperor confronted the task of creating public support for a war the public was far from demanding. Public celebrations had an important role to play in this effort.

One of his first steps was to reassure Catholics of his abiding support for the Church. Within weeks of the Plombières agreement, and months before word of the possibility of an Italian war had been made public, the emperor and empress set off on an impressive official tour of Normandy and Brittany, the most solidly Catholic area of the country. As might be expected, the tour had a stronger religious component than was usually the

case. They seemed to visit every church and prelate on their route, frequently promised financial help for church repairs, and raised the bishop
of Rennes to the rank of archbishop in a ceremony attended by some 700
clergy. They ended up on 15 August at Sainte-Anne-d'Auray, Brittany's
chief pilgrimage site. Louis Veuillot, the most outspoken ultramontane jour
nalist of the Empire, was ecstatic:

> The sovereign of France on pilgrimage, on his knees before the altar of
> Sainte-Anne-d'Auray, under the eyes of an attentive, respectful, and moved
> Europe; around him, full of enthusiasm and love, as at the solemnity of a
> *sacre,* the people who gave the last blood shed for the throne and for the
> cross; at his side, the empress, her face streaming with tears from her heart
> of a Christian, a wife, and a mother, felt that force, that glory, understood
> that future that no pomp could better reveal to her![35]

Veuillot's enthusiasm, however, was destined to be short-lived.

In the next step in the preparations, the regime began making overt
hints of impending conflict, hints that were presumably intended to plant
the idea of war in the public mind and to measure reaction to it. Here too,
celebrations played a key role. At the official New Year's reception at the
Tuileries in 1859, the Austrian ambassador arrived to pay his respects to
the emperor, as custom dictated. Instead of greeting the ambassador with
the usual polite niceties, however, the emperor voiced his regret that relations between their two countries were not as good as in the past. To that
point, as far as anyone knew, relations between the two powers had been
fine, but the emperor's words made it clear that the situation might soon
change. According to historian Lynn Case, the general reaction to this
unexpected and well-publicized revelation was decidedly negative.[36] Nonetheless, the preparations continued with another testing of the waters just a
month later.

To cement the alliance with Piedmont, the emperor had married off his
troublesome, crypto-republican cousin Jerome to the Princess Clotilde, the
daughter of Victor Emmanuel II. Although the actual agreement was not
made public, the marriage, coming as it did on the heels of the New Year's
reception, was correctly perceived as another sign of an approaching conflict with Austria over Italy. The newlyweds returned to France at the
beginning of February and received a mixed reception. The prosecutor at
Aix reported that a large and sympathetic crowd was on hand to greet
them in Marseille,[37] but the Parisians seem to have given them a much
cooler welcome. Officials, including Magnan and Haussmann, met the couple at the station and escorted them through the decorated streets to the
Tuileries, where the emperor and empress were waiting. As for the populace, however, the correspondent for the London *Times* reported that

nothing could be more indifferent, or even colder, than the demeanour of the crowd. What surprised most people, no cries were heard, and hardly even was the silent courtesy of taking off the hat paid. None of the official shouters in the service of the police appeared to be present; and if there were any, they certainly did not perform their peculiar duty—they were mute and motionless.[38]

The official newspaper, *Le Moniteur universel,* seems to bear this out; in contrast to its usual high-flown rhetoric about wildly enthusiastic crowds, in this case it noted blandly that a "considerable crowd pressed together along the route" gave the newlyweds "a most attentive and sympathetic welcome."[39] All this—and especially the apparent absence of the official cheerleaders—indicates that in this case the regime wanted to use the arrival as a sounding board for popular feelings about the possibility of war rather than as a way of manipulating such feelings.

At the opening of the legislative session a few days later, the emperor responded ambiguously to the fears of war. He declared the situation in Italy to be "abnormal" but called the war rumor a "false alarm" and misleadingly claimed that the marriage of his cousin to Princess Clotilde was not the product of a "hidden reason, but the natural consequence of the community of interest of these two countries and of the friendship of the two sovereigns."[40] The next month saw the international pressures for peace grow stronger. With neither domestic nor foreign support for intervention, it appeared that peace might carry the day. In March, when the Russians proposed an international congress to settle the problem, the emperor accepted and forced Cavour to accept too. The Plombières agreement seemed dead in the water.

Miraculously, however, bumbling Austrian diplomats saved the day for their enemies. Instead of assenting to a conference in which they would have had both Prussia and Great Britain on their side, the Austrians decided to settle the problem with unilateral threats. On 22 April they delivered an ultimatum to Piedmont demanding disarmament. Piedmont rejected the ultimatum on 26 April, and on 29 April, Austrian troops invaded. Here was the justifiable cause for war that Napoleon III and Cavour had been trying to contrive at Plombières. Four days later the emperor proclaimed that in this act of hostility against a French ally, Austria had also declared war on France. He would soon, he said, playing on the memory of the First Empire, put himself at the head of the army and lead it toward "that classic land, famous through so many victories, to find once again the footprints of our fathers."[41]

The emperor brought to war the same flair for spectacle that he brought to so much else. Departing Guard units from Paris, for example, took a very public leave:

Each of them paraded on the Place du Carrousel, band leading, then stopped amid a considerable crowd; an officer stepped forward and entered the palace to get the standard that was kept there.

After he had returned to the regiment, the emperor appeared at one of the windows of the Marsan Pavilion along with the empress and the little Prince Imperial. The regiment presented arms, the band played the national hymn, and then cries of *Vive l'Empereur!* came from all mouths, hats went flying in the air, and handkerchiefs were waved. It was one of those spectacles that moved you profoundly and brought tears to your eyes.[42]

In the provinces too, the troop sendoffs had a festival-like atmosphere, though attitudes seem to have varied somewhat from group to group and region to region. The prosecutors' reports from Brittany, for example, describe less enthusiasm than those from less Catholic areas, and several reports described the war as more popular with urban workers than with other groups.[43]

Whatever enthusiasm the troop departures may have generated, however, was mild compared with that of the departure of the emperor from Paris on 10 May. According to one witness,

> It is not possible to get an idea of the enthusiasm with which he was welcomed when, in campaign uniform, tunic, and kepi, he appeared beneath the main entrance to the Louvre facing the Palais-Royal. I found myself the first one next to the door, in the first row, as usual, at the risk of getting myself crushed. An immense acclamation of *Vive l'Empereur! Vive l'Italie!* rang out; the figure of the sovereign beamed with joy. An immense crowd struck up the "Marseillaise"; I was moved down to the bottom of my soul and I ended up sharing the common joy and hope.[44]

The emperor was dressed in a campaign uniform, as if he were going immediately into battle, and rode in an open coach accompanied by the empress. A squadron of his Cent-Gardes accompanied the procession, which turned east on the Rue de Rivoli after leaving the Louvre. "Never has the emperor received a better ovation than that of today," said Horace de Viel Castel. "It was a *furia* that will never be understood by those who did not see it."[45] "He was driven to the train by an immense crowd and frenetic acclamations," wrote Prosper Mérimée, and "is now more popular than he has ever been."[46] The crowd cheered "Vive l'Empereur!" and "Vive l'Italie!" and, according to another witness, threw rosaries and medals of Notre-Dame-des-Victoires into his carriage.[47]

This enthusiasm reached its apogee on the Place de la Bastille. According to Viel Castel:

> I saw the moment when that same people who made the barricades and the insurrections, who chased out two royal families, and twice proclaimed

the Republic, unharnessed the carriage of Napoleon III and pulled it themselves to the Gare de Lyon.

I am exaggerating nothing, I am trying to describe what I saw and I am
unequal to the reality.

The people of Paris were moved and enthusiastic, they were entirely
Bonapartist.[48]

To be sure, despite Viel Castel's testimony, it is still not entirely clear that
the workers really did pull the carriage to the station as he states. Not only
is Viel Castel one of the least trustworthy observers of the period, but the
incident was not mentioned in the principal newspaper reports.[49] All
sources seem to agree, however, that there was great enthusiasm, though
the correspondent for the London *Times* seemed a bit skeptical about its
sincerity. His report, sprinkled with theatrical metaphors, concluded that "it
cannot be denied that there was a very strong feeling, evanescent it may
be, but which looked very like enthusiasm. The thing was got up well, and
it had more than a *succès d'estime*."[50]

Effective stage management and, in particular, the "official shouters"
who were almost certainly out in force for the occasion must have played
an important role in generating this enthusiasm. But, for once, the result
seems to have surpassed the expectations even of the Bonapartists. "Friends
were as surprised as enemies," Emile Ollivier later noted. "The passion of
French democracy for the emancipation of peoples manifested itself once
again. Even those who since December had cold-shouldered the emperor
of the coup d'état bore him off to war in triumph."[51] Indeed, a war for
the emancipation of Italy, the seemingly tolerated singing of the "Marseillaise," the climax of the departure on the Place de la Bastille all seemed
specifically designed to appeal to the left. And at least as far as the immediate success of the departure, the tactic seems to have worked. As one liberal
Bonapartist journalist said of the departure a few years later:

> Never had a conqueror at the apogee of his power had a triumphal entry
> comparable to that departure of Napoleon III for Italy: those who saw the
> enthusiasm of that day cannot forget it. On the Place de la Bastille, it arrived
> at a paroxysm. It was here that the pride of the past joined the enthusiasm
> of the present; it was here above all that each felt that France had once
> again become France and that France still meant the Revolution.[52]

The emperor had been gone scarcely ten days when news of victories
began pouring in: Montebello, 20 May; Palestro, 30 May; Magenta, 4 June;
Solferino, 24 June. As regent, Eugénie decided to celebrate the two major
battles, Magenta and Solferino, with *Te Deum* ceremonies in Notre-Dame
and throughout the country. Viollet-le-Duc (now without the assistance of

Lassus, who had died in 1857) once again decorated the cathedral for the pompous ceremonies, which the empress herself attended.[53] As usual, the Bonapartist press made the celebrations into moments of unity between nation and dynasty. One sympathetic paper, for example, pronounced that "all France united itself wholeheartedly with the empress under the antique vaults of Notre-Dame to sing the *Te Deum* for Magenta. The people's joy and that of the sovereigns met in the same hymn of gratitude to God and gave expression to the same triumphal cry."[54] The ceremonies in Paris went off without a hitch, but problems arose in the provinces when the clergy in a number of areas either neglected to sing the *Te Deums* or sang them poorly.[55] The emperor's worries about the Catholic reaction to the war were proving well founded.

Equally vexing, though the French won the battles, the war was a far cry from the glorious campaigns of the First Empire. At Solferino, as one historian put it, "two antiquated military machines, both rusty, competed in incompetence, and the French, mostly by accident, held the field."[56] Moreover, the battles were extremely bloody by any standard. At Solferino alone, the Austrians lost 22,000 men and the French lost 17,000. Facing the prospect of more losses of this magnitude, growing Catholic dissatisfaction at home, and the possibility of Prussian interference on the side of Austria, Napoleon III requested an armistice. On 11 July he met the Austrian emperor Francis Joseph at Villafranca, and the two signed a peace agreement.

But this hasty and seemingly premature termination to the war was, as one diplomatic historian put it, "the first really disastrous mistake of [the] reign."[57] Many were glad the war was over, but the end came too late for the right and too early for the left. The prosecutor at Besançon reported that many of the "heads of the demagogic party" who had rallied to the emperor during the war "today are splitting off with an *éclat* that is a fairly significant indication of the current dispositions of this party."[58] Perhaps sensing the dissatisfaction, the emperor did not return to Paris in the conquering-hero style he had used for his departure. He crossed France quickly and quietly, arriving at Saint-Cloud without fanfare on 17 July.

The troops, by contrast, received a spectacular welcome on their return on 14 August.[59] Like a Hollywood studio that repeats successful movie plots almost without alteration, the Empire used the same scenario for the return of the troops from Italy that it had used four years earlier for the return of the troops from the Crimea. The emperor once again met the soldiers on the Place de la Bastille and returned by way of the *grands boulevards* to the Place Vendôme, where they paraded past him to the cheers of the crowd. On the Place de la Bastille, city architect Victor Baltard had erected a large triumphal arch representing the gothic façade of the cathedral of Milan.[60] Spectators crowded along the boulevards and into the stands erected around the Place Vendôme. Many of them had arrived the night before to get good places; others climbed into the basin of the Château-d'Eau or rented space on ladders erected by small-time entrepreneurs behind the crowd.[61]

The troops once again paraded in their worn campaign uniforms and bore the battered eagles and torn standards they had taken into combat (figure 7.3). "His Majesty the Emperor Napoleon III, the generals, and the soldiers were the objects of inexpressible enthusiasm," said one account, "but it was above all the flags, torn into strips and completely shredded by grapeshot, that were acclaimed by the hurrahs and the bravos of the crowd."[62] "As the flags passed, burned and pierced by the shots received," said another witness, "everyone felt electrified."[63]

But glory goes hand in hand with tragedy. As before, the wounded and mutilated soldiers marched at the heads of their columns, attracting a great deal of sympathetic attention. "A young officer who had lost both of his arms and a young soldier supported by two of his friends, scarcely walking on two legs of wood drew particular attention."[64] But these very real and very poignant symbols of the war had a different effect than the tattered flags. The Prince Imperial, then in his third year, supposedly had to be

Figure 7.3. The return of the troops from Italy, 14 August 1859. (Bibliothèque Nationale, Paris)

removed from the balcony from which he was watching the parade with his mother because "he could not stand the spectacle of our heroic wounded, pale, lame, mutilated." [65] Others of a less impressionable age were also moved. "I was seized with pity," said one spectator on the Place Vendôme. "That vision of the miseries of war cooled my ardor for the marvelous mise-en-scene of the triumph." [66]

The return of the troops from Italy was the last of the great victory celebrations of the Second Empire. Perhaps for that reason many later saw it as a high point of the Empire but also linked it with the military disaster that was to come. Eleven years later, Edouard Drumont, better known as the Third Republic's most virulent anti-Semite, declared the return to be the "true *fête nationale* under Napoleon III" but also lamented that an ungrateful Italy did not later think of coming to France's aid as France had hers.[67] General du Barail said, "We acclaimed the victorious eagles but wondered why they were back so soon. . . . We felt in a confused way that the emperor no longer had his hand on the tiller of Europe." [68] Even some of those most closely associated with the regime claimed to have sensed that something was amiss. "In the midst of those exhilarating cheers, which even the wisest find intoxicating, I felt my heart tighten," said General Fleury, for whom the "unachieved victory" and the "painful comparison with the past of the First Empire" seemed to presage ill. Haussmann himself said that he "would never forget the truly triumphal entry of the army into Paris" but concluded with a *cri de coeur* of regret that "if the war of 1870 had been better conceived, better prepared, better conducted, we would perhaps have seen once again a similar National Solemnity instead of watching the most lamentable, the most irreparable of catastrophes!" [69]

Second Empire military spectacles, then, were not merely excuses for parading about in colorful uniforms. They tapped into and helped to perpetuate both the memory of the glorious days of the First Empire and a compelling image of the nation as a fraternity, a unified community worthy of great sacrifice. But even when, as they often did, these spectacles placed their emphasis on the troops, it was still the emperor who emerged as the central figure. It was he who distributed the eagles, he who reviewed the troops, he who commanded the maneuvers, he who welcomed the soldiers back after service in the Crimea and in Italy. In these celebrations, we see a man whose only real connection to the military prior to coming to power was his uncle place himself at the center of the deeply felt complex of images that surrounded the army. But this style of leadership, this "playing soldier," was bound to be most effective when combined with military victory and was entirely incompatible with military defeat such as that of Sedan.

EIGHT

The Fête Impériale
in the Provinces

Histstory, like good detective fiction, sometimes has its dogs that do not bark in the night—its moments when events that fail to occur as expected provide important clues to what really did happen. We can see one such incident (or nonincident) in the Second Empire's failure to formally inaugurate the new statue of Napoleon I that it erected on the Vendôme Column in 1863. What might be called the "curious incident of the statue in the daytime" does not allow us to solve any long-standing murder mysteries, but it does offer an interesting perspective on the political changes of the 1860s.

Erected during the First Empire and made from cannons captured at Austerlitz, the Vendôme Column was originally decorated with a statue by Antoine-Denis Chaudet depicting the emperor in Roman garb and holding a winged victory, or Nike, in one hand. After the fall of the Empire, however, having an imperial image dominate one of the most important corners of Paris did not sit well with the newly restored monarchy. Chaudet's statue soon found itself removed from its perch, melted down, and, in an extraordinary act of monumental politics, used to make a new statue of Henry IV for the Pont-Neuf, the old one having been turned into revolutionary cannons.

Twenty years later, however, the First Emperor was back in fashion. Attempting to bask in a bit of reflected glory, the July Monarchy commissioned the sculptor Emile Seurre to make a new statue of him for the column. Unlike Chaudet, Seurre portrayed the emperor not in antique clothes but in a military uniform and with his hand tucked into his jacket in the now famous gesture. Generally known as the "Little Colonel," this statue, inaugurated in 1833, grew into one of the most widely recognized and well-loved images of Napoleon I. It remained on the column until 1863, when Napoleon III decided to replace it with a statue modeled on Chaudet's original, a decision made after he quite fortuitously found himself in possession of the original Nike from that statue. It turned out that the group of workers who had removed the statue from the column during the Restoration had kept the Nike rather than melting it down with the rest of the statue and had then left it in a wine shop in lieu of payment. The owner of the wine shop turned the Nike over to the government, but the symbolic moment must have passed, since instead of destroying the figure, the government sold it to a collector. The collector's heirs eventually passed it on to Napoleon III, who commissioned the sculptor Augustin Dumont to make a new statue modeled on that of Chaudet and using—despite Dumont's objections—the original Nike. In 1863, the new statue was placed atop the column and the "Little Colonel" was demoted to a less significant location at Courbevoie, outside Paris.[1]

Given its history and location, the new Napoleon was the single most important public statue erected during the Second Empire, at least from a political point of view; yet the government failed to stage the sort of inauguration that the history of the *fête impériale* would lead us to expect. Nor did the ceremonial lapse pass unnoticed by contemporaries. "Frankly," said *L'Illustration,* "after all that, we might have expected at least a fireworks show, an illumination, and a review of the National Guard. But nothing of the sort happened; one day, without letting anyone know, they took down the little fellow and hoisted up another in his place, and that was that."[2]

One missed opportunity for a celebration does not necessarily indicate a major change of policy, yet given the general dearth of Bonapartist extravaganzas in Paris during the period following 1863, the curious incident of the Vendôme statue seems at least prophetic. Until that year, big celebrations in the capital were frequent and lavish; after it, with the exception of the Universal Exposition of 1867, they were few and far between. Thus, the last of the major military celebrations, the return of the troops from Italy, took place in 1859, and the last of the big public works inaugurations, that of the Boulevard du Prince Eugène, in late 1862.

This shift away from large celebrations in the capital roughly corresponds with two other major political developments: the move from a "repressive" to a "liberal" Empire and the decline of imperial popularity in Paris, as demonstrated in legislative elections. Beginning in 1860, the Empire began to implement a series of legal measures providing greater political freedoms, including far more liberal laws on the press and on political associations. These measures culminated in the formation of a quasi-parliamentary government under Emile Ollivier in January 1870, just in time to be destroyed along with the rest of the Empire in the Franco-Prussian War.

Historians have long debated whether the liberalization of the 1860s was part of the imperial program from the beginning or an accommodation to the rising opposition to the regime during the 1860s. It is true that Napoleon III's rhetoric had always included a more liberal dimension, and he may have been merely awaiting a modicum of prosperity and stability to implement a more liberal program. And the changes were not directly forced on him, since legislative elections in the country as a whole, as well as the plebiscite of 1870, indicate that he continued to enjoy wide popularity. At the same time, however, the opposition was clearly growing in Paris and in several other regions. Most striking in this respect, opposition candidates in the legislative election of 1863 garnered no less than 63 percent of the vote in Paris. That the emperor carried out a series of liberal measures at the same time that the liberal opposition was showing itself to be the most dynamic political force in the country would hardly seem to be entirely fortuitous.

Growing opposition to the Bonapartist regime in Paris made the supposed enthusiasm of the crowds at Parisian celebrations described in the official press increasingly suspect. During the 1850s, the big Parisian spectacles had been reassuring assertions of imperial legitimacy. Bonapartists, as we have seen, consistently saw the cheering crowds that turned out for these events as proof of the continuing popularity of the emperor and Empire. Such claims became progressively more questionable after the 1863 elections, especially in Paris. While direct evidence for why the regime decided not to formally inaugurate the new statue on the Vendôme Column is lacking, given the timing it seems likely that such considerations may have played a role. But while open opposition to the regime was growing in Paris and some other areas, the same cannot be said for the provinces generally. And it was to the provinces that the regime turned more and more frequently during the 1860s.

Paris, of course, has never been all of France, and it was even less so during the Second Empire than today. At that time only some 5 percent of the population lived in the capital (compared to more than 15 percent today). And while the press actively spread word of Parisian celebrations throughout the country, the logic of universal suffrage demanded that 95 percent of the population receive something more than vicarious experiences.

Moreover, the bulk of Louis-Napoleon's support came from rural areas. Throughout the Second Empire, it should be noted, France remained a predominantly rural country. With almost 70 percent of the population in 1866 still living in rural areas,[3] it was clear that those areas would have greater political weight than urban areas in a system of universal suffrage. Of course, social, economic, and political life varied widely from region to region in the nineteenth century, and it is difficult to generalize. The 1851 peasant uprisings against the coup d'état studied by Ted Margadant, for example, stand in marked contrast to the peasants of the Limousin studied by Alain Corbin, who particularly underscores "the intensity of the enthusiasm demonstrated by the people of the countryside on the occasion of the festivities that marked the birth of the Empire."[4] On the whole, however, Bonapartism seems to have been both more widespread and longer lasting in rural areas than among city-dwellers. Even areas that had been in violent revolt in 1851 generally settled down—with the help of severe repression to be sure—to vote for Bonapartist candidates for the duration of the Empire. And some rural areas—in Normandy and in the southwest, for example—continued to vote Bonapartist even during the Third Republic.[5]

The close ties between Louis-Napoleon and the peasantry were not, at least initially, the product of any particular policy but rather part of the heritage of the First Empire. According to Frédéric Bluche, one of the most astute historians of Bonapartism, "The plebiscites of the Consulate and above all that of 1815 already show the city/country opposition."[6] And clearly the heavy rural vote for Louis-Napoleon in the presidential election of 1848 demonstrates that neither the candidate's prorural policies nor his system of official candidates and prefectorial influence—neither of which yet existed in 1848—can alone explain the peasant support.

For Karl Marx, Louis-Napoleon was the representative *par excellence* of the conservative peasantry, who saw him as the guardian of all that was traditional and retrograde against all that was new and progressive. But many peasants saw in Louis-Napoleon—according to Réné Rémond's now-classic argument—a means of emancipation from the traditional domination of the local nobility that did not at the same time put power into the hands of the Parisian republicans.[7] Whatever the underlying reasons for the peasant support, Louis-Napoleon did not take it for granted. Indeed, the persistence and growth of rural Bonapartism throughout this period would probably have been very different without what Bluche has called "the seduction exercised on the rural majority by a political regime that addressed it directly."[8]

In this wooing of the provincial masses, as in so many other areas, ceremonies and celebrations played an important role. On orders from the central government, all of the major official festivals were celebrated everywhere in France. Prefects, subprefects, and, at the village level, mayors organized the same kinds of activities that took place in Paris. Soldiers back from the wars, for example, marched through the streets of some provincial cities as they had through those of Paris or were fêted with mass banquets, such as that at Versailles in 1859. And for the 15 August celebrations, illuminations, imperial decorations, martial music, distributions of charity, greased poles that contestants had to climb to retrieve prizes, and the rest, were all usually on the agenda everywhere in France. These activities generally took place on an appropriately reduced scale, of course, but in the larger cities like Lyons and Marseille they were still often quite lavish. And in smaller communities it was probably more difficult than in Paris to avoid such celebrations. Nor was it only amusements that all shared. When the government ordered a special *Te Deum* in Notre-Dame, it almost always ordered *Te Deums*—or their equivalents—for every church in the country, Protestant and Jewish congregations included. In this manner, the regime attempted to ensure that all of the central celebrations of the regime—the imperial marriage, the baptism of the Prince Imperial, the victory parades, and the rest—filtered down to even the most insignificant of country hamlets.

In addition to ensuring that the provinces shared in national celebrations, the government also made its presence felt in local festivities. Regional officials regularly attended ceremonies like inaugurations and school prize ceremonies, where they gave speeches that included praise for the emperor. Officials were so much a part of such celebrations that one guest at an 1857 school anniversary found their absence worth noting: "Not one weapon, not one official uniform; all was free, all was private in this imposing reunion."[9]

Of all the local festivals, the regime seemed to have a special predilection for agricultural fairs. The two major types of agricultural fairs, the *comices agricoles* and the *concours régionaux*, were held during the summer months and included such activities as plowing competitions and livestock shows. The *comices*, the local flavor of which is perhaps best evoked in Gustave Flaubert's famous seduction scene in *Madame Bovary*, were by far the smaller and more numerous of the two, with more than 500 held each year.[10] The *concours*, on the other hand, of which there were only twelve each year, were larger, regional fairs established by the government in 1851 in order to help speed agricultural progress. These fairs usually took place in constructions specially built for the occasion (figure 8.1) and were often paired by the municipal authorities with other festive activities. The one at Le Mans in 1865, for example, included a *cavalcade historique,* or historical parade, depicting scenes from the history of the city.[11]

The use of agricultural fairs for political purposes predated the Empire. In *Sentimental Education,* Flaubert (who seems to have been particularly fond of these events) had one of his characters write to another in 1848 to say that his candidature for the Assembly stood no chance because he had not visited the region he was up for: "We didn't even see you at the *comices agricoles!,*" he wrote, as if that were a disastrous political error.[12] The politicians of the Second Empire, however, proved more adept than Flaubert's hero. Not only did local and even national officials regularly attend, but the emperor and empress themselves put in appearances from time to time. In May 1868, for example, 150,000 spectators reportedly turned out to greet the imperial couple on a visit to the *concours régional* at Orléans.[13] A month later, the couple made a similar excursion to the *concours régional*

Figure 8.1. Emperor and empress visiting the regional fair at Auxerre, from *L'Illustration,* 6 June 1866. (Doe Library, University of California, Berkeley)

at Rouen.[14] Although they only stayed about three hours, the visit included a procession through the center of the city, where the Rouennais had to crowd along the narrow and picturesque street to get a glimpse of their sovereign.

The high point of the fairs were the awards distributions, ceremonies at which politics as well as prizes were the order of the day. Like school prize ceremonies and inaugurations, both *concours* and *comices* awards ceremonies were occasions for speeches. The speeches by the political dignitaries almost always included at least a short mention of the emperor, and many praised him effusively for being the first to truly understand the problems of the provinces. One speaker at a *concours régional* called him "the first farmer of the Empire." [15] And another (Michel Chevalier) told his audience that the emperor was "the first to understand the extent of the task that lay before the government with respect to the population of the countryside." [16]

Guarded praise for the French Revolution was another leitmotif of many of these speeches. The conservative Bonapartist Raymond-Théodore Troplong, for example, declared:

> In 1789, a formidable revolution broke out under the regime of privileges and restrictions, and it was the inhabitants of the countryside that were its most passionate instruments! . . . In 1848, another revolution erupted, this one threatening the monarchy, property, and the traditional bases of social order; and it was the peasants associated with property [*associés à la propriété*] and inspired by conservative principles who gave the most solid support to the reestablishment of the monarchy, calling back with enthusiasm the imperial dynasty, that symbol of modern times and glorious flag of the conquests of 1789![17]

Such evocations of 1789 *and* conservative principles demonstrate that here too, as in the more explicitly historical celebrations, the regime presented itself as the synthesis of the two central strands of French history, monarchy and Revolution. Nor was this essential part of Bonapartism's self-representation out of place in the countryside. On the contrary, it demonstrates the regime's sense that peasants saw the Empire as, in René Rémond's words, "the maintenance of the Revolution's victories over the evil designs of the nobles. It was the guarantee of equality, it was the peasantry's revenge against the age-old domination by the notables." [18]

Agricultural fairs and other local celebrations provided important conduits for the regime to reach out to provincial audiences with messages tailored especially for them. As spectacles, however, such festivities did not have the same capacity to impress as the lavish shows like the imperial marriage and baptism. But the more lavish aspects of the *fête impériale* were not always reserved for Parisians alone. Indeed, the imperial tours through the provinces can be counted among the most spectacular political events of the age. And they were at their most frequent during the 1860s, the same years when imperial spectacle in Paris was on the downswing, and the Empire itself was in its most politically troubled period.[19]

In touring the provinces in the grand manner, Napoleon III was following well-trodden paths. Many sovereigns before him, including his uncle, had made such excursions. People at the time often saw the imperial trips as part of this tradition of monarchical voyages, or "progresses" as they were usually called. "It is necessary to remember," said an education official at Caen reporting on preparations for the emperor's arrival in his region in 1858, "that the voyages of sovereigns in Normandy have always been genuine political events. The tradition of the voyage of Louis XVI to Cherbourg is still alive in this country. The passage of the Emperor Napoleon I left a profound impression that should be continued by Napoleon III."[20] And Napoleon III himself sometimes emphasized that he was following in others' footsteps. His speech at Cherbourg, for example, explicitly evoked both Louis XVI and Napoleon I.[21] The published accounts of the trips (which he seems to have financed) also played up the historical dimension. Félix Ribeyre's account of the imperial visit to the Massif Central is typical in this respect. According to Ribeyre, "In order to find in the annals of the Auvergne the memory of an exultation so unanimous and so spontaneous, it would be necessary to go back to the Council of Clermont and to the crusade preached by Peter the Hermit."[22] This search for historical antecedents to the voyages served, as we have seen with other celebrations, to link Napoleon III to the tradition of great French monarchs. At the same time, it also served to make these visits, most of which had only minimal real political importance, seem like major occurrences.

Despite the copycatting, the last emperor of France was as innovative as he was imitative. Anthropologist Clifford Geertz has noted that royal progresses generally help to "locate the society's center and affirm its connection with transcendent things by stamping a territory with ritual signs of dominance." According to Geertz, "When kings journey around the countryside, making appearances, attending fêtes, conferring honors, exchanging gifts, or defying rivals, they mark it, like some wolf or tiger spreading his scent through his territory, as almost physically part of them."[23] This is certainly true in many ways of both the trips of the sovereigns of the Old Regime and those of Napoleon III. The eagles, the "N"s, the triumphal arches that greeted the emperor on these trips were clearly "ritual signs of dominance" that had their origins in the similar signs used by previous occupants of the throne of France. At the same time, however, as David

Kulstein has noted, "Louis-Napoleon's use of the royal tour was so different from that of his predecessors that it became a new and original propaganda technique."[24]

The difference stems from the fact that over the course of the nineteenth century, society's center had shifted, at least from a political standpoint. Under the monarchical system, the signs of dominance acted principally to connect the king to a cosmology of divine right and a rule that transcended his physical body.[25] Such themes, for example, were often evoked in the allegories on the temporary triumphal arches that greeted the king; yet they are almost entirely absent from the voyages of Napoleon III. Instead, the chief signs of Napoleon III's dominance were the massive crowds that turned out to welcome him in every corner of the Empire, crowds that were extensively described and illustrated in the various forms of mass media at Napoleon III's disposition. What is interesting, then, is that while the exterior form of Napoleon III's voyages remained in many ways that of the monarchical progresses, the inner character of those voyages had been profoundly altered by the advent of plebiscitarian democracy.

As president of the Second Republic, Louis-Napoleon had used provincial trips as a tool for drumming up support for himself in an uncertain political situation. After the coup d'état, he had again turned to a provincial tour to build up popular support for the reestablishment of the Empire. As emperor, he continued in the same vein, making some six major provincial voyages, voyages that can be compared with the royal progresses of the monarchs of the Old Regime in both length and symbolic importance, as well as numerous shorter and/or less lavish excursions. Strikingly, only two of the six major trips (to the north in 1853 and to Normandy/Brittany in 1858) occurred during the most stable period of his rule—that is, between the reestablishment of the Empire in December 1852 and the Italian campaign of 1859. The other trips were all undertaken during the 1860s—the southeast and Algeria in 1860, central France in 1862, the south and Algeria again in 1865, and the north again in 1867. In addition, in 1866 the empress and Prince Imperial made an official trip through eastern France that was no less elaborate for the absence of the emperor, and in 1869 the empress made a well-publicized trip to Egypt for the inauguration of the Suez Canal that also included stops in southern France.

Although by far the most spectacular, the big, official voyages in no way exhausted the imperial penchant for travel. Indeed, in the final years of the Empire, Napoleon III's declining health made long trips difficult, yet as Bernard Ménager has noted, he seemed to multiply the number of shorter excursions—as an "antidote" to his political problems, Ménager argues.[26] These shorter journeys served the same basic function as the long trips—

that of affirming the links between the regime and the popular masses outside of Paris and of making it clear to all that those links continued to be strong. The trips were often one-day affairs, visits by railroad to inaugurate hospitals or to attend agricultural fairs, for example, though if one includes the court's yearly peregrinations to such places as Biarritz, many were longer.

The official who oversaw the arrangements for all official displacements was General Emile-Félix Fleury, originally Napoleon III's First Equerry, later promoted to Grand Equerry.[27] For the longer trips in particular, Fleury's task was of major proportions. After the decision to undertake one of these voyages had been made, Fleury drew up a preliminary program in accordance with the wishes of the emperor and the various requests from cities and towns who desired to welcome him.

Once this general program had received imperial approval, Fleury contacted the prefects of the relevant departments and "worked out with them the details of the fêtes, the composition of the guest lists, the visits promised by the emperor or empress to public or industrial establishments, or to houses of charity."[28] He also got in touch with local bishops and archbishops to plan the church services that were an important part of every trip and contacted other authorities for the list of persons to receive decorations or medals during the trip. Prior to departure, copies of the itinerary were made and distributed to the members of the party accompanying the emperor.[29] In addition, Fleury assembled a special notebook for the emperor containing details about the local notables they would meet at the various receptions along the way. This information, according to Fleury, "was precious for the emperor and empress" since it not only allowed them "to single out individuals and to treat them according to their merits" but also provided them with "the opportunity to say a pleasant word to each."[30] Clearly the man who was supposed to be above politics was not above acting like a politician.

Preparations for these trips also had a dimension that had little to do with pleasant words. Local and national officials greatly feared that someone, either a local revolutionary or an outsider, would try to disrupt the visit or even attempt to assassinate the emperor. When the emperor and empress passed through the just-annexed province of Savoy on their voyage of 1860, for example, the fear was that one of the French exiles in Geneva would make a bomb and smuggle it across the border.[31]

Such meditations led to a great emphasis on security. Prior to the emperor's arrival in any given location, the local authorities increased their surveillance of individuals they suspected of harboring malice toward the imperial family and had political exiles, if any were present, transported to other cities.[32] If they could, they arrested known opponents of the regime and held them until after the tour had passed through. "Prudence," as the prosecutor at Rennes candidly instructed his subordinates shortly before the emperor and empress arrived there in 1858, "leads us to suppose that there may be some isolated cases of ill will among the locals or attempts [to disrupt] by outsiders. Speech that is obviously seditious or that demonstrates hostile sentiments must be promptly investigated; the persons charged will be placed in custody and their pasts carefully researched." The prosecutor did not ask his men to go outside the law in these efforts, but he did recommend using "systematic delays" in making inquiries in order to "ensure that the dangerous men that you will have picked up are not released during Their Majesties' passage." If that were not enough and the suspected revolutionary was acquitted, "file an appeal, [even] in the presence of serious doubt. Later, judicial leniency or imperial clemency can intervene."[33]

In addition to such preventive measures, the police also had to keep a close and watchful eye on the crowd after the imperial party had arrived. On her way to Egypt for the inauguration of the Suez Canal in 1869, for example, Eugénie stopped in Lyons, where, to ensure her a warm welcome, the authorities hired special agents to mingle surreptitiously with the spectators. The task of these agents was to watch for any signs of trouble and to yell pro-imperial slogans in order to whip up popular enthusiasm.[34] All of this security seems to have been fairly effective. Although occasionally there were minor problems, no serious disturbances were reported on any of the trips during the Empire.

Other aspects of the trips were no less tightly regulated than security, although here ceremony rather than prudence set the standard. According to the official ceremonial guide, when a voyage was announced ministerially, the prefect, accompanied by a detachment of gendarmes and National Guardsmen from the canton, were to receive the emperor at the border of the department. Subprefects received him at the border of the arrondissement, and mayors at the borders of their communes. Mayors were to be accompanied by their adjuncts, municipal councils, and a detachment of the National Guard. The guide further specified that "upon the entry of the emperor into each commune, all the bells will be rung. If the church is on his route, the curé or priest in charge will wait before the entrance with his clergy." It also decreed that "keys to the city will be presented to him by the municipal bodies."[35]

These visits generally followed a set pattern. When the emperor arrived in a city, usually by train, most of the local officials, military units, and a crowd of spectators met him in the decorated station. Someone, generally the mayor, read a prepared address of welcome. After the emperor returned the compliment, the party left the station and boarded court carriages, the arrangements for which were one of Fleury's chief headaches. Normally rows of soldiers were stationed along both sides of the route of the cortege, which generally took the emperor first to the local cathedral for a mass and then to the town hall or prefecture for an official reception. Often the empress held a special ladies' reception while the emperor took care of the various officials, military officers, and businessmen important enough to merit an invitation to greet him personally.

The provincial visits also included occasions for demonstrations of more popular support. In a style of politics similar to the American "whistle-stop" tours, the imperial train often halted very briefly for a short receptions in small towns and villages before continuing on. The emperor and empress would step out to acknowledge the acclamations of the local populations, and the train would continue on its way. In a similar way, crowds often gathered to cheer in the streets outside the balls and official receptions. The emperor and empress would then step out onto a balcony for a few moments to acknowledge their supporters. And no visit was complete without a procession, often through the more narrow streets of the city centers, where even a relatively small number of spectators could appear to be an immense crowd.

Longer stops at larger cities often also included more formal occasions that put emperor and people together. Sometimes this took the form of a long procession before the emperor of various local groups—rural delegations, veterans of the wars of the First Empire, workers' corporations with their banners, and so forth. At Valenciennes in 1853, for example, a vast procession of miners filed through the city's central square before the imperial newlyweds (see figure 8.2). Such events, especially when disseminated in the illustrated press, seemed to make palpable the emperor's massive support in the provinces. If time permitted, the visits included other events designed to attract a large crowd of spectators: military reviews, fireworks, illuminations of public buildings, and visits to factories and charitable institutions, for example. These spectacles were often tailored to local interests, as in the visit to Sainte-Anne-d'Auray on the trip through Brittany.

Entertaining the emperor did not, of course, come cheaply, and almost all expenses were borne locally. This could mean financial disaster for prefects, who were expected to spend their own money on these affairs, though local public finances were usually tapped for most of the expenses, and the emperor stepped in to help out in extreme cases.[36] Among the more onerous expenses were decorations. Local officials worked with city architects to provide the most lavish embellishments they could afford for train sta-

Figure 8.2. Miners parading before emperor and empress at Valenciennes, from *L'Illustration*, 1 October 1853. (Doe Library, University of California, Berkeley)

tions, streets, public buildings, and anywhere else the emperor or empress was likely to set foot. Sometimes successful decorations could lead to bigger things for architects, just as successful visits on the whole could lead to bigger things for prefects. Adolphe Alphand, for example, one of the most important French landscape architects of the nineteenth century, first came to Haussmann's attention when he planned much of the decoration for Louis-Napoleon's visit to Bordeaux in October 1852, the same occasion when Haussmann, then prefect of the Gironde, came to the attention of Louis-Napoleon.[37] When Haussmann arrived in Paris as prefect of the Seine, he brought Alphand with him.

One of the most common decorations on these visits was the triumphal arch. So many arches were erected on the 1858 trip to Brittany, for example, that one journalist could describe the trip as "an almost continuous triumphal arch from Paris to Cherbourg, Cherbourg to Brest, Brest to Auray, Auray to Rennes, and Rennes to Paris."[38] The practice of erecting temporary arches dates from the Old Regime, but it had undergone distinct alteration by the Second Empire.[39] Often designed by the most important artists of the day, the arches of the sixteenth, seventeenth, and eighteenth centuries generally had been decorated with complicated and elaborate allegories praising the monarch. The arches of the Second Empire, by contrast, were much simpler and more easily understood by the masses than those of the Old Regime—or even those of the Revolution. They bore short inscriptions, in French rather than in Latin, and they usually included easily understood political symbols such as eagles, tricolor flags, and perhaps a few imperial crowns and "N"s.

Arches came in all shapes and sizes and might be erected by any group who wished to catch the imperial eye. For the emperor's official entrance into a city, the municipal authorities usually erected a large and pompous traditional arch festooned with imperial symbols and an appropriate slogan or two. But other local groups also put up arches to welcome the visitor. Workers' corporations, fire companies, horticultural societies, and other groups often erected arches of a more fanciful nature than the staid models of the municipal authorities. In Dunkerque in 1853, for example, the cod fishermen erected an arch made of fish barrels and nets, and in that same city in 1867, the civil engineering service erected an arch out of life-saving equipment.[40] Sometimes these groups erected the arches themselves, and sometimes they commissioned private entrepreneurs to do the job for them. After one of these entrepreneurs, Alexis Godillot, advertised that he could provide arches "within the reach of all pocketbooks," a journalist sarcastically remarked that soon people would even be putting them up for their family celebrations: "Here is progress: in the past the government had a monopoly on triumphal arches; today grocers and hosiers can aspire to such luxuries." [41]

The chance to see the emperor on one of his trips drew large numbers of spectators from the surrounding countryside. Peasants often lined the railroad tracks where the imperial train passed and flocked to the cities and towns where it stopped. Clearly the visits drew large and enthusiastic crowds, and, as usual, the Bonapartist press played those crowds for all they were worth and then moved easily to comforting generalities about the overwhelming popularity of the Empire. Of the 1858 Brittany trip, for example, *Le Constitutionnel* wrote: "Acclaimed with an indescribable enthusiasm by the entire population of these two ancient provinces, the emperor and empress must come away from this triumphal tour with . . . the firm conviction that their throne can rest on the devotion and affection of the nation." [42] Or as Auguste Marc put it in a fully illustrated account of the 1860 trip to the south: "From the cathedral, the emperor and empress directed themselves toward the prefecture amid an immense throng of people from every part of the department, and on the whole way they were able to witness the devoted and patriotic sentiments that animate the department of the Côte-d'Or." [43]

Nor was such rhetoric solely for public consumption. In his official report to the minister of justice, one prosecutor wrote a glowing and entirely typical account of the effect of the same 1858 trip: "The emotions that have agitated the country found themselves suddenly pacified by the grand and triumphal voyage now coming to an end. Never has the strength of a sovereign manifested itself by more striking signs, never has it aroused more ardent sympathy." [44] Given the fact that the prosecutor probably believed that his career prospects depended to some degree on telling the minister what he wanted to hear, we should not place too much faith in such statements as reflections of reality. More important, however, the fact that the same kind of overblown rhetoric that pervaded the newspapers also found itself in nonpublic government reports indicates, I think, that the regime officials believed that rhetoric—or at least very much wanted to believe it. Thus they clearly found it immensely reassuring when the emperor received a warm welcome and interpreted whatever welcome he did get in the best possible light.

In order to spread the "ardent sympathy" the voyages aroused as widely and deeply as possible, the regime's publicists made a special effort to get descriptions and illustrations of the voyages into circulation. In addition to the usual heavy press coverage—especially in the official and subsidized press—journalists on the imperial payroll published books devoted to the trips. One author of two such works, Florian Pharaon, received, apparently on the personal orders of Napoleon III, both a monthly 2,000-franc stipend and another 150,000-franc subsidy for his newspaper, *L'Etincelle*.[45] Copies of the books may have been distributed in the regions visited to serve as lasting reminders of the imperial concern demonstrated on the trips. Such was the case at any rate with a special issue of *L'Illustration* devoted to the tour through Brittany. According to Jean-Noël Marchandiau, *L'Illustration*'s chief historian, Napoleon III personally authorized funding for 18,000 copies of this issue to be printed and passed out to notables in the region.[46]

What the trips of the Second Empire most forcefully expressed—or at least attempted to express—was the emperor's interest in provincial France and the return of that interest in the form of his continuing popularity. This underscored almost every aspect of the voyages—the numerous triumphal arches, the long parades of various civic groups, the large and enthusiastic crowds, and the reporting in the Bonapartist press. And while the particular locality visited was clearly the area most affected by the tour, each tour also became a powerful manifestation of the close relationship between the emperor and the people of France and therefore also had a much wider appeal. More than any previous voyages, according to one contemporary, the voyages of Napoleon III appealed to "general popular opinion" and excited "that enthusiasm and that emotion that form characters, give birth to devotion, and strengthen the ties of affection which for monarchists of every country are called patriotism, and which for sovereigns take the noble name of love of their subjects."[47]

After the advent of universal male suffrage in 1848, provincial France, with its vast rural population, began to come into its own. One of the first gestures of independence of this new political force was the election and support of Louis-Napoleon Bonaparte. As British historian F. A. Simpson pointed out: "Every other regime in the history of modern France had been imposed by Paris on the provinces; under the Second Empire alone, in the person of Louis Napoleon, the provinces imposed a ruler upon Paris."[48] Throughout the length of his reign, Louis-Napoleon cultivated this support through agricultural fairs and imperial voyages no less than through pro-agricultural policies such as the drainage of swamplands—indeed, more so since the regime actually reduced real support for agriculture in a number of areas, including farm credit and agronomic education.[49] And although there were notable exceptions that should not be overlooked, provincial, and especially rural, support for Louis-Napoleon continued throughout the Empire. As Alain Corbin's recent study of a young nobleman brutally murdered by a rural Bonapartist mob in 1870 demonstrates, in certain circumstances, that support could reach fanatical proportions, even during Napoleon III's final days as emperor of France.[50]

But the situation in Paris by the end of the Empire was very different from that in Corbin's "village of cannibals," as the later history of the 15 August celebrations demonstrates. Despite the administration's best efforts, in the long run the 15 August festival in Paris failed to find that "genuine popular resonance" that has correctly been seen as necessary for successful public holidays.[51] Crowds continued to turn out for the spectacle, it is true, but already in 1861, one pro-imperial observer complained of a "want of novelty,"[52] and Parisians like the young François Coppée tended more and more to use the day off to get out of the city.[53] This dissatisfaction grew stronger over the course of the 1860s, and by 1869, the year of the last 15 August celebration, even the government could not seem to work up much enthusiasm.

Yet 15 August 1869 was the 100th anniversary of the birth of Napoleon I. Such an event, had it occurred during the 1850s or early 1860s, would clearly have resulted in a lavish celebration. But by 1869 the political temper of the capital had decidedly changed. The Empire was liberalizing; the press was almost free, and oppositional meetings and demonstrations in Paris were becoming common. The government spent the usual amount of money on the celebration, but no more. And though the decorations of that year did refer to the emperor, as in the illumination of his name atop the Arc de Triomphe, it was merely a theme, as the Chinese decoration of 1861 had been. According to one witness: "I . . . was much impressed by its lack of animation and brilliancy. It was not such as I had seen in the early days of my career. . . . The people, for their part, seemed indifferent and gloomy."[54]

Another new development was the hostile press. Previously, because of censorship, even the republican and legitimist press had carried accounts of the festivities or, at most, refrained from mentioning them. But in 1869, the floodgates of criticism of the celebration opened. *L'Opinion nationale*, for example, complained about spending exorbitant sums of money on a celebration when some cities did not have libraries; *La Vie Parisienne* characterized the affair as "bread and circuses" and called on the organizers to "invent something new."[55] The strongest attack of all came in the Legitimist newspaper, *La Gazette de France*, which published a long and virulent anti-Napoleonic poem and two scathing historical articles on the First Emperor, claiming that he was neither French nor even born on 15 August![56] By the late 1860s, then, the Second Empire, which earlier had jumped on even the slightest pretext to self-confidently strut and swagger through the streets of Paris, was no more. Instead, the regime, like Napoleon III himself, seemed more like an old, sick man, a man who now could only watch as others began to swagger.

NINE

Rituals of Opposition

I f the Second Empire found public spectacle a useful political tool, so too did its opponents, both republican and legitimist alike. But in contrast to the regime's freedom to mount whatever celebrations it liked whenever it liked, throughout most of the period the opposition had to work in the face of extremely severe restrictions. Until 1868 almost all public political assemblies were illegal and the press was tightly controlled. And even after the liberalizations of 1868, many limitations remained. Speaking derogatorily of the imperial family, for example, was defined throughout the period as a "seditious cry" and punished by fines and prison terms. As late as October 1869, for example, the prosecutor at Metz was reporting such infractions to Paris.[1] But even with these restrictions, the opposition still often managed to use celebrations to challenge the *fête impériale* and to call into question its underlying message of quasi-unanimous national support for the emperor.

The groups who opposed the Empire challenged the politics of imperial festivity in two ways: they directly subverted imperial spectacles, and they put on a variety of public manifestations of their own, manifestations that served not only to publicize their principles but also to demonstrate their continuing political viability. This two-pronged approach seems to be true not only of the Second Empire but of oppositional festivity generally. According to anthropologist David Kertzer, "Attempts to undermine the rituals of political support can themselves be one of the means of bringing into question the legitimacy of the political order." But Kertzer also notes that "any insurgent political force has need of its own system of ritual legitimation. No revolutionary force has ever gotten far without creating such a ritual nexus of legitimation."[2] This schema was somewhat complicated during the Empire by the fact that opposition to the Second Empire came from two different groups: legitimists and republicans. The two groups both used similar tactics, but the "ritual nexus" of the legitimists remained tied to the Church, while that of the republicans focused on the memory of great men. In the end, the republicans proved themselves the stronger of the two. Indeed, republican oppositional festivity reached a crescendo in Paris after the liberalizations of 1868 and helped to make the republicans the most dynamic political force of the day.

One way opponents of the regime undermined imperial celebrations was by not participating in them as expected or required. Failing to illuminate one's house at a moment of official rejoicing would seem a subtle means of opposition, but not so subtle that it would go unnoticed by the regime.[3] It was often similarly noticed if a municipal council—even in a tiny commune—neglected to send the emperor an address of congratulation for his marriage or after the Italian campaign.[4] Other opponents of the regime who had some official standing (especially legitimists)[5] might make themselves conspicuous by their absence at official festivals. The prefects' reports on the celebration of 15 August in 1857, for example, include complaints of magistrates skipping the religious procession in the Lot-et-Garonne, legitimist functionaries neglecting to attend the soirée at the prefecture in Poitiers, and the "refusal" of the Municipal Council of Marchenoire (Loire-et-Cher) to attend the *Te Deum*.[6] The regime took these absences and omissions quite seriously, since they tended to undercut its pretension to be above politics, a pretension, as we have seen, that was especially on display in celebrations.

The religious dimension of so many celebrations placed Catholic priests in a particularly sensitive position. Many priests disapproved of the Empire and its policies, and some let their political sentiments influence their actions. The most common complaint was that they neglected to sing the required prayers for the Emperor in *Te Deum* services—a major offense in the eyes of the government.[7] Other typical complaints made to the authorities in Paris include a curé's refusal to begin mass on 15 August 1865 until the Sapeurs-Pompiers removed their flag from the church and another curé's refusal to let the mayor put a flag on his bell tower and denigration of the government on 15 August 1867, according to the mayor.[8] Politics may make strange bedfellows; it does not make happy marriages.

Opponents of the regime also overtly interrupted celebrations by yelling out oppositional slogans or worse. At a banquet held to celebrate the declaration of Empire in one southern town in 1852, for example, the official revelers were supposed to be treated by local workers to a rendition of a traditional Provencal chain dance, the farandole. Instead, the workers subjected the officials to cries of "Vive la République!," "Vive Ledru Rollin!," and "A bas Napoléon!" And for the same celebration in the Drome, someone burned down the stage from which the proclamation was to have been read.[9] At the other end of the Empire in 1869, students at the Ecole des Beaux-Arts staged a "scandalous" demonstration as the funeral procession for Raymond Troplong, president of the Court of Cassation, passed in front of their courtyard in the Rue Bonaparte.[10] A less noisy way to demonstrate ongoing opposition to the *fête impériale* was to surreptitiously put out either an oppositional placard or some other symbol of opposition on the night before an official celebration. In 1857, for example, someone slipped a republican flag bearing the words "Liberty, Equality, Fraternity" (presumably a relic from 1848) into the official decoration of a train station before an inauguration.[11] Such efforts rarely accomplished much, however, since the authorities usually found and removed them before the crowds arrived the next morning.[12]

However, one disruption of an official celebration—the refusal of a young student to accept a school prize from the Prince Imperial—stands out from the rest. Parisian students were a fractious bunch during the Second Empire. In December 1865, they caused an uproar by booing the opening of Edmond and Jules de Goncourt's *Henriette Maréchal* at the Théâtre Français because they believed the play had only been accepted at the behest of the Princesse Mathilde. On occasion, they also shouted down professors they considered too close the regime and participated in manifestations such as the one that disrupted the funeral of Troplong. To alleviate some of this "spirit of opposition," in 1867 Victor Duruy, the minister of education, invited the Prince Imperial to distribute the prizes won in the *concours général*, the most important academic competition of the year for lycée students in the Paris region.[13] The success of that ceremony led him to try to repeat the performance in 1868. It was a mistake.

Hundreds of students, their parents, and various dignitaries, including the prefect of the Seine and the archbishop of Paris, filled the decorated amphitheater of the old Sorbonne for the gala event. As their names were called, the student prize winners clambered down from the banks of seats and went to the stage to receive the books and paper crowns they had earned. But when the name of the fifteen-year-old son of republican leader General Cavaignac was called, the boy remained in his seat instead of coming forward to receive his second-place prize for Greek composition. The announcement of the well-known republican name alone was enough to warrant extra cheers from the assembled adolescents. The cheers, later characterized as "hostile manifestations" by one school official,[14] rang out even louder when the name was called out a second time, for it became obvious that the young Cavaignac was remaining in his seat as a silent protest against the presence of the Prince Imperial. On stage, Duruy stood with the crown in his hand for what must have seemed a very long moment before the next name was called.[15] The Prince Imperial did not return for the *concours général* distribution in 1869.

Even those who were far away from the location of imperial spectacles sometimes tried, in their own ways, to voice their opposition. As historian Susanna Barrows has noted of the seditious cries during the 1850s, they "were voiced like a counterpoint to the official music of the Empire. Each imperial fête triggered an anti-fête, each laudatory image, its derisory reception."[16] The imperial marriage in 1853, for example, spawned a number of pointed if somewhat vulgar responses from people who were clearly unhappy with the new regime. The prosecutor in Bordeaux reported the arrest of a man who claimed that "the empress is a whore. She had two children before her marriage."[17] And the prosecutor in Grenoble reported the arrest of two people who made similar statements—a man who asserted that "the emperor had married a whore, after having two children before his marriage" and a woman who claimed that it was "the marriage of a whore with a thief."[18]

But conspicuous absences and gut reactions were only part of the story. The opposition to the regime also had a more constructive approach to challenging the hegemony of the *fête impériale:* it used its own ceremonial occasions as public shows of strength and defiance. Because of the repression, such ceremonies could not be overtly political manifestations such as election rallies or anniversaries of revolutionary *journées.* Instead, they took the form of traditionally accepted ceremonial moments that the government had more difficulty controlling. For the legitimists, this usually meant religious holidays, while for the republicans it generally meant funerals. In addition to their convenience as occasions for public demonstrations, these preferences were rooted in the histories and ideologies of the two movements.

Belief in the divine anchoring of monarchical authority had been a key pillar of the Old Regime state, and it continued to be a central precept of legitimist thought in the nineteenth century.[19] Allied with the closely related fact that many members of the clergy were themselves legitimists, this made it likely that some legitimist politics would sometimes creep into ceremonies that were ostensibly of a purely religious nature. At the ceremonial crowning of a statue of the Virgin and child in Avénières in 1860, for example, the prefect reported legitimist overtones in the sermons and a white flag among the window decorations. The festival, he concluded, "hid its political meaning beneath a religious exterior."[20] Similarly, reporting on the memorial services held for the volunteers killed defending the Papal States from Italian nationalists at Castelfidaro later that same year, prosecutors said that they were legitimists and generally perceived to be so by the populace.[21] Sometimes these ceremonies could be almost as spectacular as official ceremonies, as, for example, the inauguration of the church of Notre-Dame-de-la-Garde in Marseille in 1864. In reporting on this ceremony, Senator Charlemagne-Emile de Maupas declined to enumerate "all the eccentricities, almost borrowed from Paganism, which are put to work by the clergy in order to pique public curiosity" about this celebration, but he did maintain that "the real end of this religious manifestation, which will attract no less that 200,000 outsiders to Marseille, is for the bishop to give proof of his sympathy to the ardent clerical party of the region."[22]

Perhaps because it was afraid of interfering too dramatically in the affairs of the Church, the government does not seem to have gone to great lengths to control these ostensibly religious events. At least one newspaper, however, *L'Union de l'Ouest*, received an official warning for reporting on one of them,[23] and they were sometimes the concern of important officials. Apropos of a beatification ceremony at Thouars (Deux-Sèvres), for example, the minister of the interior wrote to the minister for religion *(Cultes)* that "this ceremony, while conserving in appearance a purely religious character, had in the thought of its organizers a political goal," that of rallying noble and legitimist families in order to strengthen the influence of their party.[24]

The authorities were less shy about ruffling republican feathers than those of Church authorities, though republican ceremonies, too, could prove slippery. Popular republican opposition to the regime was expressed in a variety of ceremonial activities: by quietly observing the republican anniversary of 24 February, for example, or through traditional celebrations such as Carnival. Early on, however, probably because they were fairly easy to control, these efforts began to give way to the funeral as a particularly privileged locus of public dissent. In a century that venerated the dead, funerals held a certain moral force that made their prohibition difficult. In France, moreover, funerals and other ceremonies involving the dead were also a long-established part of the revolutionary tradition. Ceremonies such as the funeral of Jean-Paul Marat and the moving of the remains of Voltaire and Jean-Jacques Rousseau to the Pantheon stand among the most important events of the Revolution of 1789 and the two succeeding revolutions carried on in a similar vein. Those killed in the Revolution of 1830 were solemnly entombed beneath the July Column on the Place de la Bastille, and in 1848 the carting of the bodies of those killed in the initial skirmish through the streets of Paris helped precipitate full-scale revolt. Later, in a funerary gesture that symbolically linked the three revolutions, those killed in February 1848 were buried alongside the dead of 1830 beneath the Place de la Bastille. But the republican funerals looked not only to the past. Their intrinsic emphasis on sacrifice and struggle for the eventual victory of the Republic linked participants to future generations as well as to those who had gone before.

Bonapartists, of course, also had funerals, but, with the significant exception of the return of the body of the First Emperor to France in 1840, their ceremonies never approached those of the republicans in symbolic importance for the movement. The problem—a key problem for both Bonapartism and its variants in other countries—was that Bonapartist ideology was predicated on the particular right of one individual to represent the nation. Only the emperor truly counted, and "great men" were great primarily by virtue of their association with him. For republicans, by contrast, the nation was embodied in the people, and numerous individuals who had made significant contributions to it (martyrs of the revolutions, great poets, statesmen, and so forth) could be honored as truly great in their own right. Thus state funerals during the Second Empire were not even officially called "state" funerals but funerals "at the expense of the public treasury."[25] The most important of them tended to be for men closely associated with the emperor such as the Duc de Morny, the emperor's illegitimate half-brother and political confederate who died in 1865, and Jérôme Bonaparte, the last surviving brother of Napoleon I who died in 1860. These funerals consisted primarily of long processions followed by colorless official speeches in praise of men few would miss. They seem to have been, as Alphonse Daudet put it in a thinly veiled description of the funeral of Morny, "even more tedious than gloomy."[26] The emperor and empress never attended such ceremonies, and though they were clearly intended to impress, they neither generated nor sought to generate much popular enthusiasm, especially when compared with some of the republican opposition funerals or with the state funerals of the Third Republic.[27]

The republican opposition funerals of the Second Empire were likely to occur in small towns as much as in large cities. After the death of a prominent local republican, often an ex-representative or mayor of the Second Republic, other republicans from the area would attend the funeral in large numbers, thus turning the ceremony into a demonstration of the continuing force of republican sympathies as well as a homage to their deceased comrade. The simple presence of these men and women provided the chief expression of republicanism in these ceremonies, but red ribbons and flowers seem to have been used in some funerals.[28] Republicans also tended to skip the religious parts of the ceremonies. Sometimes the deceased's will requested that he be taken directly to the cemetery without going to the church for the traditional service. Such *enterrements civils*, as Thomas Kselman has pointed out, were not merely statements of anticlericalism but could also be political statements and attempts "to define an appropriate ritual for death and burial outside the sacramental system of the Catholic church."[29] But even religious burials could be politically subversive. In some cases, the republicans simply waited outside the church and then rejoined the cortege for the trip to the cemetery. And at one ceremony in the Yonne, the more than 250 republicans attending went to a cabaret during the religious service.[30]

Although geographically concentrated in traditionally republican areas, in terms of timing, these ceremonies occurred fairly frequently throughout the period—including the repressive 1850s—and they almost always seem to have been entirely peaceful. Nonetheless, they did not fail to worry the local authorities. A typical prosecutor's report on one such "regrettable manifestation" that took place at the funeral of "an individual known for the exaltation of his political opinions" in a village in the Var in 1853 recorded that "more than a hundred members of the former secret society of this commune, preceded by their principal leaders, attended as a body the burial of this demagogue. The public order was not troubled, but the gathering of all of these individuals produced a deplorable effect."[31]

The government's ability to control these ceremonies was limited. It could not deny the dead their right to a decent burial or make attending a funeral into a prosecutable offense without running the risk of more serious disturbances. It did, however, see the funerals as a serious problem, and it attempted to prevent them from becoming too large and unwieldy. Police Minister Maupas set out general regime policy toward the funerals in an 1853 circular to the prefects. Maupas warned that "the socialist party seems to want to stir itself up again" and was using funerals as a means to that end. In contrast to this "exploitation" of the respect and veneration attached to these ceremonies, the government's motives, Maupas claimed, were entirely virtuous. The government, he said, was "disposed to give full latitude to reunions that are formed under the inspiration of familial affection or relations of friendship." At the same time, however, it had to "show itself attentive to the prevention of that sort of profanation that seizes as pretext the mortal remains unknown to the crowd following them in order to simulate a respect that is nothing but a lie and to hold a political demonstration whose meaning is lost on no one." [32]

Maupas clearly feared the possible results of republican funerals. "We are no longer at the point," he continued, "when one could, without obstacle and without repression, spread fear or agitation in public, and the administration should prevent and suppress everything that tends to compromise tranquillity and harm good order." Maupas instructed prefects to "take the necessary dispositions to prevent such manifestations." The best means to achieve this, he said, was "to prevent too large a reunion from gathering at the mortuary, to dissipate any gathering that may have the character of a mob, to prohibit entrance into the cemetery of too many persons unknown to the family, and to forbid any kind of speech." [33]

Soon after Maupas issued his instructions, the cunning, preventive measures he outlined began to be put to use. When Michel de Bourges, a prominent attorney and left-wing republican of legendary ugliness, died in 1853, the government ordered that the funeral take place at 7:30 in the morning, ensured that plenty of troops were on hand, and allowed only family members to attend. [34] Things went a bit further at the 1854 funeral of an ex-deputy to the 1848 Legislative Assembly in the Gard. The local police commissioner noticed that among the parents and friends of the deceased there was "a rather large number of individuals who, for the most part, belonged to the party of disorder." At the head of a squad of infantry, the commissioner then cut off the cortege and forbade anyone not related to the deceased to accompany the body. "No resistance was put up," noted the official report, "no cries were made, and everyone retired without giving rise to the least disorder." [35]

In Paris, perhaps because the possibility of unrest was perceived to be greater, a more tolerant attitude reigned. But even though the authorities generally seem to have been less ready to actually step in than in the provinces, they still detailed large numbers of troops to potentially disruptive ceremonies in case such action became necessary. When Pierre-Joseph Proudhon died in 1865, for example, a very large crowd attended the ceremony. The two regiments of troops detailed to the area almost precipitated a crisis when the crowd objected to the music of the military bands. But the colonels of the regiments wisely did not insist on continuing their inappropriate fanfares and actually switched to the respectful drumroll used for military funerals. The entirely nonreligious ceremony was permitted to continue without further interruption, even though it included an anticlerical speech by a freemason.[36]

In certain cases, the government used an even more adroit method of combating republican manifestations at funerals. Fearing that the funerals of François Arago in 1853 and Pierre-Jean Béranger in 1857 would turn into demonstrations, it simply declared that the ceremonies would be held at the expense of the public treasury, that is, that they would be state funerals, entirely ordered and organized by the government.[37]

Béranger's funeral was the more worrisome of the two. An immensely popular songwriter whose verses had contributed significantly to the resurgence of the cult of the First Emperor during the Restoration and July Monarchy, Béranger had never rallied to Napoleon III. Indeed, the liberal sympathies of the seventy-seven-year-old poet were well known despite his avoidance of overt politics during the Second Empire. Thus, after Béranger's death in July 1857, more than a few Gallic eyebrows must have been raised when the official newspaper announced that "the emperor, wanting to honor the memory of this national poet whose works have so powerfully contributed to maintaining the cult of patriotic sentiments in France and to popularizing the glory of the Empire, has decided that the expenses of his funeral will be paid for by the imperial civil list." An order from Prefect of Police Pietri further declared that the funeral would take place the following day and that the funerary cortege would be "composed exclusively of official deputations and of persons provided with letters of invitation."[38]

Troops were, of course, well in evidence at the funeral, but so were 200,000 to 500,000 predominantly working-class spectators.[39] Prosper Mérimée, for whom the spectators were reminiscent of "the terrible days of 1848," was relieved that the emperor had taken over the funeral and had held it "with lots of pomp, which is to say with lots of *sergents-de-ville* and soldiers."[40] A local lawyer, Henri Dabot, noted that certain people had wanted to "make a little noise" at the funeral but found no way around the large military force. "The emperor is a sly one," Dabot concluded; "he honors Béranger in his own *manner*, which is to say in a *manner* that prevents any demonstrations."[41] "In a word," wrote the correspondent of the London *Times*, "the arrangements were of such a nature as to crush instantly the slightest attempt at disturbance."[42]

But security alone did not dictate the imperial action. In addition to the heavy military presence, the funeral included all of the official honors, and both the emperor and empress sent representatives to follow in the cortege, which went from Béranger's home in the Rue Vendôme to the church of Saint-Elisabeth and then to the Père Lachaise Cemetery. At the sight of the imperial carriages, claimed the official newspaper, "cries of *Vive l'Empereur!* joined with acclamations in honor of the immortal bard of the First Empire." [43] Paying Béranger such high honors, then, as his biographer Jean Touchard noted, was also an attempt "to turn his funeral to the greater glory of the regime." [44] Living, Béranger had rejected the regime's advances, its offers of money and position; dead, he no longer had a choice in the matter, and his family did not try to stand in the regime's way. The fact that his verses had contributed to the Napoleonic legend combined with his silence vis-à-vis the Second Empire enabled the regime to claim him as its own. The funeral and the eulogies in the official press that followed it sought to link Béranger, perhaps the most popular poet of the nineteenth century, to a ruler he wanted no part of. [45]

Funerary manifestations provided a limited but important means for republicans to demonstrate publicly their continuing opposition to the regime even during its most repressive years. Nor did the significance of funerals diminish with the advent of the "liberal" Empire of the 1860s, not even when the liberalization brought an alternative means of public political opposition by lifting the ban on public meetings in 1868. Although the government continued to monitor political meetings closely and retained the right to adjourn any assembly that "appears of a nature such as to trouble order or compromise public security," [46] as Alain Dalotel, Alain Faure, and Jean-Claude Freiermuth have demonstrated, the meetings provided—in Paris at least—a forum for the airing of radical and even revolutionary socialist opinions. [47] The press liberalization of the same year, as we have seen, also made it easier for republicans to criticize the regime and its spectacles. But instead of fading from the picture with the arrival of these new and far more flexible means of oppositional communication, the funerary motif in republican opposition grew even more significant. Indeed, two of the most important public oppositional manifestations of the last years of the Empire—the Baudin memorial demonstration and the funeral of Victor Noir—clearly fit into the funerary tradition.

The Baudin memorial demonstration did not turn a funeral into a political manifestation, but it did something very similar. It used All Souls' Day (2 November), the traditional French day for remembering the dead by visiting cemeteries—and thus a day when cemeteries were filled with people—for the same purpose. [48] An almost forgotten radical republican deputy of the Second Republic, Alphonse Baudin, received the homage due him only in 1868, after Eugène Ténot, an editor of the republican newspaper *Le Siècle*, published an account of the coup d'état of 2 December 1851. According to Ténot, Baudin was attempting to rally resistance to the coup among workers when one of them remarked that they had no wish to die for the 25 francs a day paid to the deputies. Baudin replied that they would soon "see how one dies for 25 francs!"—a statement that rang prophetically true when he was killed by government troops a few moments later.[49] This martyr's death made Baudin a fit hero for the republican opposition; it allowed him to stand as both a symbol of resistance to the regime and, at the same time, as a reminder that the Napoleonic regime was founded on an illegal act of force.

On All Souls' Day in 1867, a small demonstration leading to several arrests took place at the tombs of Italian nationalist Daniele Manin and Godefroy de Cavaignac in the Montmartre Cemetery.[50] The next year a larger crowd gathered at the cemetery and, after leaving garlands on Cavaignac's monument, sought out (with some difficulty) the grave of Baudin, who had become famous through the recent publication of Ténot's book. Although the demonstration included speeches "of a very exciting nature," as well as cries of "Vive la République!," no arrests were made at the time.[51] The next day, however, some republican newspapers decided to open a subscription to erect a monument on Baudin's grave.

News of the subscription was a red flag for the regime. The moderately important demonstration had been bad enough, but a permanent monument to a man killed resisting the Bonapartist state went too far. Moreover, erecting the monument would retroactively legitimate the demonstration itself as a significant act of resistance. As Pierre de la Gorce put it, "Subscription and manifestation mutually reinforced each other; and what had been just a more or less factious gathering would take on by virtue of the commentary that would follow the character of an imposing commemoration."[52]

The government's decision to get tough, however, was a serious miscalculation. Despite the fact that the seven men prosecuted for either speaking at the demonstration or heading the subscription were all convicted, their trial did more than any monument to advance the republican cause. The regime had reckoned without a heavily bearded, thirty-year-old defense attorney named Léon Gambetta. Gambetta did not so much defend his client as put the Napoleonic regime itself on trial. His fiery rhetoric followed the logic of memorializing Baudin: it challenged the legitimacy of the Bonapartist regime by focusing attention on the regime's foundation. The imperial state, Gambetta declared, was founded on an illegal act, and its spectacles, he implied, were a lie. The true anniversary of the regime, he boldly declared, was not 15 August but 2 December, the date of the coup d'état. He told the men of the Second Empire:

What judges you best is that you have never dared to say: We will celebrate, we will put with the solemn commemorations of France, the Second of December as a national anniversary. And yet all of the regimes that have succeeded each other in this country have honored the day that gave them birth. . . . There are only two anniversaries, 18 Brumaire and 2 December, that have never been raised to the rank of solemnities of origin because you know that if you tried to put them there they would be rejected by everyone's conscience. Well then, this anniversary you do not want, we claim it, we will take it for ourselves: we will celebrate it always and unceasingly; it will be the festival of our dead every year until the day the country, once again [its own] master, will force upon you a great national expiation in the name of Liberty, of Equality, and of Fraternity![53]

This thrilling denunciation of the Bonapartist regime made what had been just another radical demonstration into a political event of major significance and helped to galvanize the republican opposition into a more overtly revolutionary stance. Troubles in Paris began mounting again in the spring and early summer of 1869, with crowds of people gathering at the Place de l'Hôtel de Ville to sing the "Marseillaise," riots put down by force, and mass arrests.[54] And it was no real surprise when the legislative elections held six months later brought the opposition its most important victory yet. The government candidates received only some 4.5 million votes—down almost a million from 1863—while the republicans garnered some 3 million. Among the men the republicans elected in Paris was Léon Gambetta.

Worse was to come for the regime, and soon. Just half a year after the 1869 election came the largest truly oppositional manifestation of the Empire, one that needed no court trial to push it into public attention. Indeed, at the end of Victor Noir's funeral, the imperial government congratulated itself on merely having survived. According to Emile Ollivier, then prime minister of the new quasiparliamentary government: "Everyone recognized at the time that the funeral of Victor Noir would have lost the Empire if it had not been for our government. The emperor told me so formally and with thanks."[55]

Noir, whose real name was Yvan Salmon, worked as a journalist for the *Marseillaise*, a satirical republican scandal sheet edited by Henri Rochefort. On 10 January 1870, while arranging a duel between Prince Pierre Bonaparte and an editor at the *Marseillaise*, Noir was shot and killed by the prince after a brief argument. Having a member of the imperial family kill a republican provided the radical opposition with an unparalleled offensive opening. The morning after the incident occurred, Rochefort published a virulent attack on the government in which he declared (among much else in the same vein) that he was no longer "so weak as to believe that a Bonaparte could be other than an assassin!" The article was strongly worded enough to earn Rochefort a six-month prison sentence (despite the new liberal press law), but sympathy for Noir probably drew the masses to the funeral more than Rochefort's call to arms. The republicans, as one observer noted, had "their classic instrument, a young corpse with whom one could not help but sympathize."[56]

Moving from tragedy to spectacle, the funeral took place the next day, the 12 January.[57] A large crowd gathered outside the Noir house in Neuilly, while inside, the family and various radical leaders, including Rochefort, argued about where the body would be buried. Some of the more radical leaders favored defying the government order not to take the body to the Père Lachaise Cemetery on the other side of Paris, a course that would have meant a long procession through the center of the city and almost certain clashes with the authorities. The Noir family and some of the other leaders argued instead for the cemetery at Neuilly, where they could proceed with their demonstration without interference. In democratic fashion, even the crowd was asked its opinion, it opted for Neuilly. Nonetheless, disorder persisted. Some of those who wanted to go to Père Lachaise tried to harangue the crowd and had to be restrained; they continued their efforts even after the procession had begun by forcibly trying to turn the hearse toward Paris.

Despite pouring rain, an enormous crowd of spectators thronged the procession's route, perhaps 200,000 strong. "Looking at that crowd," said a witness, "one is astonished that there is anyone left in the interior of the city."[58] Rochefort himself collapsed in the press of people and had to retire. Hunger, lack of sleep, and overwork since Noir's death were the causes, he said, and not lack of nerve as others maintained. After a brief ceremony at the grave, the crowd dispersed peacefully. On the way back into central Paris, however, Rochefort reappeared with some followers. The troops, massed at the Palace of Industry on the Champs-Elysées in case of trouble, scattered the group with an inconsequential charge but allowed Rochefort himself to pass unmolested because of his parliamentary immunity.

Victor Noir's funeral not only demonstrates the continuity of the funerary theme in the manifestations of the regime's republican opponents but also illuminates the divisions in the ranks of those opponents. As Roger Williams noted, "Those who marched behind Noir's coffin, Delescluze, Flourens, Vermorel, Millière, and Raoul Rigault, among others, were those who rose again on March 18, 1871. In other words, the men of the Commune were mustered for revolutionary action fourteen months before they would seize control of Paris."[59] The more moderate republican leaders, by contrast, were nowhere to be seen that day. The divisions between the more conservative republicans and the radical republicans, divisions that had helped destroy the Second Republic and would mar the beginnings of the Third, continued beneath the surface of the Empire.

But it is really only in retrospect that such divisions seem either evident or important. At the time, the lesson of Victor Noir's funeral for republicans and Bonapartists alike was that the capital—and presumably many other places in France as well—contained enormous reserves of people who opposed the regime and who could no longer be cowed into a semblance of acquiescence in its right to rule. Many French people in the cities and most in rural areas clearly continued to support the emperor in 1870, at least in a general way. But Bonapartist pretensions to represent any kind of real national consensus were wearing very thin indeed.

The idea of "unity," as historian Raoul Girardet has shown, has long been a powerful myth in French political life, and it has long been associated with the idea of the "fête" or "festival." Rousseau, the men of the French Revolution, and Michelet all saw festivals as particularly appropriate moments for the expression of what held a people together.[60] The same might be said of the Bonapartists, except for them that unity could only take place under the leadership of the emperor. Napoleon III's appeal stemmed to a large degree from his seeming ability to unify the nation— his apparent embodiment of a general national consensus. And imperial festivals, as we have seen a number of times in this study, projected this image of national unity behind the emperor in a powerful and well-publicized way. In the provincial tours, for example, the cheering crowds that met him in every corner of France, the delegations of workers, the peasants lining the railroad tracks to see his train pass, and the hundreds of triumphal arches erected along his routes all attempted to show that the entire nation was unified behind its emperor.

In the face of this apparently overwhelming popularity, it was easy for the regime and its supporters to write off the republicans as a fringe minority, a dangerous group of intractable revolutionary demagogues. The politicized funerals of the republicans denied the validity of this notion. Tens, hundreds, or even thousands of republicans marching peacefully behind the casket of one of their deceased comrades bespoke not only republican perseverance in spite of repression but also respect for the dead, reverence for the virtue of "great men," and belief in the eventual triumph of the Republic. In the 1860s, as the Empire eased the severe repression of its first decade, new opportunities for opposition became available. Yet funerals and other memorial ceremonies remained in the republican repertoire and in some ways even took on an increased importance.

Nor were funerals forgotten by the men of the Third Republic. Not only did Alphonse Baudin and Victor Noir finally receive memorials (Noir in Père Lachaise, where the Empire had denied him permission to be buried), but they also made state funerals a key ritual of the new polity. Republican funerals, then, were much more than just an astute manipulation of popular sympathies. In this respect, Emile Ollivier expressed only half the truth when he described revolutionaries profiting "from the immunity that covers grieving processions in order to organize their seditious manifestations." [61] The oppositional, "seditious" funerals of the Second Empire linked republicans with the long French revolutionary tradition. At the same time, the funerary ethos of admiration for the achievements of common men was rich enough, enough in tune with its age, to find favor with the next generation of republicans as well. [62]

Conclusion

If France can be guided to peace and kept tranquil by shows,
shows may in the end be as useful to them as Parliaments.
—"Government by Shows,"
Illustrated London News,
supplement, 21 August 1852

The period of Louis-Napoleon's rule represents a pivotal moment in
the modern history of political ritual. Louis-Napoleon was the first
leader to pursue a cohesive and concerted politics of public spectacle that
used modern forms of mass dissemination to portray one man as the embodiment of the national will. Moreover, his systematic use of repression
to secure control over the public arena in which the celebrations took place
has a strikingly modern flavor, as do many of his specific themes. The use
of a romanticized past, the trumpeting of prosperity and progress, the self-
serving solicitude for the downtrodden, the images of suffering and sacrifice
for the national community, the military playacting, the supposedly wildly
enthusiastic crowds, and the organized demonstrations of mass support have
all become the stock-in-trade of modern authoritarian rulers. Louis-
Napoleon did not, of course, invent these themes out of nothing; they were
all present in some form or another before he came to power. But he was
the first to put them together in a coherent package that transformed a
mass electorate into support for his own personal rule.

The *fête impériale* was designed, first and foremost, to reach and influence as many people as possible. From this stemmed the regime's concerted
effort to publicize its festivals by every means possible, but especially

through the press. From this also stemmed the regime's attempts to strike the imagination of the masses. "Spectacles," as one Bonapartist newspaper remarked apropos of the fireworks show at the first 15 August celebration, "are never better understood than when they are addressed to the impressionable imagination of the masses, and are, so to speak, an instruction and a lesson. . . . It is a good thing that our popular festivals stir up great memories of national glory in the heart of the crowd."[1]

When they discussed such matters, Bonapartists often emphasized the felicitous effect of Second Empire festivals on average French people, and sometimes the superiority of their celebrations over those of previous regimes. The journalist Emile Begin, for example, maintained that while festivals from 1789 to 1851 had all somehow been lacking in popular appeal, during the Second Empire they had "taken on a character of universality, we would even say of intimacy." Far from being mere *divertissements*, in Begin's view, these events helped to "spread a taste for the beautiful, to rekindle the national spirit, and to establish the rapid development of a host of happy ideas that rest, sleeping, in the heart of the proletarian."[2] An official, the public prosecutor for the Paris region, similarly remarked, apropos of the inauguration of the Boulevard du Prince Eugène in late 1862, that such spectacles had a positive impact on the common people of the country by arousing "their best instincts" and "their most noble sentiments." The people responded, he said, with "universal adhesion" and then "returned more confident to their daily labor."[3]

In these spectacles, Louis-Napoleon acted out various roles. Sometimes he was a military leader, the defender of the freedom and glory of France. Other times he played the modernizing sovereign, taking his country proudly into a secure and profitable future by providing it with railway lines and streets. On yet other occasions, he was the heir of the First Emperor who healed the historical cleavage between revolutionary and monarchical France. And both he and Eugénie often played the solicitous benefactor providing for the poor and sick. The ultimate goal of this play-acting was to put both emperor and Empire above politics. Since the central justification for the Empire was, as Albert Guérard has remarked, "to be above parties, the integration of all truly *national* energies,"[4] the celebrations strove to paint the emperor as the representative of the will of the entire nation—as France incarnate.

This idea found its fullest and clearest articulation in the descriptions of celebrations in the Bonapartist press. Often written by men close to Louis-Napoleon, these descriptions constantly reiterated the theme of national unity represented by and embodied in the person of Louis-Napoleon, recognized, of course, by the crowd. "All of the classes of society were there," said a typical description of a military review, "and since the same sentiment filled every heart, the same cry came from every mouth."[5] "The people and the sovereign so identify with each other," read the same paper's account of the arrival of Queen Victoria in 1855, "that they now have only the same interest, the same thought, the same soul."[6] Through celebrations, then, the regime expressed a political relationship in which one man stood as privileged representative of the popular will. Just as the Universal Expositions provided a positive model of the economic and social relations of modern industrial capitalism, so the celebrations more generally helped to popularize and give form to a political order that made Louis-Napoleon the embodiment of the will and even the "soul" of the nation.

For particular ceremonies, artists and architects in the service of the state transformed the city into an ephemeral wonderland. The elaborate and seductive festival architecture, the brilliant illuminations, the lavish fireworks, and the multifarious popular amusements drew large crowds of spectators. Moreover, the regime had at its disposal an evocative and eclectic repertoire of symbols and symbolic actions, which it used to heighten the emotional quality of the celebrations. Emblems of the national community such as the tricolor flag had an important place in almost all celebrations, as did eagles, bees, and other symbols reminiscent of the First Empire. Even more stirring were the dramatic moments created for particular celebrations—the curtain opening to reveal the Boulevard de Sébastopol, for example, or the wounded soldiers marching in their tattered campaign uniforms after returning from the Crimea and from Italy.

Paris itself added symbolic depth to these shows. Many of its streets, buildings, and squares, for example, had meaningful historical associations, which might be evoked by using that location in a particular celebration. The Place de la Bastille recalled the French Revolution, just as the Arc de Triomphe had a clear association with the First Empire. New Paris also played a role, since Haussmann's rebuilding of the city with broader boulevards and wider sidewalks allowed it to better serve as a setting for imperial celebrations. In addition to making the new streets the centerpieces of lavish inaugurations, the regime often used them for its processions, even when more traditional routes were available. In this manner, it both put one of its major accomplishments on display and allowed access to greater numbers of spectators.

But all of the "happy ideas," "noble sentiments," and "universal adhesion" supposedly elicited by Second Empire celebrations did not enable the regime to survive military defeat in 1870—a defeat that included the capture of the emperor. This does not mean, however, that the *fête impériale* failed. What is surprising about Napoleon III is not, after all, that he finally fell but that he survived as long as he did. That an undistinguished adventurer who had spent little time in France and who had no military victories to his credit could not only overthrow the Second Republic but also reestablish the Empire, dominate France longer than any other leader of the past two centuries, and only fall at the hands of a foreign military power demonstrates that Napoleon III was doing something right.

In the final analysis, Louis-Napoleon owed his longevity not to what he actually accomplished for France but to the fact that he successfully managed to present himself as the embodiment of the people. His spectacles provided an interpretation of French history in which he was made to seem the only true representative of the nation as a whole; they portrayed him as bridging the social and political chasms that had divided Frenchmen since the Revolution, as bringing the country peace, prosperity, and national glory, and as receiving overwhelming popular approval. Packaging? Public relations? Of course. But in an age unjaded by long and close experience with the rough-and-tumble of democracy, these themes could work a powerful chemistry.

As Benedict Anderson has pointed out, "The 'nation' proved an invention on which it was impossible to secure a patent."[7] The Bonapartist vision of the national community did not manage to supplant either the legitimist or the republican visions. Indeed, Louis-Napoleon's attempt to appropriate the nation, to make himself its privileged representative, pushed his opponents to respond. Despite heavy repression, they called out "Vive la République!" at the imperial celebrations. And they worked to find holes in the repressive machinery, such as funerals and church festivals, where they could elaborate their own, very different ideas of who represented the true people. In the long run, then, France was neither "guided to peace" nor "kept tranquil" by shows. Instead, shows themselves became what they have remained: the chief battlefields for the new politics of a democratic age.

Notes

ABBREVIATIONS

AD   Archives Départementales
AN   Archives Nationales, Paris
BHVP Bibliothèque Historique de la Ville de Paris, Paris
BN   Bibliothèque Nationale, Paris

INTRODUCTION

1. See especially Mona Ozouf, *La Fête révolutionnaire, 1789–1799* (Paris, 1976); Michel Vovelle, *Les Métamorphoses de la fête en Provence de 1750 à 1820* (Paris, 1976); M.-L. Biver, *Fêtes révolutionnaires à Paris* (Paris, 1979); Françoise Waquet, *Les Fêtes royales sous la Restauration ou l'Ancien Régime retrouvé* (Paris, 1981); Charles Rearick, *Pleasures of the Belle-Epoque: Entertainment and Festivity in Turn-of-the-Century France* (New Haven, 1985); Rosemond Sanson, *Les 14 juillet, 1789–1975: Fête et conscience nationale* (Paris, 1976); Valérie Noëlle Jouffre, ed., *Fêtes et Révolution* (Paris, 1989); Alain Corbin, Noëlle Gérôme, and Danielle Tartakowsky, eds., *Les usages politiques des fêtes aux XIXe–XXe siècles* (Paris, 1994); and Olivier Ihl, *La Fête républicaine* (Paris, 1996).

2. Bernard Ménager, *Les Napoléon du peuple* (Paris, 1988). See also Jean Tulard,

"Le Retour des Cendres," in Pierre Nora, ed., *Les Lieux de mémoire, II: La Nation* (Paris, 1986), 3:81–110.

3. Clifford Geertz, *The Interpretation of Cultures* (New York, 1973), p. 312.

4. David Cannadine, "The Context, Performance and Meaning of Ritual: The British Monarchy and the 'Invention of Tradition,' c. 1820–1977," in Eric Hobsbawm and Terence Ranger, eds., *The Invention of Tradition* (Cambridge, 1983), p. 105.

5. George L. Mosse, *The Nationalization of the Masses: Political Symbolism and Mass Movements in Germany from the Napoleonic Wars through the Third Reich* (New York, 1975), pp. 1–2.

6. George L. Mosse, "Caesarism, Circuses, and Monuments," *Journal of Contemporary History* 6 (1971): 169.

7. According to the official formula used in all decrees, Napoleon III was emperor "by the grace of God and the national will."

8. S. de Naurois, "Les Fêtes du pouvoir avant 1789," in Jouffre, *Fêtes et Révolution,* p. 36.

9. Maurice Agulhon, "Fête spontanée et fêtes organisées à Paris en 1848," in Jean Ehrard and Paul Viallaneix, eds., *Fêtes de la Révolution* (Paris, 1977), p. 260.

10. See Maurice Agulhon, *The Republic in the Village: The People of the Var from the French Revolution to the Second Republic,* trans. Janet Lloyd (Cambridge, 1982), pp. 254–60; Peter McPhee, *The Politics of Rural Life: Political Mobilization in the French Countryside, 1846–1852* (Oxford, 1992), pp. 188–93, 212–16; Robert Bezucha, "Masks of Revolution: A Study of Popular Culture during the Second French Republic," in Roger Price, ed., *Revolution and Reaction: 1848 and the Second French Republic* (London, 1975), pp. 236–53.

11. *L'Illustration,* 29 November 1851.

12. J. Lesguillon, in *Gazette municipale: Revue municipale,* 1 September 1853. See also the introductions to La Jus, *Recherches historiques sur le service des cérémonies à la cour de France et dans les principales cours de l'Europe* (Paris, 1857); and *Le Cérémonial officiel* (Paris, 1865).

13. Jean-Marie Apostolidès, *Le Roi-machine: Spectacle et politique au temps de Louis XIV* (Paris, 1981), p. 8.

14. Gustave Flaubert, *Dictionnaire des idées reçues* (Paris, 1913), p. 59.

15. Emile Durkheim, *The Elementary Forms of the Religious Life,* trans. Joseph Ward Swain (New York, 1915), p. 251. See also Raymond Firth, *Symbols Public and Private* (Ithaca, 1973); Murray Edelman, *The Symbolic Uses of Politics* (Urbana, 1964) and *Politics as Symbolic Action* (Chicago, 1971); and Charles D. Elder and Roger W. Cobb, *The Political Uses of Symbols* (New York, 1983).

16. David I. Kertzer, "The Role of Ritual in Political Change," in Myron J. Aronoff, ed., *Culture and Political Change* (New Brunswick, N.J., 1983), p. 63.

17. Alexis de Tocqueville, *Democracy in America,* ed. J. P. Mayer, trans. George Lawrence (Garden City, N.Y., 1969), p. 643.

18. See the lists of names in AD, Gironde, 1M 730.

19. F. Dutacq, "Les Dessous d'un voyage officiel: Visite de l'Impératrice à

Lyon, en 1869, d'après les rapports de police," *Revue du Lyonnais* 15 (July–September 1924): 337–40.

20. According to an English observer, the "official shouters" were "sent in small bands to shout, and it is easy to distinguish their fabricated enthusiasm from the spontaneous signs of contentment or approval." *The Times* (London), 7 February 1859.

21. [Jean-Eugène] Robert-Houdin, *Life of Robert-Houdin, the King of the Conjurors,* trans. R. Shelton MacKenzie (Philadelphia, 1859), pp. 317–19.

22. Daniel J. Boorstin, *The Image: A Guide to Pseudo-Events in America* (New York, 1961), pp. 11–12.

23. In the first half of 1866, the circulation of the four major illustrated papers totaled more than 170,000 copies. Pierre Guiral, "La Presse de 1848 à 1871," in Claude Bellanger et al., eds., *Histoire générale de la presse française* (Paris, 1969), 2:302.

24. John B. Thompson, *Ideology and Modern Culture: Critical Social Theory in the Era of Mass Communication* (Stanford, 1990), p. 15.

25. For general accounts of the regime's use of repression, see Howard C. Payne, *The Police State of Louis Napoleon Bonaparte, 1851–1860* (Seattle, 1966); McPhee, *Politics of Rural Life;* John Merriman, *The Agony of the Republic: Repression of the Left in Revolutionary France, 1848–1851* (New Haven, 1978).

26. Geertz, *Interpretation of Cultures,* p. 315.

27. Timothy Garton Ash, "Eastern Europe: The Year of Truth," *New York Review of Books,* 15 February 1990, p. 18.

28. Guiral, "La Presse de 1848 à 1871," p. 252.

29. *Le Constitutionnel,* 5–6 April 1858.

30. *The Times* (London), 6 November 1868.

ONE

1. Maurice Agulhon, *The Republican Experiment, 1848–1852,* trans. Janet Lloyd (Cambridge, 1983), p. 119.

2. See *Le Moniteur universel,* 21 December 1848; *Journal des débats,* 21 December 1848; and Victor Hugo, *Napoléon-le-petit,* in *Oeuvres complètes: Histoire* (Paris, 1987), pp. 3–6.

3. [Victor-Fialin] de Persigny, *Mémoires du Duc de Persigny* (Paris, 1896), pp. 5–6.

4. Accounts of witnesses vary on this point. Both Barrot and Maupas, for example, maintain that Cavaignac refused Louis-Napoleon's hand, while the newspapers, Hugo, Ollivier, Castellane, and Quentin-Bauchart all record that the two men did shake hands. The relevant texts are excerpted in André Lebey, *Louis-Napoléon Bonaparte et la Révolution de 1848,* 2 vols. (Paris, 1907–8), 2:325–28. See also Frederick A. De Luna, *The French Republic under Cavaignac* (Princeton, 1969), pp. 396–97.

5. Good descriptions of the ceremony are found in *La Patrie* and the *Journal*

des débats, both 25 December 1848, and in André Lebey, *Louis-Napoléon Bonaparte et le ministère Odilon Barrot* (Paris, 1912), pp. 32–35.

6. Lebey, *Louis-Napoléon Bonaparte et le ministère Odilon Barrot*, pp. 34–35; Hippolyte Thirria, *Napoléon III avant l'Empire*, (Paris, 1895), 2:10–13.

7. *Le Moniteur universel*, 15 February 1849.

8. Gabriel Vauthier, "Cérémonies et fêtes nationales sous la seconde République," *La Révolution de 1848* 18(1921–22): 59–60.

9. *Le Moniteur universel*, 16 February 1849.

10. At least this was the way it was supposed to work according to the official program published in the *Moniteur*, 23 February 1849. Descriptions of the ceremony published the next day do not mention the lifting of the mourning decorations. See *Le Moniteur universel*, 25 February 1849; *La Patrie*, 24 February 1849; *La Liberté*, 25 February 1849.

11. The government had prescribed prayers for the sovereign since the seventeenth century. The practice was halted during the Revolution but was brought back by article 8 of the Concordat of 1801 and continued under the successive regimes of the nineteenth century. "Note sur les prières publiques pour le chef de l'Etat," 23 November 1852, in AN, F19 5566.

12. Charles Merruau, *Souvenirs de l'Hôtel de ville de Paris, 1848–1852* (Paris, 1875), p. 239.

13. Alexander Herzen, *Lettres de France et d'Italie (1847–1852)*, trans. N. H. (Geneva, 1871), p. 244.

14. Ibid., pp. 250–51. According to Martin Malia, for Herzen, "in a republic the sanctions of religion are secularized as the 'will of the people,' 'popular sovereignty,' or 'parliamentary supremacy,' but they remain nonetheless absolute sanctions for the tyranny of the state and society over the individual and hence, as a practical matter, are the same as divine right." *Alexander Herzen and the Birth of Russian Socialism, 1812–1855* (Cambridge, 1961), p. 377.

15. Agulhon, *Republican Experiment*, p. 104 (emphasis in original).

16. See Bernard H. Moss, "June 13, 1849: The Abortive Uprising of French Radicalism," *French Historical Studies* 13 (Spring 1984): 390–414.

17. John Merriman, *The Agony of the Republic: The Repression of the Left in Revolutionary France, 1848–1851* (New Haven, 1978), p. 86. See also Peter McPhee, *The Politics of Rural Life: Political Mobilization in the French Countryside, 1846–1852* (Oxford, 1992), chapters 6 and 7.

18. Raymond Huard, *Le Suffrage universel en France, 1848–1946* (Paris, 1991), pp. 54–59.

19. *Le Dix Décembre*, 8 May 1849.

20. Napoleon III, *Oeuvres* (Paris, 1869), 3:83.

21. Ibid., p. 89. Republicans and legitimists alike strongly objected to such formulations. See, for example, *La Liberté*, 25, 28 July 1849, and *La Gazette de France*, 26 July 1849, on the president's speech at Ham.

22. *Le National*, 14 August 1849.

23. Napoleon III, *Oeuvres*, 3:35–6, 89, 107–8.

24. *Le Dix Décembre*, 24 July, 14 August 1849.

25. *Le Dix Décembre*, 14 June 1849.

26. George L. Mosse, *The Nationalization of the Masses: Political Symbolism and Mass Movements in Germany from the Napoleonic Wars through the Third Reich* (New York, 1975), p. 4.

27. Maréchal de Castellane, *Journal, 1804–1862* (Paris, 1896), 3:185.

28. Jean-Noël Marchandiau, *L'Illustration 1843/1944: Vie et mort d'un journal* (Toulouse, 1987), p. 86.

29. *Le Moniteur universel*, 14 August 1849.

30. *Le National*, 15 August 1849; *La Liberté*, 18 August 1849.

31. See, for example, *La Liberté*, 7, 8 July 1849, on the president's visit to Chartres.

32. The society was brought to public attention by *La Liberté*, 29 September, 1 October 1849.

33. *La Presse*, 13 August 1850. Karl Marx, for whom the society epitomized the *lumpenproletariat*, also focused on the part it played in arranging "popular" receptions for Louis-Napoleon. Marx, *The Eighteenth Brumaire of Louis Bonaparte* (New York, 1963), pp. 75–76.

34. *Le Dix Décembre*, 30 September 1849, 10 March 1850. This newspaper was closely connected with the society. See also *Le Pouvoir*, 13 August, 17, 30 September 1850.

35. *L'Opinion publique* and *La République*, 14 September 1850.

36. *Le Constitutionnel*, 14, September 1850; *Le Pouvoir*, 14, 17 September 1850.

37. See the account of the Allais Affair in the *Gazette des Tribunaux*, 25 December 1850, for the testimony of a police spy that he had been hired by the society for these purposes.

38. *Le National*, 30–31 July 1849.

39. Lebey, *Louis-Napoléon et le ministère Odilon Barrot*, pp. 591–92.

40. AN, BB18 1479, no. 7876.

41. A cabinetmaker, for example, received four months for having yelled it in a café in August 1850. *Gazette des Tribunaux*, 22 December 1850.

42. In *La Presse*, 22 February 1850.

43. *Journal des débats*, 25 February 1850.

44. *La Presse*, 24 February 1850, for example, warned that any manifestation might be used against the people and advised abstaining from such actions. *La Voix du peuple*, 24–25 February 1850, issued similar counsels and noted that the funerary character of the day was fitting since "au lieu d'être à la liberté, le présent est au despotisme."

45. See the reports in *La Presse*, *La Voix du peuple*, and *Le National*.

46. Miscellaneous correspondence between mayors and prefect, AD Gironde, 1M 706.

47. This hostility was confirmed in June when the Assembly refused to vote a compensation for those wounded during the February Days. See "Chronique de la Quinzaine," *Revue des deux mondes*, 15 June 1850, pp. 1133–34.

48. *La Voix du peuple* and *Le National*, 5–6 May 1850.

49. BN, Collection de Vinck, t. 129, no. 15,865.

50. Napoleon III, *Oeuvres*, 3:131–34.

51. *Le Moniteur universel*, 18 August 1850.

52. *Le Pouvoir*, 18 August 1850.

53. Letter of 21 August 1850, in AD Marne, 31M 6.

54. See, for example, subprefect of Vitry-le-François to prefect of the Marne, 26 August 1850, in AD Marne, 31M 6.

55. *Le Moniteur universel*, 22 August 1850. *Le Pouvoir*, 22 August 1850, similarly stressed that the incident was a "plot" against the president rather than a popular outcry.

56. Napoleon III, *Oeuvres*, 3:137.

57. Ibid., pp. 140–41.

58. Ibid., p. 142.

59. This was controversial because it was widely seen as a civil list, and "voter une list civile au président, c'est le faire presque roi." V. de Mars, "Chronique de la Quinzaine," *Revue des deux mondes*, 15 June 1850, p. 1130.

60. On these reviews and the controversy, see Thirria, *Napoléon III avant l'Empire*, 2:321–49.

61. *Gazette des Tribunaux*, 30 November, 25, 27 December 1850; Odilon Barrot, *Mémoires posthumes* (Paris, 1876), 4:62–67; Chaix d'Est-Ange, *Discours et Plaidoyers*, ed. Edmond Rousse (Paris, 1862), 1:361–87.

62. Barrot, *Mémoires posthumes*, 4:60–61.

63. Count [Joseph Alexander] von Hübner, *Neuf ans de souvenirs d'un ambassadeur d'Autriche à Paris sous le Second Empire, 1851–1859* (Paris, 1904), 1:10.

64. *L'Illustration*, 10 May 1851. Most of the following description is drawn from this article.

65. Maurice Agulhon, *Marianne into Battle: Republican Imagery and Symbolism in France, 1789–1880*, trans. Janet Lloyd (Cambridge, 1981), pp. 102–103.

66. Hübner, *Neuf ans de souvenirs*, 1:18. Nassau William Senior estimated that some 200,000 to 300,000 people turned out even in the rain. Nassau William Senior, *Journals Kept in France and Italy from 1848 to 1852*, 2nd ed. (London, 1871), 2:172.

67. Napoleon III, *Oeuvres*, 3:220–21.

68. Thirria, *Napoléon III avant l'Empire*, 2:526.

69. Merruau, *Souvenirs*, pp. 442–43. See also David H. Pinkney, *Napoleon III and the Rebuilding of Paris* (Princeton, 1958), p. 38.

70. Napoleon III, *Oeuvres*, 3:222, 259–65.

71. Ibid., p. 268.

72. Claude Lefort, *Democracy and Political Theory*, trans. David Macey (Minneapolis, 1988), p. 17. For a somewhat different take on the same transformation, see Pierre Rosanvallon, *Le Sacre du citoyen: Histoire du suffrage universel en France* (Paris, 1992).

TWO

1. Quoted in Howard Payne, *The Police State of Louis Napoleon Bonaparte, 1851–1860* (Seattle, 1966), p. 56.

2. Letter of 29 December 1851, in George Sand, *Correspondance,* ed. Georges Lubin (Paris, 1964–86), 10:612–17.

3. On the 1851 plebiscite, see Maurice Agulhon, *The Republican Experiment, 1848–52,* trans. Janet Lloyd (Cambridge, 1983), pp. 172–73; Philippe Vigier, *La Seconde République,* 3rd ed. ("Que sais-je?" collection; Paris, 1967), pp. 118–20; Payne, *Police State,* pp. 49–57; Peter McPhee, *The Politics of Rural Life: Political Mobilization in the French Countryside, 1846–1852* (Oxford, 1992), pp. 245–48.

4. A. de la Gueronnière, in *Le Constitutionnel,* 9 December 1853.

5. AN, F21 721. Materials found here include payment orders, descriptions of decorations, and correspondence.

6. Letter of 28 December 1851, AN, F19 5579.

7. AN, F19 5579 and 6434. A certain amount of confusion was created by the seemingly conflicting orders concerning the dates for the ceremonies, and as a result, in many places the ceremony was not held on the date projected by the government.

8. Viollet-le-Duc and Lassus to Morny, 24 December 1851, in AN, F21 721.

9. AN, F21 721.

10. Good descriptions of the decorations and ceremony are found in *Le Moniteur universel,* *Le Constitutionnel,* and *Le Journal des débats* (reprinted from *La Patrie*), 2–3 January 1852. Illustrations can be found in *L'Illustration,* 3, 10 January 1852, and in BN, Collection de Vinck, t. 132, no. 16,090. See also Jean-Michel Leniaud, *Jean-Baptiste Lassus (1807–1857) ou le temps retrouvé des cathédrales* (Paris, 1980), pp. 181–82.

11. Rodolphe Apponyi, *Vingt-cinq ans à Paris (1826–1852): Journal du comte Rodolphe Apponyi,* 4 vols. (Paris, 1913–26), 4:385–86.

12. According to one newspaper of legitimist leanings, the cold kept away many of the invited guests, especially ladies. *La Gazette de France,* reprinted in *Le Journal des débats,* 2 January 1852.

13. Circular from Fortoul to the bishops of France, 29 December 1851, in AN, F19 5579. A minor crisis ensued when the legitimist bishop of Luçon refused either to use the prescribed formula or to instruct his priests to do so. See Jean Maurain, *La Politique ecclésiastique du Second Empire* (Paris, 1930), pp. 12–13, and Jean Maurain, *Le Saint-Siège et la France de décembre 1851 à avril 1853: Documents inédits* (Paris, 1930), pp. 23–41.

14. Louis Girard, "La Cour de Napoléon III," in *Hof, Kultur und Politik in 19. Jahrhundert: Akten des 18. Deutsch-französischen Historikerkolloquiums* (Bonn, 1985), p. 156.

15. Constitution of 14 January 1852, article 14. A copy of the Constitution is found in Napoleon III, *Oeuvres* (Paris, 1869), 3:297–315.

16. See Michael Marrinan, *Painting Politics for Louis-Philippe: Art and Ideology in Orléanist France, 1830–1848* (New Haven, 1988), pp. 61–64.

17. *Le Moniteur universel,* 29 April 1852. It might also be noted that during this period a large embankment encircling the area gave spectators a better view. See Marcel de Baillehache, *Souvenirs intimes d'un lancier de la garde impériale,* 3rd ed. (Paris, 1894), p. 4.

18. I have primarily used the accounts given in *Le Moniteur universel,* 11 May 1852; *La Presse,* 11 May 1852; *Le Constitutionnel,* 11 May 1852; *L'Illustration,* special supplement to issue of 15 May 1852; and *The Times* (London), 11 May 1852. An interesting eyewitness account is found in the anonymous *Tricolored Sketches in Paris during the Years 1851–2–3,* pp. 159–63. According to this observer, there were "a million of people in the streets, and four hundred thousand of them at least in the immediate vicinity of the Champ de Mars." The author also notes that "there was but little cheering and very few cries of *Vive l'Empereur!* This is certain and contested by no one."

19. *La Presse,* 11 May 1852.

20. On the songs sung at such gatherings, see Roger Lévy, "Le Culte de Napoléon en Normandie sous la monarchie de Juillet," *La Révolution de 1848* 8 (1911–12): 379–91.

21. *Le Dix Décembre,* 18 August 1849.

22. Decree of 16 February 1852, *Bulletin des Lois,* January-June 1852, p. 345.

23. For a different view, see Rosemonde Sanson, "Le 15 août: Fête nationale du Second Empire," in Alain Corbin, Noëlle Gérôme, and Danielle Tartakowsky, eds., *Les Usages politiques des fêtes au XIXe–XXe siècles* (Paris, 1994), pp. 134–35.

24. AN, F21 721 and 722.

25. Auguste Romieu, *L'Ere des césars* (Paris, 1850), and *Le Spectre rouge de 1852* (Paris, 1851). On Romieu, see Alfred Marquiset, *Romieu et Courchamps* (Paris, 1913).

26. Romieu, *Le Spectre rouge,* p. 70. Carrousels were a flashy cavalry maneuver.

27. Good descriptions of the celebration can be found in *Le Moniteur universel,* 16–17 August 1852; *Le Constitutionnel,* 16–17 August 1852; and *L'Illustration,* 21 August 1852.

28. *Le Constitutionnel,* 16–17 August 1852.

29. Ibid.

30. An excellent description of the storm and the problems it caused is in *Tricolored Sketches in Paris,* pp. 193–98. See also *L'Illustration,* 21 August 1852.

31. See A[dolphe] L[ance], "La Fête du 15 août," *Encyclopedie d'architecture* 2(1852): 97–99.

32. *Tricolored Sketches in Paris,* p. 197; Count [Joseph Alexander] von Hübner, *Neuf ans de souvenirs d'un ambassadeur d'Autriche à Paris sous le Second Empire, 1851–1859* (Paris, 1904), 1:71.

33. Comte Horace de Viel Castel, *Mémoires* (Paris, 1883), 2:93.

34. Jean Noël Marchandiau, *L'Illustration 1843/1944: Vie et mort d'un journal* (Toulouse, 1987), p. 91.

35. *Le Constitutionnel,* 16–17 August 1852.

36. Copies of the circular are to be found in AN, F19 5578 and 6435.

37. There are a number of reports of such problems in AN, F19 5577.

38. See Prefect of Police Pietri's "Rapport," 19 August 1852, in AN, F19 5605, and the various reports in AN, F19 5577.

39. I have primarily used *Le Moniteur universel, Le Constitutionnel,* and *L'Illustration* throughout the month in question. See also AN, BB30 404, no. 768P, and F. Laurent, *Voyage de sa Majesté Napoléon III* (Paris, 1853).

40. Ted W. Margadant, *French Peasants in Revolt: The Insurrection of 1851* (Princeton, 1979), p. 8.

41. Quatrelles l'Epine, *Le Maréchal de Saint-Arnaud d'après sa correspondance et des documents inédits* (Paris, 1928–29), 2:215, 218–33.

42. AN, BB30 404, contains a number of prosecutors' reports concerning Louis-Napoleon's visit. These reports often note the arrest of "demagogues" or others, either because of threats against the president or as a general preventive measure. See especially folder no. 768P. In the same carton is a file (no. 784P) of some 196 documents concerning the "complot de Marseilles."

43. [Charlemagne-Emile] de Maupas, *Mémoires sur le Second Empire* (Paris, 1885), pp. 611–12.

44. [Victor Fialin] de Persigny, *Mémoires du Duc de Persigny* (Paris, 1896), pp. 172–82.

45. A[dolphe] Granier de Cassagnac, *Souvenirs du Second Empire* (Paris, 1881–84), 2:145–47. Cassagnac claims that his account is based on the testimony of the son of the prefect of the Cher.

46. *Journal du Loiret,* 14 September 1852; *L'Orléanais,* 15 September 1852.

47. *Le Constitutionnel,* 16 September 1852.

48. *Le Courrier de Bourges,* 15 September 1852 (emphasis in original).

49. Quatrelles l'Epine, *Le Maréchal de Saint-Arnaud,* 2:219.

50. Napoleon III, *Oeuvres,* 3:336–37. The statue being inaugurated was the one that had been placed on the rond-point of the Champs-Elysées on 15 August.

51. See the two letters from Feuillet de Conches to Fortoul of 14, 15 October in AN, 246AP 16. Some official correspondence is also found in AD, Seine, VD6 524.

52. AD, Seine, VD4 2599.

53. *Le Moniteur universel,* 17 October 1852.

54. Marius Riollet, ed., "Le Journal de Romain Bouquet (1848–1853)," *La Révolution de 1848* 8 (1911–12): 372–73 (emphasis in original).

55. Letter from Amadée Bocher to his brother Charles, printed in Charles Bocher, *Mémoires, 1816–1907* (Paris, n.d.), 2:180–82 (emphasis in original).

56. Hübner, *Neuf ans de souvenirs,* 1:78.

57. *Tricolored Sketches in Paris,* p. 224.

58. François-Louis Poumiès de la Siboutie, *Souvenirs d'un médecin de Paris* (Paris, 1910), p. 340.

59. *Le Moniteur universel,* 2 December 1852.

60. *Le Moniteur universel,* 3 December 1852; *L'Illustration,* 11 December 1852. For other illustrations, see BN, Collection de Vinck, t. 134, nos. 16,264–66.

61. *Le Moniteur universel,* 3 December 1852.

62. H. R. C. W. Cowley, *The Paris Embassy during the Second Empire,* ed. F. A. Wellesley (London, 1928), p. 13. The newspapers, of course, carried the usual reports of enthusiastic crowds: "Never has this generous population shown such lively and sympathetic enthusiasm. Its acclamations were from the heart; it was the cry of recognition and affection." *Le Moniteur universel,* 3 December 1852.

63. On the tradition of thaumaturgic kingship, see Marc Bloch, *Les Rois thaumaturges* (Paris, 1961).

64. The ceremonies were all to have taken place on 5 December, but in some places, they were postponed to 12 December because the prefects did not have time to make all of the necessary arrangements. See the reports to the minister of the interior in AN, F1C I 108, and the reports to the minister of justice in AN, BB30 406, no. 835P. See also AN, BB30 383, 384, and 406, no. 857P.

65. The ceremonies had been requested by a circular from Fortoul, minister of public instruction and religious sects, to the bishops of France, 1 December 1852. See also the responses of the bishops to this circular in AN, F19 5579.

THREE

1. Descriptions of the ceremony can be found in *Le Moniteur universel,* 15 August 1857; *Le Constitutionnel,* 15 August 1857; *L'Illustration,* 22 August 1857; and the *Revue des beaux-arts,* 1 September 1857. AN, 64AJ 205, contains some incoming correspondence concerning the ceremony.

2. On the completion of the Louvre, see Christiane Aulanier, *Histoire du Palais et du Musée du Louvre,* vol. 4; *Le Nouveau Louvre de Napoléon III* (Paris, n.d.); Albert Babeau, *Le Louvre et son histoire* (Paris, n.d.), pp. 297–304; Louis Hautecoeur, *Histoire du Louvre: Le château—le palais—le musée, des origines à nos jours, 1200–1928* (Paris, n.d.), pp. 95–104; David H. Pinkney, *Napoleon III and the Rebuilding of Paris* (Princeton, 1958), pp. 80–82; Maurice Vachon, *Le Louvre et les Tuileries: Histoire monumentale nouvelle* (Lyons, 1926), pp. 206–16; and *The Second Empire, 1852–1870: Art in France under Napoleon III* (Philadelphia, 1978), pp. 59–61.

3. *L'Illustration,* 31 July 1852; Aulanier, *Histoire du Palais,* pp. 13–14.

4. The persistence of the classical tradition in Parisian architecture is excellently surveyed in Anthony Sutcliffe, *Paris: An Architectural History* (New Haven, 1993).

5. *Gazette municipale,* 16 August 1854. The work went so quickly that contemporaries sometimes likened it to magic. See A. Etex, *Essai d'une revue synthétique sur l'exposition universelle de 1855* (Paris, 1856), pp. 11–12; *Le Moniteur universel,* 19 August 1854.

6. The speech is reprinted in Napoleon III, *Oeuvres* (Paris, 1869), 3:39–41.

7. Peter Paret, "Continuity and Discontinuity in Some Interpretations by

Tocqueville and Clausewitz," *Journal of the History of Ideas* 49 (January–March 1988): 163–64.

8. A[dolphe] Granier de Cassagnac, *Histoire des causes de la Révolution française* (Paris, 1850), 3:6/8.

9. See his speech at the inauguration of the statue of Napoleon I and his brothers at Ajaccio, reprinted in *Le Siècle*, 19–20 May 1865.

10. David S. Landes, *The Unbound Prometheus: Technological Change and Industrial Development in Western Europe from 1750 to the Present* (Cambridge, 1969), p. 193. See also David H. Pinkney, *Decisive Years in France, 1840–1847* (Princeton, 1986), pp. 23–49.

11. See especially Ted W. Margadant, "Tradition and Modernity in Rural France during the Nineteenth Century," *Journal of Modern History* 56, no. 4 (December 1984): 667–97.

12. Napoleon III, *Oeuvres*, 3:357–60.

13. Count [Joseph Alexander] von Hübner, *Neuf ans de souvenirs d'un ambassadeur d'Autriche à Paris sous le Second Empire, 1851–1859* (Paris, 1904), 1:102.

14. AN, FIC I 108.

15. In addition to the usual press accounts of these ceremonies, see *Relation générale des cérémonies relatives au mariage de Sa Majesté l'Empereur Napoléon III avec son excellence Mademoiselle Eugénie de Gusman, comtesse de Teba* (Paris, 1853), a copy of which can be found in BHVP, 399106; and Ferdinand Bac, *Le Mariage de l'Impératrice Eugénie* ([Paris], 1928).

16. Fould's *aide-mémoire* for the evening is now in the Bibliothèque Nationale. BN, Collection de Vinck, t. 136, no. 16,486.

17. Hübner, *Neuf ans de souvenirs*, 1:104.

18. For example, see the decoration of Lecointe and Hittorff for the baptism of the Duc de Bordeaux in 1821 described in Françoise Waquet, *Les Fêtes royales sous la Restauration ou l'Ancien Régime retrouvé* (Paris, 1981), pp. 72–78.

19. Jean-Michel Leniaud, "Archéologie pratique et décors de cérémonies religieuses: Le mariage de Napoléon III à Notre-Dame," in *100e Congrès national des sociétés savantes: Archéologie* (Paris, 1975), p. 314.

20. The Bibliothèque Historique de la Ville de Paris has an excellent photograph of this portico that is reprinted in *Paris des illusions: Un siècle de décors éphémères, 1820–1920*, exposition catalog (Paris, 1984), p. 44.

21. *Le Constitutionnel*, 31 January 1853.

22. The Montijo arms were obtained with some difficulty. They were not important enough to be generally known, and Eugénie, according to her friend Prosper Mérimée, was "pas forte sur son blason." Mérimée to Viollet-le-Duc, January 1853, in Prosper Mérimée, *Correspondance générale*, ed. M. Parturier, 2nd series (Toulouse, 1953–64), 1:14.

23. *Illustrated London News*, 5 February 1853.

24. Lassus and Viollet-le-Duc to Cambacérès, 15 March 1853, in AN, F21 1464. See also AN, O5 2301.

25. [Emile Félix] Fleury, *Souvenirs du général comte Fleury*, 3rd ed. (Paris, 1897), 1:234.

26. *The Times* (London), 5 February 1853.

27. Fleury, *Souvenirs*, 1:235–36.

28. *Tricolored Sketches in Paris during the Years 1851–2–3* (New York, 1855), p. 281.

29. *Le Moniteur officiel*, 31 January 1853; Thomas W. Evans, *The Memoirs of Dr. Thomas W. Evans: Recollections of the Second French Empire* (London, 1905), 1:95–96.

30. *Illustrated London News*, 5 February 1853.

31. *Tricolored Sketches in Paris*, p. 282.

32. Hübner, *Neuf ans de souvenirs*, 1:106.

33. Hector Berlioz, *Correspondance Générale*, ed. Pierre Citron (Paris, 1983), 4:273 (emphasis in original).

34. According to the official ceremonial instructions, based on similar instructions from earlier royal births, the empress was accompanied throughout her labor only by her mother, the Grande-Maitresse of her household, her lady-of-honor, and the new governess. However, "Au moment où se feront sentir les dernières douleurs," the ministers of state and justice were to enter, as well as "all of the princes and princesses that his Majesty judges convenient to admit." AN, F70 634.

35. A copy of the official ceremonial instructions, based on similar instructions from earlier royal births, can be found in AN, F70 634.

36. The prefects' reports on the celebrations in AN, FIC I 111[1] have a few complaints of dissatisfaction but on the whole report widespread popularity.

37. Sibour to the minister of public instruction and religion, 24 March 1856, in AN, F19 5579.

38. Maurice Paléologue, *The Tragic Empress: A Record of Intimate Talks with the Empress Eugénie, 1901–1919*, trans. Hamish Miles (New York, 1928), pp. 12–13.

39. The budget for the ceremony was originally projected at 400,000 francs. It was soon raised to 520,000, but in the end a 900,000 franc credit was required. Of this, a bit over 250,000 francs went to the decoration of the cathedral. See AN, F21 723, F70 249, and O5 22 (1856), no. 533. The city of Paris also spent a significant amount of money for decorations and a banquet.

40. Prosper Mérimée, "Baptême du Prince Impérial. Décoration de Notre-Dame," *Le Moniteur universel*, 13 June 1856.

41. Description of the decorations and ceremony drawn primarily from *Le Moniteur universel*, 13, 15 June 1856; *Le Constitutionnel*, 15 June 1856; *L'Illustration*, 21 June 1856; and the printed program for the ceremony found in AN, F19 5579, no. 222. A number of bills and payment orders are found in AN, O5 2303, and an interesting letter of complaint from the archbishop of Besançon can be found in AN, F19 7805. Zola wrote an evocative description of the celebration in chapter 4 of *Son Excellence Eugène Rougon* (Paris, 1961), but he was not present at the

ceremony. See also Pierre Marie Auzas, "Viollet-le-Duc et Notre Dame de Paris: Le baptême du Prince Impérial," *Bulletin de la Société de l'histoire de l'art français* (1965), pp. 231–37.

42. AN, F70 251.

43. These were ceremonial items carried in by high-ranking ladies of the court; they consisted of a candle, the holy oil, salt, a towel, the basin, and the ewer. Their use dates from the Old Regime.

44. There is a good discussion of the religious politics of the baptism in Jean Maurain, *La Politique ecclésiastique du Second Empire* (Paris, 1930), pp. 112–15.

45. Research into the earlier baptisms was done by the minister of public instruction and religion and presented to the emperor at a ministerial council meeting, 16 April 1856. See AN, F19 5608; AN, 154Mi 1; AN, 400AP 70.

46. Edmond Rousse, *Lettres à un ami* (Paris, 1909), 1:257.

47. Hübner, *Neuf ans de souvenirs*, 1:435.

48. Hôtel-de-Ville de Paris, *Fêtes et cérémonies à l'occasion de la naissance et du baptême de Son Altesse le Prince Impérial* (Paris, 1860), p. 8. A copy of this is found in BHVP, 92893.

49. AD Seine, V.K3 77.

50. In many areas, severe rains and flooding seriously dampened the celebration. See prefects' reports in AN, FIC I 111[1.]

51. *Illustrated London News*, 5 February 1853.

52. BN, Collection de Vinck, t. 146, no. 17469.

53. The painting is analyzed at length in Albert Boime, *Thomas Couture and the Eclectic Vision* (New Haven, 1980), pp. 263–81.

54. Louis Girard, *Nouvelle histoire de Paris: La Deuxième République et le Second Empire, 1848–1870* (Paris, 1981), p. 266.

55. See Jean Maurain, *Le Saint-Siège et la France de décembre 1851 à avril 1853: Documents inédits* (Paris, 1930), and le Marquis de Ségur, *Souvenirs et récit d'un frère*, 6th ed. (Paris, 1882), 1:183–93.

56. Even the *sacre* of Charles X in 1825 had been widely ridiculed, most prominently by Béranger in his "Le sacre de Charles le simple." See Adrien Dansette, *Histoire Religieuse de la France contemporaine* (Paris, 1948), 1:252–53.

57. Quoted in Comte Fleury, *Mémoires of the Empress Eugénie* (New York, 1920), 1:313.

58. Norbert Elias, *The Court Society*, trans. Edmund Jephcott (New York, 1983), p. 1.

59. Philip Mansel, *The Court of France, 1789–1830* (Cambridge, 1988), p. 85. On the court of the First Empire, see also Philip Mansel, *The Eagle in Splendour: Napoleon I and His Court* (London, 1987), and Otto Zieseniss, *Napoléon et la Cour Impériale* (Paris, 1980).

60. The best introduction to imperial politics is still Theodore Zeldin, *The Political System of Napoleon III* (New York, 1958).

61. An excellent source for details about the court is Duc de Conegliano, *La*

Maison de l'Empereur (Paris, 1897). A good, short overview is Louis Girard, "La Cour de Napoléon III," in *Hof, Kultur und Politik in 19. Jahrhundert: Akten des 18. Deutsch-französischen Historikerkolloquiums* (Bonn, 1985).

62. Quoted in H. Montgomery Hyde, *Mexican Empire: The History of Maximilian and Carlota of Mexico* (London, 1946), p. 53.

63. Eugénie to the Duchess of Alba, 14 February 1856, in *Lettres familières de l'Impératrice Eugénie* (Paris, 1935), 1:127.

64. Princess Pauline de Metternich, *Souvenirs (1859–1871)*, 18th ed. (Paris, 1922), pp. 93–94.

65. Albert Verly, *De Notre-Dame au Zululand* (Paris, 1896), p. 96.

66. On Worth, see Henriette Vanier, *La Mode et ses métiers: Frivolités et luttes des classes, 1830–1870* (Paris, 1960), pp. 193–98.

67. Emile Ollivier, *Journal* (Paris, 1961), 1:218.

68. For a general overview of court dress, see Vanier, *La Mode et ses métiers*, pp. 155–63. On the earlier history of court dress, see Philip Mansel, "Monarchy, Uniform, and the Rise of the *Frac*, 1760–1830," *Past and Present* 96 (August 1982); 103–32.

69. Bayle St. John, *Purple Tints of Paris: Character and Manners in the New Empire* (London, 1854), 1:119–20.

70. Architects of the Imperial Palaces to the Minister of the Imperial Household, 3 August 1853, AN, O5 97.

71. AN, F70 251.

72. The official regulations were quite specific about the size and shape of the trains. They were published in the *Moniteur de la mode*, December 1853.

73. Hübner, *Neuf ans de souvenirs*, 1:197.

74. Ibid., p. 171.

75. Fleury, *Mémoires of the Empress Eugénie*, 1:332–33.

76. The hunt included Prince Murat, the Spanish ambassador, and the Prince de Moscowa and took place on 8 November 1862. AN, 400AP 71.

77. Elias, *Court Society*, pp. 83–86.

78. 'Le lever est le moment où Sa Majesté sort de son appartment intérieur pour entrer dans son appartement d'honneur." *Le Cérémonial officiel* (Paris, 1865), pp. 28–29.

79. There is a short discussion of the painting in *The Second Empire, 1852–1870*, pp. 307–8.

80. Mérimée, *Correspondance générale*, 4:311–13. Mérimée used words like "ridicule" and "pénible" to describe the ceremony and noted that the actual prostration lasted only a brief moment.

81. For good descriptions and illustrations of the visit, see *Le Moniteur universel*, 19–29 August 1855; *L'Illustration*, 25 August, 1 September 1855; Edouard Gorges, *Revue de l'Exposition universelle* (Paris, 1855–56), 2:6–14; Queen Victoria, *Leaves from a Journal* (New York, 1961); Hôtel-de-Ville de Paris, *Fête donnée in l'honneur de S. M. B. La Reine Victoria* (Paris, 1856). See also AN, BB30 412, F21 519, O5 21–22, and AD, Seine, V.K3 76. AN, O5 2309 contains bills and payment

orders for everything from powdered wigs for the coachmen to new bathtubs installed for the visits of monarchs. The visit is also mentioned in numerous journals and memoirs of the period.

82. Guy de Maupassant, *Contes et nouvelles,* ed. Albert-Marie Schmidt (Paris, 1956), 1:284.

83. *La Vie Parisienne,* 18 May 1867.

84. Girard, "Cour de Napoléon III," p. 161.

85. E. J. Hobsbawm, *The Age of Revolution, 1789–1848* (New York, 1962), p. 218.

86. Jean Tulard, "Le retour des Cendres," in Pierre Nora, ed., *Les Lieux de mémoire, II: La Nation* (Paris, 1986), 3:107. For an excellent treatment of the July Monarchy's use of Napoleonic imagery, see Michael Marrinan, *Pointing Politics for Louis-Philippe: Art and Ideology in Orléanist France, 1830–1848* (New Haven, 1988), pp. 141–200.

87. See *Revue des beaux-arts,* 1 September 1856.

88. The two he inaugurated were at Lyons in 1852 and at Cherbourg in 1858. The only other statue he inaugurated was Jeanne Hachette at Beauvais in 1851.

89. Approximately 40 percent of the figures memorialized on public statues were from before 1789, 2 percent from the Revolution, and 31 percent from the period after 1815. I make no claims for the definitiveness of my figures, which were collected primarily through newspapers and in Ministère de l'Instruction publique et des Beaux-Arts, *Inventaire général des richesses d'art de la France: Paris—Monuments civils* (Paris, 1879), 1:294. I have not included statues of biblical figures, statues erected in churches or cemeteries, or statues on buildings such as the Louvre. I have, however, included busts. For a general treatment of public statuary in the nineteenth century, see Maurice Agulhon, "La 'statuomanie' et l'histoire," *Ethnologie française* 8 (1978): 145–72.

90. Louis-Napoleon did not personally attend these services (except in 1852), but he did usually attend another special commemorative mass held in the chapel of the Tuileries on the same day.

91. *Le Moniteur universel,* 3 April 1858. See also J. M. Gilis, "Le Centenaire de la Médaille de Sainte-Hélène," *Souvenir Napoléonien,* May 1957, pp. 1–2. On Second Empire medals generally, including the Saint Helena Medal, see Musée Monétaire, *Ordres de Chevalerie et Récompenses nationales,* exposition catalog (Paris, 1956), pp. 310–19.

92. See Rosemonde Sanson, "Le 15 août: Fête nationale du Second Empire," in Alain Corbin, Noëlle Gérôme, and Danielle Tartakowsky, eds., *Les Usages politiques des fêtes au XIXe–XXe siècles* (Paris, 1994), pp. 117–36.

93. AN, F21 726.

94. *Revue des beaux-arts,* 1 August 1855. In the end, the celebration was not entirely canceled since the city went ahead with its plans, although it only spent half of what it usually did.

95. Haussmann to minister of state, 7 August 1861, in AN, F21 725.

96. Lefuel to Vaillant, 9 July 1867, in AN, F21 727.

97. On Visconti's festival work, see Barry Bergdoll, "Metteur en scène des fêtes du juillet et des fastes du IIe Empire," in Françoise Hamon and Charles MacCallum, eds., *Louis Visconti, 1791–1853* (Paris, 1991).

98. See payment records in AN, F21 725–26 and F70 248–49.

99. Lefuel and Galand to minister of state, 4 July 1861, in AN, F21 725.

100. *L'Opinion nationale*, 16–17 August 1864.

101. See the program in AN, F21 726.

102. Escudier, "Les fêtes du 15 août," *Le Reveil*, 21 August 1858.

103. Rossini, for example, apparently wrote the music for the cantata sung at the Opera in 1867. In AN, AJ13 505. (The series of cartons from AJ13 500 to AJ13 506 contains numerous similar works written for the 15 August celebrations and other celebrations. AJ13 527 to AJ13 529 also contain a number of documents and programs for special performances.)

104. AN, AJ13 501, no. 659 ter.

105. Edouard Drumont, *Les Fêtes nationales à Paris*, 2nd ed. (Paris, 1879), unpaginated.

106. Henri Maret, *Le Tour du monde parisien* (Paris, 1862), pp. 42–47.

107. AN, F70 250.

108. For examples, see AN, O5 298, and the reports to the prefect of the Gironde in AD, Gironde, 1M 707.

109. AN, F1C I 111.

110. AN, BB30 384. See also Sanson, "Le 15 août," p. 135.

111. Arno Mayer, *The Persistence of the Old Regime: Europe to the Great War* (New York, 1981).

112. Eric Hobsbawm, "Introduction," in Eric Hobsbawm and Terence Ranger, eds., *The Invention of Tradition* (Cambridge, 1983), p. 1. On commemorative ceremonies, see also Paul Connerton, *How Societies Remember* (Cambridge, 1989), pp. 41–71.

113. Hobsbawm, "Introduction," p. 10.

114. Martin J. Wiener, *English Culture and the Decline of the Industrial Spirit, 1850–1980* (Cambridge, 1981). See also Charles Dellheim, *The Face of the Past: The Preservation of the Medieval Inheritance in Victorian England* (Cambridge, 1982).

115. Lionel Trilling, *Sincerity and Authenticity* (Cambridge, Mass., 1971), p. 138. See also Karl Mannheim's analysis in *Conservatism: A Contribution to the Sociology of Knowledge,* ed. David Kettler, Volker Meja, and Nico Stehr (London, 1986), pp. 55–56.

FOUR

1. Napoleon III, *Oeuvres* (Paris, 1869), 3:344.

2. Theodore Zeldin, *France, 1848–1945: Politics and Anger* (Oxford, 1979), p. 188.

3. These trowels were often made of gold or silver and engraved in honor of the event. They can still sometimes be seen in French museums.

4. *Revue des beaux-arts,* 1 September 1855. The new Opera also received a box with coins and commemorative medals, which seem to have been the standard items placed in these stones. On the ceremony at the Opera, see *Le Constitutionnel,* 23 July 1862.

5. Louis Girard, *Nouvelle histoire de Paris: La Deuxième République et le Second Empire, 1848–1870* (Paris, 1981), p. 250.

6. *L'Opinion nationale,* 23 July 1861.

7. *L'Illustration,* 14 October 1865.

8. AN, 246AP 24.

9. *La Vie parisienne,* 24 August 1867.

10. "Il entre par la pensée dans vos prières et dans vos espérances." Napoleon III, *Oeuvres,* 3:339.

11. This was the case, for example, with one of the regime's chief Episcopal critics, Msg. Dupanloup of Orléans. See Christianne Marcilhacy, *Le Diocèse d'Orléans sous l'époscopat de Monseigneur. Dupanloup, 1848–1878* (Paris, 1962), p. 217.

12. Sibour to Fortoul, 21 December 1852, in AN, 246AP 24.

13. There are descriptions of the ceremony in most newspapers, including *Le Siècle,* 5 January 1853. For a more personal account, see letter of 3 January 1853, in Henri Dabot, *Lettres d'un lycéen et d'un étudiant de 1847 à 1854* (Péronne, n.d.).

14. Minister of justice to minister of public education and religion, 11 September 1858, in AN, F19 5547. The *cours impériaux* were what are now called *cours d'appel.* By 1863, eleven of them attended the Corpus Christi processions and sixteen did not—not including Paris or Algiers, where the question did not arise.

15. Excellent discussions of railroads as symbols are found in Leo Marx, *The Machine in the Garden: Technology and the Pastoral Ideal in America* (New York, 1964), esp. pp. 191–92; and Wolfgang Schivelbusch, *The Railway Journey: The Industrialization of Time and Space in the Nineteenth Century* (Berkeley, 1986).

16. *L'Illustration,* 4 August 1849.

17. For the Dijon inauguration in 1851, for example, 1,200 guests from Paris were brought in by train the day before the ceremony. *L'Illustration,* 7 June 1851.

18. *L'Illustration,* 26 September 1863.

19. Evêché de Nantes, "Bénédiction du chemin de fer" (Nantes, [1851]).

20. The growing dissatisfaction with the railroads was due to a combination of factors, including high rates and poor service (especially for third-class travel), the perception of profiteering by a few already wealthy investors, and fear of crime in the enclosed carriages. See articles on the future of railway travel by Félix Mornand, *L'Illustration,* 23 August, 13 September 1856; Louis Girard, *La Politique des travaux publics du Second Empire* (Paris, 1952), pp. 209–13; and Schivelbusch, *Railway Journey.*

21. *L'Illustration,* 3 November 1855, 18 July, 19 September 1857.

22. For an example, see *L'Illustration,* 1 December 1855.

23. *Le Constitutionnel,* 25 September 1862.

24. See T. J. Clark, *The Painting of Modern Life: Paris in the Art of Manet and His Followers* (New York, 1985), pp. 66–68. On the way this might work within a

Parisian department store, see Michael B. Miller, *The Bon Marché: Bourgeois Culture and the Department Store, 1869–1920* (Princeton, 1981), pp. 165–78.

25. Philip G. Nord, *Paris Shopkeepers and the Politics of Resentment* (Princeton, 1986), p. 104.

26. François Loyer, *Paris au XIXe siècle: L'Immeuble et la rue* (Paris, 1987), p. 238.

27. The boulevard inaugurations have been recently and well treated in David Van Zanten, *Building Paris: Architectural Institutions and the Transformation of the French Capital* (Cambridge, 1994), pp. 204–11.

28. Jeanne Gaillard, *Paris, la Ville (1852–1870)* (Paris, 1976), p. 561.

29. David H. Pinkney, *Napoleon III and the Rebuilding of Paris* (Princeton, 1958), pp. 183–84.

30. The text of the law is found in *Le Moniteur universel*, 7 April 1858. Among other things, it calls for the construction of what were to become the Boulevards Prince-Eugène and Malesherbes, and the widening of the Boulevard du Sébastopol where it crosses the Ile de la Cité.

31. Emile Ollivier, *L'Empire libéral* (Paris, 1899), 4:74.

32. It had been announced that the emperor and empress would inaugurate the boulevard on 10 December (a symbolic date for Bonapartists). The street was decorated with flags, banners, venetian masts, and a triumphal arch, and the crowds were waiting, but the imperial couple did not arrive. After what seemed a sufficiently long delay, the authorities called off the ceremony; workers began taking down the decorations, and the crowd of spectators began to disperse. Then, in the midst of the chaos Minister of Interior Persigny arrived, and a belated and disorganized ceremony took place amid the half-disassembled decorations. See *Revue municipale/Gazette municipale*, 16 December 1853, pp. 1129–30. *L'Illustration*, 17 December 1853, carried an illustration of the inauguration that shows no signs of disorder. The only mention of the inauguration in *Le Moniteur universel* was a description picked up from the Bonapartist newspaper *La Patrie*, which noted no problems whatsoever (13 December 1853).

33. Donald Reid, *Paris Sewers and Sewermen: Realities and Representations* (Cambridge, Mass., 1991).

34. The description of the ceremony and decorations and the text of the emperor's speech (quoted below) have been drawn primarily from newspaper accounts. See especially the 5–6 April 1858 issues of *Le Moniteur universel*, *Le Constitutionnel*, *La Patrie*, *Le Pays*, and *L'Estafette*, as well as *L'Illustration*, 10 April 1858.

35. L. Marchand, in *L'Estafette*, 5–6 April 1858.

36. Count [Joseph Alexander] von Hübner, *Neuf ans de souvenirs d'un ambassadeur d'Autriche à Paris sous le Second Empire, 1851–1859* (Paris, 1904), 2:134.

37. "Comme dans une féerie," Henri Dabot, *Souvenirs et impressions d'un bourgeois du quartier Latin de mai 1854 à mai 1869* (Péronne, 1899), p. 38.

38. Walter Benjamin, *Reflections*, trans. Edmund Jephcott (New York, 1978), p. 159.

39. *Le Constitutionnel*, 5–6 April 1858.

40. Hübner, *Neuf ans de souvenirs,* 2:134.

41. On this law, see Vincent Wright, "La loi de sûreté générale de 1858," *Revue d'histoire moderne et contemporaine* (July–September 1969), pp. 414–30.

42. See, for example, the *Gazette de France, L'Union,* and *L'Univer,* 5–6 April 1858.

43. A.-M. Desnoyers, in *Le Courrier de Paris,* 5–6 April 1858.

44. *Le Moniteur universel,* 5–6 April 1858.

45. *Le Pays,* 5–6 April 1858.

46. *La Patrie,* 7 April 1858.

47. *Le Constitutionnel,* 8 April 1858.

48. Hübner, *Neuf ans de souvenirs,* 2:134.

49. Pinkney, *Napoleon III and the Rebuilding of Paris,* pp. 184, 190–92.

50. For illustrations and criticism of these decorations, see *L'Illustration,* 6 December 1862; *Illustrated London News,* 13 December 1862.

51. *Le Moniteur universel,* 8 December 1862.

52. Paul Veyne, *Bread and Circuses: Historical Sociology and Political Pluralism,* trans. Brian Pearce (London, 1990), p. 1. See also ibid., pp. 347–76.

53. *La Vie parisienne,* 24 April 1869.

54. Alexis de Tocqueville, *Democracy in America,* ed. J. P. Mayer, trans. George Lawrence (Garden City, N.Y., 1969), p. 435. A similar discussion is found in ibid., p. 643.

FIVE

1. No full-scale study of either exposition currently exists, although they are treated in a number of works. See especially John Allwood, *The Great Exhibitions* (London, 1977), pp. 33–48; Linda Aimone and Carlo Olmo, *Les Expositions universelles, 1851–1900,* trans. Philippe Olivier (Paris, 1993); Philippe Bouin and Christian-Philippe Chanut, *Histoire Française des foires et des Expositions Universelles* (Paris, 1980), pp. 56–71, 74–93; Barrie M. Ratcliffe, "Paris 1855," and Arthur Chandler, "Paris 1867," in John E. Findling, ed., *Historical Dictionary of World's Fairs and Expositions, 1851–1988* (Westport, Conn., 1990), pp. 16–22, 33–43; Frank Anderson Trapp, "The Universal Exhibition of 1855," *Burlington Magazine,* June 1965, pp. 300–305, and " 'Expo' 1867 Revisited," *Apollo* 89 (1969): 112–31. On art at the expositions, see Patricia Mainardi, *Art and Politics of the Second Empire: The Universal Expositions of 1855 and 1867* (New Haven, 1987).

2. Eugene Rimmel, *Recollections of the Paris Exhibition of 1867* (Philadelphia, [1868]), pp. 1–2.

3. On this aspect of the railroad, see Wolfgang Schivelbusch, *The Railway Journey: The Industrialization of Time and Space in the Nineteenth Century* (Berkeley, 1986), pp. 33–44. According to Leo Marx, the phrase "annihilation of space and time" was extremely common during the nineteenth century and comes from a minor poem of Alexander Pope. Marx, *The Machine in the Garden: Technology and the Pastoral Ideal in America* (New York, 1964), p. 194.

4. Claude Lévi-Strauss, *The Savage Mind* (Chicago, 1966), p. 23.

5. On the role of what he calls "specular dominance" at the expositions, see Tony Bennett's excellent article, "The Exhibitionary Complex," *New Formations* 4 (Spring 1988): 73–102.

6. Richard Terdiman, *Discourse/Counter-Discourse: The Theory and Practice of Symbolic Resistance in Nineteenth-Century France* (Ithaca, 1985), pp. 61–62.

7. According to Bourdieu, "These mental structures . . . contribute at least as efficaciously as the provisions of custom towards defining and maintaining the delimitation of powers between the sexes and generations. . . . The theory of knowledge is a dimension of political theory because the specifically symbolic power to impose the principles of the construction of reality—in particular, social reality—is a major dimension of political power." *Outline of a Theory of Practice,* trans. Richard Nice (Cambridge, 1977), p. 165.

8. Paris Exposition universelle de 1867, *Guide de l'exposant et du visiteur* (Paris, 1866), p. 45.

9. Speech at the award ceremony in 1867, reprinted in Napoleon III, *Oeuvres* (Paris, 1869), 5:286.

10. "Art Journal," *The Illustrated Catalogue of the Universal Exposition* (London, 1868), p. 4.

11. "Let us compete through art / Let us compete through industry / Progress will come through rivalry / And we will each enrich our country / By always working for its prosperity / By always working for its prosperity." This was itself an entry for a competition to write words for a cantata to the exposition. In AN, F12 3097.

12. This aspect of the expositions is underscored by Raymond Isay's marvelous study, *Panorama des expositions universelles* (Paris, 1937), which remains the best synthetic work on the French expositions. See also Pascal Ory, *Les Expositions universelles de Paris* (Paris, 1982).

13. On Chevalier, see Jean Walch, *Michel Chevalier, économiste Saint-Simonien, 1806–1879* (Paris, 1975).

14. Michel Chevalier, "Introduction," in Michel Chevalier, ed., *Exposition universelle de 1867: Rapports du jury international* (Paris, 1868), 1:viii–xxxiv. Chevalier expressed similar, although less fully articulated, views in 1855. See his article in the *Journal des débats,* 15 May 1855. Frédéric Le Play, another chief organizer of the expositions, held very much the same ideas about the limited role of the state. See his *Réforme sociale en France* (Paris, 1866), 2:523–24.

15. Siegfried Kracauer, *Orpheus in Paris. Offenbach and the Paris of His Time,* trans. Gwenda David and Eric Mosbacher (New York, 1972), p. 64. Walch argues that Chevalier arrived at an "original synthesis" of Saint-Simonian socialism and liberal capitalism. Walch, *Michel Chevalier,* p. 260.

16. It is interesting in this respect that the medals were valued at specific amounts of money. In 1855, for example, the four Fine Arts medals were worth 5,000, 750, 650, and 550 francs. See S. A. I. Le Prince Napoléon, *Rapport sur l'Exposition universelle de 1855* (Paris, 1857), p. 109.

17. Charles Baudelaire, "The Exposition Universelle, 1855," in *Mirror of Art*, trans. and ed. Jonathan Mayne (London, 1955), p. 196.

18. Ernest Renan, "La Poésie de l'Exposition," in *Oeuvres complètes* (Paris, n.d.), 2:250.

19. Victor Fournel, "Voyage à travers l'Exposition universelle," *Le Correspondant*, 71 (25 July 1867): 623.

20. *Bibliothèque universelle et Revue suisse* 30, no. 120 (5 December 1867): 624–25.

21. Napoleon III, *Oeuvres*, 5:185.

22. Ibid., p. 287.

23. Prince Napoléon, *Rapport*, p. 130.

24. Whitney Walton, *France at the Crystal Palace: Bourgeois Taste and Artisan Manufacture in the Nineteenth Century* (Berkeley, 1992), pp. 199–220.

25. Ibid., pp. 199–201. It is also worth noting that Minister of State Rouher himself attributed much of the impetus toward free trade in the late 1850s to the good showing of French industry at the Exposition of 1855. Rouher, "Note lue au Conseil," AN, 45 AP 1.

26. Mainardi, *Art and Politics of the Second Empire*, p. 33.

27. Ibid., p. 2.

28. This aspect of the expositions is evoked in Guillemette Delaporte, "L'Exposition universelle de 1855 à Paris: Confrontations de cultures et prises de conscience," *L'Ecrit-Voir*, no. 6 (1985): 5–10; Marie-Noëlle Pradel de Grandry, "Découverte des civilisations dans l'espace et dans le temps," in Robert Bordaz et al., eds., *Le Livre des expositions universelles, 1851–1989* (Paris, 1983), pp. 289–96.

29. Emile Zola, *L'Argent*, in *Oeuvres completes* (Paris, n.d.), p. 272.

30. On workers at the expositions, see Madeleine Réberioux, "Les ouvriers et les expositions universelles de Paris au XIXe siècle," in Bordaz et al., *Le Livre des expositions universelles*, p. 198.

31. Prince Napoléon, *Rapport*, p. 83.

32. Ibid., pp. 99–101.

33. See the report by A. Saint-Yves and A. Vitu on class 94, "Produits de toutes sortes fabriqués par des ouvriers, chefs de métier," in Chevalier, *Rapports du jury international*, 13:953–84.

34. *L'Exposition universelle de 1867 illustrée*, 7 October 1867.

35. See the report by Darimon and Van Blarenberghe on class 95, "Instruments et procédés de travail spéciaux aux ouvriers chefs de métier," in Chevalier, *Rapports du jury international*, 13:985–1012, esp. pp. 991–92.

36. Jeanne Gaillard, *Paris, la ville (1852–1870)* (Paris, 1977), p. 562.

37. Charles de Linas, *L'Histoire du travail à l'Exposition universelle de 1867* (Paris, [1868]), p. 2.

38. Paris Exposition universelle de 1867, *Catalogue général: Histoire du Travail* (Paris, n.d.); Burton Benedict, *The Anthropology of World's Fairs* (Berkeley, 1983), p. 30.

39. The reports are collected in Arnould Desvernay, ed., *Exposition universelle*

de 1867 à Paris: Rapports des délégations ouvrières, 3 vols. (Paris, n.d.). The reports are individually paginated. An interesting discussion of the reports can be found in Edgar Saveney, "Les Délégations ouvrières à l'Exposition universelle de 1867," *Revue des deux mondes,* 2nd series, vol. 77 (October 1868); 586–621. For more recent commentary, see Jacques Rancière and Patrice Vauday, "En allant à l'expo: l'ouvrier, sa femme, et les machines," *Les révoltes logiques,* no. 1 (Winter 1975); 5–22.

40. To be fair, the reports, written by individuals, vary widely in the place accorded to workers. Nonetheless, I think my generalization is just, especially with regard to the more mechanized industries.

41. On workers and machines, see especially Rancière and Vauday, "En allant à l'expo," pp. 7–14.

42. See, for example, the reports of the piano makers and of the *mécaniciens* in Desvernay, *Rapports des délégations ouvrières,* vols. 1 and 2. Other demands included the suppression of the livret, right of association, and a revision of the *conseils des prudhommes* (courts regulating disputes between workers and bosses). See Saveney, "Les Délégations ouvrières," pp. 611–16.

43. See the reports of the *lunettiers* and the *marbriers,* both in Desvernay, *Rapports des délégations ouvrières,* vol. 2.

44. Chevalier, "Introduction," in Chevalier, *Exposition universelle de 1867,* 1:xxi.

45. Prince Napoléon, *Rapport,* pp. 59–61, 390–95.

46. Frédéric Jourdain, report on the "industries accessoires" in class 91, "Meubles, vêtements et aliments de toute origine, distingués par les qualités utiles, unies au bon marché," in Chevalier, *Rapports du jury international,* 13:842.

47. Chevalier, *Rapports du jury international,* 1:362.

48. Ibid., p. 371. Award recipients are listed in ibid., pp. 381 ff.

49. In a recent study, Tony Judt reviewed the role of women workers in the nineteenth century and concluded that their presence was so important that "in France, at least, industrialization often meant feminization." *Marxism and the French Left: Studies in Labour and Politics in France, 1830–1981* (Oxford, 1986), p. 46. This is far from the impression one gets from the expositions.

50. In favor of the workers, it might be pointed out that some of them did at least invite women to discuss questions of women's work. Saveney, "Les Délégations ouvrières," pp. 604, 608–609. Rancière and Vauday also argue that the workers' real fear was that owners would use cheap female labor to drive down wages. Rancière and Vauday, "En allant à l'expo," pp. 14–16.

51. Maxime Du Camp, *Paris, ses organes, ses fonctions et sa vie dans la seconde moitié du xixe siècle* (Paris, 1869–75), 1:12–13. Emile Zola made a similar association. During the 1867 exposition, he said, "Les trottoirs n'étaient plus assez large pour le torrent débordé de la prostitution." *L'Argent,* in *Oeuvres complètes* (Paris, n.d.), p. 272.

52. Based on my count of painters listed in Paris Exposition universelle de 1867, *Catalogue général. . . Oeuvres d'art,* 2nd ed. (Paris, [1867]).

53. A. Etex, *Essai d'une revue synthétique sur l'exposition universelle de 1855* (Paris, 1856), p. 26.

54. Walton, *France at the Crystal Palace,* pp. 49–69.

55. Albert Kaempfen, "Promenade à l'exposition," in Principaux écrivains et artistes de la France, *Paris-Guide* (Paris, 1867), p. 2020.

56. *L'Illustration,* 3 November 1855. Queen Victoria, who made a spectacular visit to Paris during the exposition, also used the chairs at the Louvre. Queen Victoria, *Leaves from a Journal* (New York, 1961), p. 106. According to the Maréchal de Castellane, Victoria had given one of the chairs to Eugénie during the latter's visit to London. Castellane, *Journal, 1804–1862* (Paris, 1896), 5:92.

57. For a general treatment of this concept at World's Fairs, see Benedict, *Anthropology of World's Fairs,* pp. 27–41.

58. In 1855, at least, Le Play claimed that he was not following any philosophic system in his classification but adopting the English system as the one best designed to "atteindre le but principal de l'Exposition universelle, celui de fournir au public et au jury international les moyens d'apprécier le mérite relatif des produits exposés." Preface to classification system, reprinted in Prince Napoléon, *Rapport,* pp. 249–54. The classification itself is in ibid., pp. 255–348.

59. Both classifications, of course, were further divided into numerous classes, sections, and subsections.

60. Mainardi, *Art and Politics of the Second Empire,* pp. 131–33.

61. Prince Napoléon, *Rapport,* p. 45.

62. Madeleine Réberioux, "Approches de l'histoire des Expositions universelles à Paris du Second Empire à 1900," *Bulletin du centre d'histoire economique et sociale de la region Lyonnaise* 1 (1979):11.

63. Le Play, in Prince Napoléon, *Rapport,* pp. 249–54.

64. According to Sigfried Giedion, the roof had "the widest vaulting attempted in the period." *Space, Time and Architecture: The Growth of a New Tradition,* 5th ed. (Cambridge, Mass., 1967), p. 257.

65. Descriptions and illustrations of all of these elements are found in *L'Illustration,* 19 May 1855.

66. *Revue des beaux-arts* 5 (1 April 1854): 108.

67. Additionally, though it was not directly connected to the decoration of the building, a life-size equestrian statue of Napoleon III stood before the entrance to the palace. The statue, by Jean Debay, depicted the emperor in the uniform of a lieutenant general. Edouard Gorges, *Revue de l'Exposition universelle,* 4 vols. (Paris, 1855–56), 1:71.

68. Maréchal, like so many others involved in the exposition, had been a Saint-Simonian in his youth. See Georges Duplessis, "Maréchal," *Revue des beaux-arts,* 10 (1 April 1859): 129–31. The following description of the allegory in the window is drawn from an article published by Maréchal himself in *Le Palais de L'Exposition,* 16 May 1855.

69. Paris Exposition universelle de 1867, *Guide de l'exposant et du visiteur,* p. 21.

70. Prince Napoléon, *Rapport,* p. 140. Although Prince Napoléon suggested the double arrangement, he envisaged neither placing the exposition in a circular building nor placing machinery and fine arts in the same building as everything else.

The accusation that Le Play stole the essential idea for the building came from George Maw, who published a design for an exposition building bearing a striking resemblance to Le Play's in 1861. His contention was rejected by the French. See AN, F12 2994, folder III:1.

71. Groups VIII and IX (Agriculture and Horticulture), however, were located on the Ile de Billancourt, and Group X (products designed to improve the condition of the population) was distributed throughout the building.

72. L. de Hegermann-Lindencrone, *In the Courts of Memory, 1858–1875* (New York, 1912), p. 154.

73. Ludovic Halévy, *Carnets* (Paris, 1935), 1:158.

74. Paris Exposition universelle de 1867, *Guide de l'exposant et du visiteur*, p. 45.

75. Dean MacCannell, *The Tourist. A New Theory of the Leisure Class* (New York, 1976), p. 6. MacCannell believes that this development is part of "modern" rather than "industrial" society. Given the interest in work at the expositions, this seems rather late, but it is far more acceptable than a more recent book, which argues that the interest is "bound up with the postmodern breaking down of boundaries." John Urry, *The Tourist Gaze: Leisure and Travel in Contemporary Societies* (London, 1990), p. 107.

76. Walter Benjamin, *Charles Baudelaire: A Lyric Poet in the Era of High Capitalism*, trans. Harry Zohn (London, 1973), p. 165.

77. Quoted in Giedion, *Space, Time and Architecture*, p. 261.

78. Rimmel, *Recollections of the Paris Exhibition*, p. 32.

79. Fournel, "Voyage à travers l'Exposition universelle," *Le Correspondant* 70 (25 April 1867): 973.

80. Kaempfen, "Promenade à l'Exposition," p. 2025.

81. François Laisney, "L'Architecture industrielle dans les expositions universelles," *Monuments historiques de la France*, no. 3 (1977): 43.

82. Alvin Kernan, *The Death of Literature* (New Haven, 1990), p. 195.

83. Pierre Bourdieu, *In Other Words: Essays towards a Reflexive Sociology*, trans. Matthew Adamson (Stanford), 1990, p. 24. Robert Darnton has similarly remarked apropos of the *Encyclopédie* that "pigeon-holing is . . . an exercise in power." *The Great Cat Massacre and Other Episodes in French Cultural History* (New York, 1984), p. 192. A highly philosophical work dealing with some of these issues is Michel Foucault, *The Order of Things: An Archeology of the Human Sciences* (New York, 1973).

84. Michel Mann, *The Sources of Social Power*, vol 1, *A History of Power from the Beginning to A.D. 1760* (Cambridge, 1986), p. 23.

SIX

1. Camille Bloch, *L'Assistance et l'Etat en France à la veille de la Révolution* (Paris, 1908), pp. 145–46.

2. Pierre d'Espezel, *Les Reines de France* (Paris, 1947), p. 26.

3. Shortly before her marriage, Eugénie wrote to her sister that she trembled "not from fear of assassins, but to appear less than Blanche of Castille and Anne of Austria in history." Letter of 22 January 1853, in Eugénie, *Lettres familières de l'Impératrice Eugénie* (Paris, 1935), 1:50. Blanche de Castille was the pious Spanish wife of Louis VIII and mother of Saint Louis. On Anne of Austria's charity, see Raymond Darricau, "L'Action charitable d'une reine de France: Anne d'Autriche," *XVIIe Siècle*, nos. 90–91 (1971): 111–25.

4. See Jean Maurain, *La Politique ecclésiastique du Second Empire* (Paris, 1930), pp. 554–67; and Amédée d'Andigné, *Armand de Melun: Un apôtre de la charité* (Paris, 1961), pp. 320–27.

5. Armand de Melun said of Napoleon III that "he seemed to me very well disposed to do good and to work toward the happiness of the people, but on condition that that good and that happiness bring him something in return, that all that is done in this genre appear to come exclusively from him, and that his power and his popularity derive all the honor and the benefit from such deeds." Cited in Jean-Baptiste Duroselle, *Les Débuts du Catholicisme social en France* (Paris, 1951), p. 493.

6. For an example of such an argument, see Armand de Melun's response to the government's attempt to organize medical services in rural areas, "Des Médecins cantonaux," in *Annales de la charité* 10 (1854): 257–65. This periodical, it might be noted, was the main voice for the interests of Catholic charities under the Empire. As such it is an excellent resource for the study of those charities but has little to say about the works of the emperor and empress, which it generally avoided mentioning.

7. Duroselle, *Les Débuts du Catholicisme social*, pp. 501–6.

8. Armand de Melun, "La Charité Catholique en France" in *Annales de la charité* (October 1864): 596; Claude Langlois, *Le catholicisme au féminin: Les congrégations françaises à supérieure générale au XIXe siècle* (Paris, 1984), pp. 479–95.

9. According to Colin Jones, between the 1740s and 1808–9, women in Montpellier went from making just over half of the wills with charitable bequests to making more than 80 percent of them. Colin Jones, *Charity and Bienfaisance: The Treatment of the Poor in the Montpellier Region, 1740–1815* (Cambridge, 1982), p. 212. The "feminization of religion" traced by Suzanne Desan during this same general period is surely not unrelated. Suzanne Desan, *Reclaiming the Sacred: Lay Religion and Popular Politics in Revolutionary France* (Ithaca, 1990), pp. 197–216.

10. Although Littré's *Dictionnaire de la langue française* (1863; s.v. "charité") cites a letter from Madame de Maintenon using the term in 1682, it was apparently not used widely, since it did not appear in the *Dictionnaire de l'Académie française* until the sixth edition came out in 1831.

11. *Chérie* (Paris, n.d.), p. 243. For Goncourt it was a sign that his heroine was severely disturbed when she began to take charity seriously and to be moved by the people she was helping.

12. Marguerite Perrot, *La Mode de vie des familles bourgeoises, 1873–1953* (Paris, 1961), pp. 98–100.

13. Langlois, *Le Catholicisme au féminin*, p. 643.

14. On women's charity in the nineteenth century, see Barbara Corrado Pope, "Angels in the Devil's Workshop: Leisured and Charitable Women in Nineteenth-Century England and France," in Renate Bridenthal and Claudia Koonz, eds., *Becoming Visible: Women in European History* (Boston, 1977), pp. 296–323; Jessica Gerard, "Lady Bountiful: Women of the Landed Classes and Rural Philanthropy," *Victorian Studies* 30 (Winter 1987): 183–209; and Bonnie G. Smith, *Ladies of the Leisure Class: The Bourgeoises of Northern France in the Nineteenth Century* (Princeton, 1981), pp. 123–61.

15. *Annales de la charité*, July–August 1862, p. 736.

16. Baron de Watteville, *Rapport à son Excellence le Ministre de l'Intérieur sur l'administration des bureaux de bienfaisance et sur la situation du paupérisme en France* (Paris, 1854), p. 24.

17. E. Knoepflin, *Annuaire de la charité* (Paris, 1863), pp. 162–67. For a description of a provincial society, see Jean-Pierre Chaline, *Les Bourgeois de Rouen* (n.p., 1982), pp. 306–7.

18. Women were accepted without religious distinction. For mothers who could not benefit from the *Sociétés de Charité Maternelle* (usually because they were unmarried), there was, at least in Paris, a separate charity, the *Association des Mères de Famille*. The empress had no official connection to this institution, but she did help it financially.

19. Decree of 26 February 1862. On the *crèche* movement, see F. Marbeau, "Les Crèches de Paris," in Principaux écrivains et artistes de la France, *Paris-Guide* (Paris, 1867), 2:1983–86; and Duroselle, *Les Débuts du Catholicisme social*, pp. 594–600. For the emperor's objections, see Albert Verly, *De Notre-Dame au Zululand* (Paris, 1896), p. 37.

20. Knoepflin, *Annuaire de la charité*, p. 147.

21. Decree of 21 March 1855.

22. *Le Moniteur universel*, 29 January 1853.

23. Georges Eugène Haussmann, *Mémoires du Baron Haussmann* (Paris, 1890–93), 2:422.

24. BN, Collection de Vinck, t. 136, no. 16,461 D.

25. Subscriptions for public monuments were often similarly limited. See Chantal Martinet, "La Souscription," in *La Sculpture française au XIXe siècle*, exposition catalog (Paris, 1986), pp. 231–39.

26. The volumes are now at AN, O5 250–87.

27. *Le Moniteur universel*, 25 May 1856.

28. *L'Illustration*, 21 May 1864.

29. *Le Constitutionnel*, 8 July 1862.

30. M. Mege, address upon the arrival of the imperial couple in Clermont-Ferrand, 8 July 1862, in *Le Moniteur universel*, 10 July 1862.

31. Horace de Viel-Castel, *Mémoires* (Paris, 1883–84), 6:147. As minister of the interior, Persigny had been responsible for the attack on the Saint-Vincent de Paul Society.

32. Decree of 8 August 1865.

33. Princess Pauline de Metternich, *Souvenirs (1859–1871)*, 18th ed. (Paris, 1922), pp. 50–54. Princess Metternich was not present at the reception, but she claims to have been told the story by the empress herself.

34. According to an American who had a small part in one of the plays, the princess "rooted up some charity as an excuse for giving a theatrical performance." L. de Hegermann-Lindencrone, *In the Courts of Memory, 1858–1875* (New York, 1912), p. 41. See also Stéphanie de Tascher de la Pagerie, *Mon séjour aux Tuileries* (Paris, 1893), pp. 174–88.

35. There is an excellent description of one of these sales by one of the aristocratic "saleswomen" in Louise de Mercy-Argenteau, *The Last Love of an Emperor* (Garden City, N.Y., 1926), pp. 43–47.

36. Emile Zola, *Son Excellence Eugène Rougon* (Paris, 1973), chap. 13.

37. Henri Rochefort, *The Adventures of My Life*, trans. Ernest W. Smith (London, 1896), 1:77.

38. Félix Ribeyre, *Voyage de Sa Majesté l'Impératrice en Corse et en Orient* (Paris, [1870]), p. 248.

39. Prosper Mérimée, *Correspondance générale*, ed. M. Parturier, 2nd series (Toulouse, 1953–64), 1:32, 34; George Sand, *Correspondance* (Paris, 1964–86), 16:385–86.

40. See, for example, the letters from Mme. Desjardins to Eugénie and the letter from the Ministry of the Interior to Mme. Desjardins, in AN, F21 1491.

41. These stories were circulated in newspapers and in hagiographical biographical accounts such as the *Almanach de l'Impératrice* (Paris, 1854 and 1855); and Hippolyte Castille, *L'Impératrice Eugénie, Portraits historiques au dix-neuvième siècle*, 2nd series, no. 15 (Paris, 1859).

42. See Madame Carette, *My Mistress, the Empress Eugénie; or, Court Life at the Tuileries* (London, n.d.), pp. 312–15. Madame Carette was one of Eugénie's ladies-in-waiting and claimed to have accompanied the empress on a number of these trips.

43. *L'Ami de l'enfance*, 3rd series, 2 (February 1865): 113.

44. Carette, *My Mistress*, pp. 316–25.

45. *Le Constitutionnel*, 15 July 1863.

46. See Ange-Pierre Leca, *Et le choléra s'abattait sur Paris, 1832* (Paris, 1982), pp. 108–12.

47. H. Thirria, *Napoléon III avant l'Empire* (Paris, 1895), 2:97–98; *Le Dix Décembre*, 17 June 1849.

48. The deaths peaked during the third week of October, then declined steadily. Altogether some 6,347 people died in Paris during the 1865 epidemic. See Prefecture du Département de la Seine, *Tableaux statistiques de l'épidémie cholerique à Paris pendant les mois de septembre, octobre, novembre et décembre 1865* (Paris, 1872), pp. 5–8.

49. Fernand Beaucour, "L'Empire et la Picardie," *Souvenir Napoléonien* (November 1959): 2.

50. *Le Moniteur universel,* 15 August 1868.

51. *Le Moniteur universel,* 24 October 1865.

52. *Le Mémorial d'Amiens,* 5 July 1866, reprinted in the *Journal des débats,* 6 July 1866.

53. See, for example, BN, Collection de Vinck, t. 153, nos. 15–18,317 and t. 157, no. 18,855; *L'Univers illustré,* 28 October 1865; and *L'Illustration,* 4 November 1865.

54. BN, Collection de Vinck, t. 153, no. 18,316 bis.

55. BN, Collection de Vinck, t. 153, no. 18,315.

56. *Journal des débats,* 25 October 1865. The story was repeated by most of the other newspapers.

57. *Le Mémorial d'Amiens,* 5 July 1866, reprinted in the *Journal des débats,* 6 July 1866.

58. Mme. Jules Baroche, *Second Empire: Notes et souvenirs* (Paris, 1921), p. 317.

59. Simon Schama, "The Domestication of Majesty: Royal Family Portraiture, 1500–1850," *Journal of Interdisciplinary History* 17, no. 1 (Summer 1986): 183. On the political implications of domestic images of royals, see also Tom Nairn's brilliant but idiosyncratic *The Enchanted Glass: Britain and Its Monarchy* (London, 1988).

60. BN, Collection de Vinck, t. 157, no. 18,855. Another popular image from the de Vinck collection, this one an allegory of Faith, Hope, and Charity, also demonstrates Eugénie's close symbolic affiliation with charity. In it, the emperor represents Faith, the Prince Imperial represents Hope, and the empress, shown with a group of children, represents Charity. BN, Collection de Vinck, t. 147, no. 17,578.

SEVEN

1. Philippe de Massa, *Souvenirs et impressions—1840–1871,* 2nd ed. (Paris, 1897), p. 36.

2. Reprinted in August Villemot, *La Vie à Paris: Chroniques du Figaro* (Paris, 1858), 2:308–9. Villemot was the pseudonym of Pierre Jules Hetzel.

3. Bayle St. John, *Purple Tints of Paris: Character and Manners in the New Empire* (London, 1854), 2:224.

4. Benedict Anderson, *Imagined Communities: Reflections on the Origin and Spread of Nationalism* (London, 1983), p. 16.

5. Jules Michelet, *The People,* trans. John P. McKay (Urbana, 1973), p. 204.

6. He also reestablished a "Garde Impériale" modeled on that of the First Empire at the same time. See *Le Moniteur universel,* 5 May 1854.

7. For accounts of the Cent-Gardes by soldiers who served with them, see General du Barail, *Mes Souvenirs,* 13th ed., 3 vols. (Paris, 1898); Marcel de Baillehache, *Souvenirs intimes d'un lancier de la garde impériale,* 3rd ed. (Paris, 1894); and Albert Verly, *L'Escadron des Cent-Gardes,* 2nd ed. (Paris, 1894).

8. According to Viel Castel, he first wore the regular army general's uniform on 31 December 1851. Horace de Viel Castel, *Mémoires* (Paris, 1883), 1:249.

9. *The Times* (London), 31 December 1855.

10. The Paris pantomime of 1854 supposedly had a cast of 1,500. See program in BN, 4-Z-Le Senne, 1042.

11. 'Program de la Fête Nationale," 15 August 1861. BN, Collection de Vinck, t. 158, no. 19,031.

12. See the outlines of these plays in AN, F21 727.

13. Napoleon III, *Oeuvres* (Paris, 1869), 3:318.

14. Maréchal de Castellane, *Journal, 1804–1862* (Paris, 1896), 5:54.

15. Baillehache, *Souvenirs intimes,* pp. 82–83.

16. *La Vie Parisienne,* 27 August 1864.

17. My description is drawn from *Le Moniteur universel,* 7 June 1867; *The Times* (London), 8 June 1867; and du Barail, *Mes Souvenirs,* 3:91–95.

18. Du Barail, *Mes Souvenirs,* 3:94.

19. For an example, see *L'Illustration,* 9 July 1853.

20. E. J. Hobsbawm, *The Age of Capital, 1848–1875* (New York, 1975), p. 74.

21. Lynn M. Case, *French Opinion on War and Diplomacy during the Second Empire* (Philadelphia, 1954), pp. 15–50.

22. Napoleon III, *Oeuvres,* 3:388.

23. Ibid., pp. 412–13.

24. *Bibliothèque universelle de Genève* 30 (October 1855): 261. News of the victory spawned similarly spontaneous manifestations throughout the country. See Case, *French Opinion,* p. 39.

25. Henri Dabot, *Souvenirs et impressions d'un bourgeois du quartier Latin de mai 1854 à mai 1869* (Péronne, 1899), p. 11. See also Count [Joseph Alexander] von Hübner, *Neuf ans de souvenirs d'un ambassadeur d'Autriche à Paris sous le Second Empire, 1851–1859* (Paris, 1904), 1:340–41; AN, F21 723. The provincial *Te Deums* were held on Sunday, 16 September, and, according to the reports of prosecutors, were popular, although false rumors and an outbreak of cholera cast a pall on the celebrations in some areas. See AN, BB30 413.

26. For descriptions of this celebration, I have used *Le Moniteur universel,* 30 December 1855; *Journal des débats,* 30 December 1855; and *The Times* (London), 31 December 1855. The emperor's speech is also reprinted in Napoleon III, *Oeuvres,* 3:431. Good illustrations can be found in *L'Illustration,* 5 January 1856.

27. *The Times* (London), 31 December 1855.

28. S. de Sacy, in *Journal de débats,* 30 December 1855.

29. A. P. Cohen, *The Symbolic Construction of Community* (Chichester, 1985).

30. See the prosecutors' reports in AN, BB30 417.

31. There was no state-sponsored festival apparently because the treaty was signed so soon after the birth of the Prince Imperial, and the regime wanted to add that rejoicing to the baptism. There was, however, widespread spontaneous celebration. See the prefects' reports in AN, FIC I 111 [1.]

32. A. Granier de Cassagnac, *Souvenirs du Second Empire* (Paris, 1881–84), 3:57.

33. Case, *French Opinion,* p. 64.

34. Cavour to Victor Emmanuel, 24 July 1858, in Mack Walker, ed., *Plombières: Secret Diplomacy and the Rebirth of Italy* (New York, 1968), p. 27.

35. *L'Univers,* 24 August 1858.

36. Case, *French Opinion*, pp. 54–56.

37. AN, BB30 422.

38. *The Times* (London), 7 February 1859.

39. *Le Moniteur universel*, 4 February 1859.

40. Napoleon III, *Oeuvres*, 5:76–77.

41. Ibid., p. 80.

42. Comtesse Stéphanie de Tascher de la Pagerie, *Mon Séjour aux Tuileries* (Paris, 1893), 2:29.

43. AN, BB30 422; Case, *French Opinion*, p. 74.

44. Dabot, *Souvenirs*, p. 51.

45. Viel Castel, *Mémoires*, 5:51.

46. Prosper Mérimée, *Correspondance générale*, ed. M. Parturier, 2nd series (Toulouse, 1953–64), 3:115–16.

47. Tascher de la Pagerie, *Mon Séjour aux Tuileries*, 2:45.

48. Viel Castel, *Mémoires*, 5:51.

49. *Le Moniteur universel*, 11 May 1859; *Journal des débats*, 11 May 1859; *The Times* (London), 12 May 1859.

50. *The Times* (London), 12 May 1859.

51. Emile Ollivier, *L'Empire libéral*, 17 vols. (Paris, 1895–1915), 4:111–12.

52. Stéphane Gachet, in *L'Opinion nationale*, 24 March 1862.

53. Some payment and other records for these ceremonies can be found in AN, F21 1955, and F70 249.

54. *Le Constitutionnel*, 8 June 1859.

55. See Jean Maurain, *La Politique ecclésiastique du Second Empire* (Paris, 1930), pp. 327–44; AD, Gironde, 1M 706.

56. A. J. P. Taylor, *The Habsburg Monarchy, 1809–1918* (London, 1948), p. 93.

57. Nancy Nichols Barker, *Distaff Diplomacy: The Empress Eugénie and the Foreign Policy of the Second Empire* (Austin, 1967), p. 208.

58. AN, BB30 422. See also Case, *French Opinion*, pp. 91–101.

59. See *Le Moniteur universel*, 15 August 1859; *Journal des débats*, 15 August 1859; *The Times* (London), 17 August 1859.

60. The arch cost over 13,000 francs. AD, Seine, V.K3 79.

61. Mme. Jules Baroche, *Second Empire: Notes et souvenirs* (Paris, 1921), pp. 129–30; Henri Maret, *Le Tour du monde parisien* (Paris, 1862), p. 94.

62. *Paris-vivant, par des hommes nouveaux: Retour de l'armée d'Italie* (Paris, 1859), p. 95.

63. Anna L. Bicknell, *Life in the Tuileries under the Second Empire* (London, 1895), p. 112.

64. *Paris-vivant*, p. 96.

65. Baroche, *Notes et souvenirs*, pp. 129–30. According to another witness, however, the Prince Imperial was seated on the saddle in front of his father. It is possible that he was moved several times during the lengthy ceremony.

66. Dabot, *Souvenirs*, p. 56.

67. Edouard Drumont, *Les Fêtes nationales à Paris*, 2nd ed. (Paris, 1879), unpaginated.

68. Du Barail, *Mes Souvenirs,* 2:252.

69. Georges Eugène Haussmann, *Mémoires du Baron Haussmann* (Paris, 1890–93), 2:234–35.

EIGHT

1. The story of the statue is found in Ministère de l'Instruction publique et des Beaux-Arts, *Inventaire général des richesses d'art de la France: Paris—Monuments civils* (Paris, 1879), 1:364–66. See also Michael Marrinan, *Painting Politics for Louis-Philippe: Art and Ideology in Orléanist France, 1830–1848* (New Haven, 1988), pp. 158–64. During the Commune, the entire Vendôme Column was pulled down, and Seurre's statue at Courbevoie was tossed into the Seine. Later, the column (with Dumont's statue) was reerected, and Seurre's statue was placed in the courtyard of the Invalides, where it remains.

2. *L'Illustration,* 12 December 1863.

3. Alain Plessis, *De la fête impériale au mur des fédérés, 1852–1871* (Paris, 1979), p. 140. A rural area here is defined as a commune of fewer than 2,000 inhabitants, a very low figure.

4. Ted W. Margadant, *French Peasants in Revolt: The Insurrection of 1851* (Princeton, 1979); Alain Corbin, *Archaïsme et modernité en Limousin au XIXe siècle, 1845–1880* (Paris, 1975), 2:842.

5. See John Rothney, *Bonapartism after Sedan* (Ithaca, 1969).

6. Frédéric Bluche, *Le Bonapartisme: Aux origines de la droite autoritaire (1800–1850)* (Paris, 1980), p. 323.

7. See Réné Rémond, *The Right Wing in France from 1815 to de Gaulle,* trans. James M. Laux (Philadelphia, 1966), pp. 125–65.

8. Frédéric Bluche, *Le Bonapartisme,* Que sais-je Collection (Paris, 1981), p. 94.

9. *Le Correspondant,* new series, 6 (September 1857): 141.

10. There were 569 of them in 1861, for example. *L'Opinion nationale,* 9 December 1861.

11. *L'Opinion nationale,* 13 May 1865.

12. Gustave Flaubert, *L'Education sentimentale* (Paris, 1961), p. 387.

13. *Journal du Loiret,* 11–12 May 1868; Louis d'Illiers, *L'Histoire d'Orléans* (Orléans, 1940), pp. 423–24.

14. *L'Illustration,* 6 June 1868; *L'Opinion nationale,* 1–2 June 1868.

15. Nelzir Allard, speech at agricultural fair in Parthenay, 1864, reprinted in Allard, *Souvenirs d'une vie militaire, politique, et administrative* (Niort, n.d.), vol. 2.

16. Michel Chevalier, at La Motte-Beuvron, 21 September 1862, in *Le Constitutionnel,* 25 September 1862.

17. At Cormeilles, reprinted in *Le Constitutionnel,* 7 October 1862. Troplong was president of the Senate and of the Court of Cassation. Both of the speeches quoted earlier by Allard and Chevalier also include praise of the French Revolution.

18. Rémond, *Right Wing in France,* p. 142.

19. Bernard Ménager, *Les Napoléon du peuple* (Paris, 1988), pp. 145–46. The

tours are also discussed in David I. Kulstein, *Napoleon III and the Working Class: A Study of Government Propaganda under the Second Empire* ([Sacramento], 1969), pp. 69–76.

20. Rapport de M. le Recteur de Caen, 21 July 1858, in AN, F19 5607.

21. In Napoleon III, *Oeuvres* (Paris, 1869), 5:65–67.

22. Ribeyre, *L'Empereur et l'Impératrice en Auvergne*, p. 12.

23. Clifford Geertz, "Centers, Kings, and Charisma: Reflections on the Symbolics of Power," in Clifford Geertz, *Local Knowledge: Further Essays in Interpretive Anthropology* (New York, 1983), p. 125.

24. Kulstein, *Napoleon III and the Working Class*, p. 69.

25. On the symbolics of Old Regime monarchical power, see especially three now-classic works: Jean-Marie Apostolidès, *Le roi-machine: Spectacle et politique au temps de Louis XIV* (Paris, 1981); Marc Bloch, *Les rois thaumaturges* (Paris, 1961); and Ernst Kantorowicz, *The King's Two Bodies: A Study in Mediaeval Kingship* (Princeton, 1957).

26. Ménager, *Les Napoléon du peuple*, p. 146.

27. See [Emile-Félix] Fleury, *Souvenirs du général comte Fleury*, 3rd ed. (Paris, 1897), 2:158–67.

28. Ibid., p. 160.

29. One of these programs for the 1860 trip south has been preserved in BN, Collection de Vinck, t. 156.

30. Fleury, *Souvenirs*, 2:162.

31. AN, BB30 423, no. 1833 P.

32. See the October 1852 correspondence between the Minister of Police and the prefect of the Indre-et-Loire concerning the political internees at Tours in AD, Indre-et-Loire, 4M 579. See also Minister of Police to prefect of the Marne, 15 July 1852, recommending "les mesures les plus energiques" and "une surveillance incessante" vis-à-vis a known radical.

33. AN, BB30 421.

34. F. Dutacq, "Les Dessous d'un voyage officiel: Visite de l'Impératrice à Lyon, en 1869, d'après les rapports de police," *Revue du Lyonnais* 15 (July–September 1924): 337–40.

35. *Le Cérémonial officiel* (Paris, 1865), pp. 59–60.

36. Bernard Le Clère and Vincent Wright, *Les Préfets du Second Empire* (Paris, 1973), pp. 234–35.

37. Georges Eugène Haussmann, *Mémoires du Baron Haussmann* (Paris, 1890–93), 3:125–32.

38. Emile Bégin, in *Le Reveil*, 21 August 1858.

39. For a general overview of triumphal arches, see Christian Dupavillon and Francis Lacloche, *La Triomphe des Arcs* (Paris, 1989).

40. *L'Illustration*, 7 September 1867.

41. Auguste Villemot, *La Vie à Paris: Chroniques du Figaro* (Paris, 1858), 2:41–42. The article originally appeared in *Le Figaro* in 1855.

42. *Le Constitutionnel*, 1 January 1859.

43. Auguste Marc, *Voyage de Leurs Majestés impériales dans le sud-est de la France, en Corse, en Algérie, 1860* ([Paris, 1860]), p. 7.

44. Procureur général, Paris, to Garde des Sceaux, 20 August 1858, in AN, BB30 383. Similar reports on this trip can be found in AN, BB30 382, 383, and 421.

45. *Documents authentiques annotés: Les papiers secrets du Second Empire* (Brussels, 1870–71), pp. 27, 38. Pharaon wrote *Voyage en Algérie de Sa Majesté Napoléon III* (Paris, 1865) and *Voyage impérial dans le nord de la France* (Lille, 1867). Félix Ribeyre wrote similar works, including *L'Empereur et l'Impératrice en Auvergne* (Paris, 1862); *Voyage en Lorraine de Sa Majesté l'Impératrice et du Prince Impérial précédé de voyage de S.M. L'Impératrice à Amiens* (Paris, 1867); and *Voyage de Sa Majesté l'Impératrice en Corse et en Orient* (Paris, [1870]).

46. Jean-Noël Marchandiau, *L'Illustration 1843/1944: Vie et mort d'un journal* (Toulouse, 1987), pp. 92–93.

47. *Journal des travaux publics,* 12 August 1858 (emphasis added).

48. F. A. Simpson, *Louis-Napoleon and the Recovery of France* (London, 1965), p. 99.

49. Plessis, *De la fête impériale,* p. 144.

50. Alain Corbin, *Le Village des cannibales* (Paris, 1990).

51. Eric Hobsbawm, "Mass-Producing Traditions, 1870–1914," in Eric Hobsbawm and Terence Ranger, eds., *The Invention of Tradition* (Cambridge, 1983), pp. 263–64.

52. Baron d'Ambès, *Intimate Memoirs of Napoleon III*, trans. A. R. Allinson (London, n.d.), 2:235.

53. François Coppée, "Souvenirs de jeunesse: Fêtes d'autrefois," *Les Annales politiques et litteraires,* 17 July 1898, p. 35.

54. Comte de Maugny, *Souvenirs of the Second Empire* (London, [1890]), pp. 168–69.

55. *L'Opinion nationale,* 21 August 1869; *La Vie parisienne,* 21 August 1869.

56. *La Gazette de France,* 14, 15, 24 August 1869.

NINE

1. Procureur général of Metz to Garde des Sceaux, 9 October 1869, in AN, BB30 389.

2. David I. Kertzer, "The Role of Ritual in Political Change," in Myron J. Aronoff, ed., *Culture and Political Change* (New Brunswick, N.J., 1983), p. 60.

3. See, for example, the report of the prefect of the Haute-Vienne, 8 December 1852, in AN, F1C I 108.

4. Prefect of the Loiret to minister of the interior, 23 February 1853, in AN, F1C I 109; Procureur général, Besançon, to Garde des Sceaux, 3 August 1859, in AN, BB30 422.

5. As local notables, the regime treated the legitimists with some deference, even sometimes naming them official candidates in the legislative elections. See

Theodore Zeldin, *The Political System of Napoleon III* (New York, 1958), pp. 34–39.

6. AN, F1C I 111[1.]

7. For examples, see the various reports in AN, F19 5566, F19 5577, and F1C I 111[1.]

8. See reports in AN, F19 5577.

9. Prefect of the Drome to minister of the interior, December 1852, in AN, F1C I 108.

10. See the anonymous report on the funeral in AN, F70 42. Despite the protest and a significant number of other problems, the funeral was reported in the official press as if everything had gone smoothly. *Journal officiel*, 7 March 1869.

11. *L'Illustration*, 18 April 1857. In another case, such a flag was inadvertently displayed by officials who had taken a rolled flag from storage without realizing what was written on it. AN, BB30 422, no. 1748 P.

12. Oppositional placards as a form of protest had been around for a long time. Their use during the Restoration is treated in Sheryl Kroen, "The Cultural Politics of Revolution and Counterrevolution in France, 1815–1830" (Ph.D. dissertation, University of California, Berkeley, 1992), pp. 46–50.

13. Duruy to General Frossard, 21 July 1867, in *Papiers et correspondance de la famille impériale* (Paris, 1870), 3:362.

14. Charles Robert to Duruy, 4 August 1868, in *Papiers et correspondance de la famille impériale*, 3:365.

15. *The Times* (London), 14 August 1868, has a good account of the ceremony. See also the letters in *Papiers de correspondance de la famille impériale*, 3:364–69. To his credit, Duruy resisted punishing Cavaignac because of evidence that the boy himself was fairly tractable and had remained in his seat at the order of his mother.

16. Susanna Barrows, "Laughter, Language, and Derision: Seditious Speech and Popular Political Culture in Mid-Nineteenth-Century France," unpublished manuscript, p. 7.

17. Procureur général, Bordeaux, to Garde des Sceaux, 18 February 1853, in AN, BB30 406.

18. Procureur général, Grenoble, to Garde des Sceaux, 7 March 1853, in AN, BB30 406.

19. An excellent study of legitimist politicians in the Third Republic is Robert R. Locke, *French Legitimists and the Politics of Moral Order in the Early Third Republic* (Princeton, 1974). See ibid., pp. 141–43, for a discussion of the place of religion in legitimist political philosophy.

20. AN, F19 5548.

21. AN, BB30 423.

22. Maupas to minister of the interior, 28 May 1864, AN, F19 5548.

23. AN, BB30 421.

24. AN, F19 5548.

25. See AN, F70 41, 42, and 251 for the relevant documents concerning these funerals.

26. Alphonse Daudet, *Le Nabab,* in *Oeuvres complètes illustrées* (Paris, 1930), 7:275.

27. On the funerals of the Third Republic, see Avner Ben-Amos, "Molding the National Memory: The State Funerals of the French Third Republic" (Ph.D. dissertation, University of California, Berkeley, 1988). Ben-Amos devotes part of a chapter to the funerals of the Second Empire (pp. 129–41).

28. The use of red decorations was punishable by law. The prosecutor at Limoges received conflicting reports as to whether the decorations for one ceremony were red or of "mixed colors," and he was forced to order a further investigation before prosecuting. Report to the Garde des Sceaux, 18 May 1852, in AN, BB30 403.

29. Thomas A. Kselman, *Death and the Afterlife in Modern France* (Princeton, 1993), p. 106.

30. AN, BB30 383.

31. Procureur général, Aix, to the Garde des Sceaux, 12 May 1853, in AN, BB30 407.

32. *Bulletin officiel du Ministère de l'Intérieur, de l'agriculture et du commerce,* 1853, p. 326, in AN, ADXIX I 144.

33. Ibid.

34. *Tricolored Sketches in Paris during the Years 1851–2–3* (New York, 1855), pp. 311–12.

35. Premier avocat général, Nîmes, to the Garde des Sceaux, 17 March 1854, AN, BB30 408.

36. *L'Opinion nationale,* 21 January 1865; Anthony B. North Peat, *Gossip from Paris during the Second Empire: Correspondance (1864–1869) of Anthony B. North Peat,* ed. A. R. Waller (London, 1903), pp. 47–48; Jean Maurain, *La Politique ecclésiastique du Second Empire* (Paris, 1930), p. 728.

37. It tried to do the same thing for Alphonse de Lamartine in 1869, but the family decided not to have a ceremony in Paris anyway. On these funerals, see Ben-Amos, "Molding the National Memory," pp. 135–41, 146, n. 64.

38. *Le Moniteur universel,* 17 July 1857. The announcement is reproduced in the best account of Béranger's funeral: Jean Touchard, *La Gloire de Béranger* (Paris, 1968), 2:342–47.

39. Touchard, *Gloire de Béranger,* 2:345.

40. Prosper Mérimée, *Correspondance générale,* ed. M. Parturier, 2nd series (Toulouse, 1953–64), 2:329.

41. Henri Dabot, *Souvenirs et impressions d'un bourgeois du quartier Latin de mai 1854 à mai 1869* (Péronne, 1899), p. 30 (emphasis in original).

42. *The Times* (London), 21 July 1857.

43. *Le Moniteur universel,* 18 July 1857.

44. Touchard, *Gloire de Béranger,* 2:343.

45. On the press eulogies, see Touchard, *Gloire de Béranger,* 2:348–52.

46. Law of 6–10 June 1868, article 13.

47. Alain Dalotel, Alain Faure, and Jean-Claude Freiermuth, *Aux origines de la Commune: Le mouvement des réunions publiques à Paris, 1868–1870* (Paris, 1980).

48. On the importance of visiting cemeteries in nineteenth-century France, see Kselman, *Death and Afterlife*, pp. 213–21.

49. Eugène Ténot, *Paris in December 1851, or, The Coup d'Etat of Napoleon III*, trans. S. W. Adams and A. H. Brandon (New York, 1870), p. 168. See also Alexandre Zévaès, *Les Débuts de la République et le procès Baudin* (Grenoble, 1935), pp. 22–24.

50. *L'Opinion nationale*, 4 November 1867. At the time, Manin's body was in the family vault of Ary Scheffer. It was returned to Manin's native Venice in 1868.

51. *The Times* (London), 9 November 1868; Zévaès, *Les Débuts de la République*, pp. 30–33.

52. Pierre de la Gorce, *Histoire du Second Empire*, 7th ed. (Paris, 1902), 5:409.

53. The speech has been widely reprinted, but the wording varies somewhat. I have used the version in Zévaès, *Les Débuts de la République*, pp. 67–68. 18 Brumaire, year VIII (9 November 1799) was the date of Napoleon I's coup d'état overthrowing the Directory.

54. *L'Illustration*, 19 June 1869; *Illustrated London News*, 19 June 1869.

55. Emile Ollivier, *Journal* (Paris, 1961), 2:418.

56. A. Claveau, *Souvenirs politiques et parlementaires d'un témoin* (Paris, 1913), 1:359.

57. Good accounts of the event are found in the press and in Roger L. Williams, *Henri Rochefort, Prince of the Gutter Press* (New York, 1966), pp. 53–54. Rochefort's own version of what happened is found in Henri Rochefort, *The Adventures of My Life*, trans. Ernest W. Smith (London, 1896), 1:238–42.

58. *L'Opinion nationale*, 13 January 1870.

59. Williams, *Henri Rochefort*, p. 54.

60. Raoul Girardet, *Mythes et mythologies politiques* (Paris, 1986), pp. 139–73. See also Mona Ozouf, *La Fête révolutionnaire, 1789–1799* (Paris, 1976), esp. pp. 336–37.

61. Emile Ollivier, *L'Empire libéral* (Paris, 1895–1915), 4:51.

62. See Ben-Amos, "Molding the National Memory."

CONCLUSION

1. *Le Constitutionnel*, 16–17 August 1852.

2. Emile Begin, "De l'art dans les fêtes publiques," *Le Reveil*, 21 August 1858.

3. Report of 3 February 1863, in AN, BB30 384.

4. Albert Guérard, *Napoleon III* (Cambridge, Mass., 1943), p. 155 (emphasis in original).

5. *Le Constitutionnel*, 29 May 1862.

6. *Le Constitutionnel*, 20 August 1855.

7. Benedict Anderson, *Imagined Communities: Reflections on the Origin and Spread of Nationalism* (London, 1983), p. 66.

Index